THE
ENCYCLOPAEDIA
OF THE
First
Peoples
of North
America

THE
ENCYCLOPAEDIA
OF THE
First
Peoples
of North
America

RAYNA GREEN

WITH

MELANIE FERNANDEZ

A GROUNDWOOD BOOK

DOUGLAS & McINTYRE

TORONTO/VANCOUVER

Rayna Green, a Cherokee from Oklahoma, is Director of the
American Indian Program at the National Museum of
American History, Smithsonian Institution

Melanie Fernandez is Community Arts Officer and
Acting First Nations Officer at the Ontario Arts Council.

© The Trustees of the British Museum

Originally published as **The British Museum Encyclopaedia
of Native North America** by British Museum Press, a division
of The British Museum Company Ltd, 1999
First Canadian edition 1999

Groundwood Books/Douglas & McIntyre
720 Bathurst Street, Suite 500
Toronto, Ontario M5S 2R4

Canadian Cataloguing in Publication Data
Green, Rayna
The encyclopaedia of the first peoples of North America
1st Canadian ed.
ISBN 0-88899-380-3

1. Indians of North America – Encyclopaedia, Juvenile.
I. Fernandez, Melanie. II. Title

E76.2.G733   1999   j970'.00497'003   C99-930391-0

Designed and typeset in Novarese by Peartree Design
Manufactured in China

Cover: A Southern Cheyenne man, 'Little Hand', photographed by
D.I. Gill in 1909. National Anthropological Archives, Smithsonian
Institution, Washington DC; a young Plains pow wow dancer.
© Tony Stone Images; a buffalo hide painted in 1992 by Dennis
Fox, Jr. (Mandan, Hidatsa and Sioux). National Museum of
American History, Smithsonian Institution, courtesy of the artist.

Half title: Portrait of Scott Bear Don't Walk (Crow and Salish), a
writer and Rhodes Scholar, at an honouring ceremony given him
on his return from Oxford University in 1996. Courtesy of Marjorie
Bear Don't Walk (Salish-Chippewa).

page vii: Iroquois embroidered burden strap.© The British Museum.

Contents

Using this book

The main entries are in A–Z order.

Often more than one version of a Native North American word exists and people may say or write it differently in different languages. In that case, the word is placed in the A–Z entries in its most widely known form, with the variations given. For example, if you look up the **Ojibwa** entry you will also see Anishinabe/Chippewa/Nipissing/Mississauga.

If you are in any doubt where to find something on the A–Z section, you can look it up in the indexes on pages 201–213.

In the encyclopaedia entries, if a word is shown in **bold type** that means it has an entry of its own that you can look up.

Use the indexes on pages 201–213 to find names, places and things that do not have a main entry of their own.

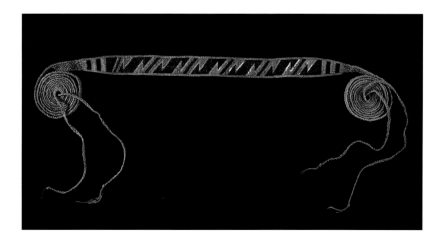

The First Nations

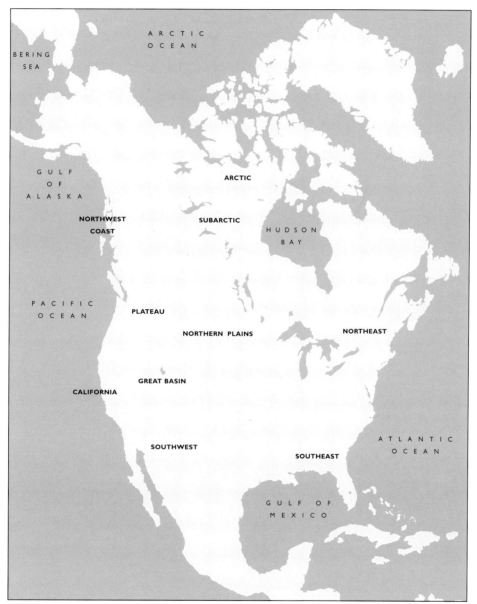

ARCTIC OCEAN

BERING SEA

GULF OF ALASKA

ARCTIC

NORTHWEST COAST

SUBARCTIC

HUDSON BAY

PACIFIC OCEAN

PLATEAU

NORTHERN PLAINS

NORTHEAST

GREAT BASIN

CALIFORNIA

ATLANTIC OCEAN

SOUTHWEST

SOUTHEAST

GULF OF MEXICO

Culture Areas

Introduction

This book is an introduction to Native North American history and culture. It does not deal with the ancient people of North America or with the indigenous peoples of South America, but with the peoples inhabiting what became Canada and the United States from about 1,000 AD. In this book, we can give descriptions of only a very few of the over 300 tribal peoples of North America as well as fragments of their histories, religions, art, languages and individual lives, but it does offer some introduction to the peoples, issues and ideas (past and present) that make up Native North American history and culture.

This introduction to Indian history comes as much through pictures and objects as through the words of native people. It represents a simple map of the history – a visual history – of Native North America. The objects, paintings and photographs show much that is painful as well as beautiful; they mean to make a reader want to go further than the pages of this book in order to understand how much more there is to know in that history.

A

Abenaki

The name Abenaki refers to the 'People of the Dawn Land', a number of **Algonquian**-speaking peoples (including Pennacook, Penobscot, Sokokis, Pigwacket, Norridgewock, Kennebec, Androscoggin and Wawenock). They lived in the area from the state of Maine to the state of Vermont, then on to the Canadian Northeast. As part of the 17th- and 18th-century Wabenaki Alliance, which included other groups from the Maritime Provinces and the American Northeast Coast, they were large in number and influential. The Abenakis in the West grew **maize** in the Champlain Valley. Those in the East were expert hunters, **basket**makers and **fish**erpeople, centred around Mount Katahdin. They were among the first Natives to experience the devastation of epidemic **disease** such as smallpox in the 17th century and also among the first to convert to **Christianity**.

When their homelands were shattered as the French and the **British** battled for control of their lands, most Abenakis moved toward French-speaking European communities. The Seven Years War (1755–63) caused most Abenakis to lose virtually everything. The Penobscot remained fairly stable in Maine, although many of their lands and rights were removed. Most Abenakis 'went underground', appearing to be assimilated (see **acculturation**) as French-American basketmakers and woodsmen.

Today, Penobscots (and their Passamaquoddy neighbours) still live in Maine. They successfully sued the US government for payments for land taken in violation of the Indian Trade and Non-Intercourse Act of 1790. Odanak Abenakis in Québec, where the Abenaki language still survives, are recognized as **status** Indians by the Canadian and Québecois government. Abenakis in Vermont still lack recognition by the US government, although they are trying to restore their recognition internally and externally as a viable Native community.[1]

Acculturation, assimilation, adaptation

The word 'acculturation' is used to describe how people undergo great changes and adapt when another culture is introduced to them or forced on them. Thus, the Native, indigenous and aboriginal Indians acculturated to the culture of the Europeans, becoming more like them in the process. An Indian who adopted Western dress and manners, learned English, French or Spanish, adopted Western **agricultural** methods, intermarried with whites, went to school and church, and apparently abandoned Native territory and detectable 'Indian' ways of behaving would be said to be acculturated into white society. The US and Canadian governments, **missionaries** and others tried to enact the 19th-century policy of '**civilization**', to force Indians into a European, American and **Christian** culture. What many saw as successful acculturation of Indians may often have been creative and clever adaptations to Western standards on a surface level in order to survive.

Mi'kmaq in Nova Scotia on the most Eastern Coast of North America, were among the first Native peoples to meet Europeans. **Inuit** peoples in the far Northwestern Arctic (Alaska) were among the last to meet Europeans. In both cases, they began to use Native materials, designs and techniques to produce objects of European form and function. This suggests an immediate understanding of a new 'market' and shows the flexibility and creativity of Native **art** and behaviour. The Indians who made these new objects had not become like white people, they had just adapted in order to survive.

For some people the only 'real' Indian is a 'traditional Indian' – clad in buffalo robes, adorned with feathers, astride a horse – the classic Hollywood stereotype. This buckskin image of the Plains Indian is indeed part of my history, but so too are suit-wearing tribal leaders. So-called Indian aficionados don't seem too happy about the suit-wearing type. They are often disappointed to learn that Indians wear [ordinary] clothes and that

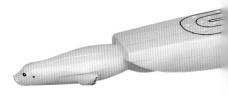

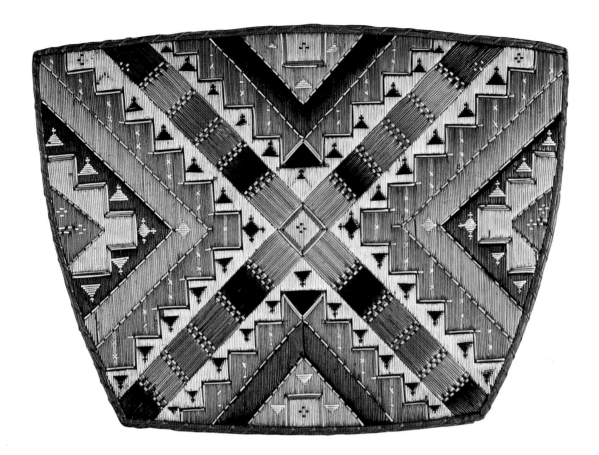

1 **Above** An 18th-century **Mi'kmaq** chair seat made from dyed porcupine quills.

2 **Below** An early 20th-century **Inuit** ivory cribbage board.

sometimes they dress more like cowboys than Indians. They are not too pleased when they learn that the majority of Indian people identify themselves as Christians… though this certainly doesn't preclude participation in Native religions. Fact is, Indians live in a multi-racial, multi-ethnic world just like everyone else in this country. They've always made alliances, intermarried, and borrowed ideas and technology from other people. This can be a productive process, a source of great vitality and innovation. Indian history didn't end in 1800. Indian cultures aren't some sort of museum piece that are frozen in time, preserved under glass. They evolve, grow and continually try to renew themselves.
Mark Trahant, Shoshone-Bannock journalist

Acoma Pueblo

Acoma Pueblo houses one of the oldest continually occupied sites in North America, in the East of New Mexico. The group of people who live here speak Keresan. Acoma (a name which is related to the people's long occupation of the place) is one of several pueblos (towns) situated on the Rio Grande River. It is linked in culture and language with the other villages of Cochiti and Laguna. Like most of the living pueblos in New Mexico, Acoma has a combination of a traditional religious government and a modern elected **tribal government**. The group has recovered about 500,000 of the several million acres of **land** it originally held when the Spanish arrived in 1539. The tribe runs a large tourism business with its spectacular setting, ancient structures and a thriving and respected tradition of **pottery** making.

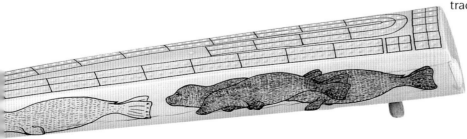

3 Above Santa Clara Pueblo, in northern New Mexico, 1900. Adobe formed most of the houses and outbuildings and all of the bread ovens. In the beehive-shaped ovens, called 'horno' and based on a Spanish design from North Africa, people baked using the wheat introduced into Indian Country by the Spanish. The wood fire made in the horno is allowed to burn up. The wood and its ash are scraped out, and the dough is put in to bake in the heat held in the mud of the high domed oven. Women in Pueblo villages bake hundreds of loaves for feast days.

Adobe

Adobe is the Spanish word meaning a clay used for building. The insulating power of adobe – cool in the summer and warm in the winter – is remarkable. It makes a perfect modern building material, and is still used by Hispanics and Indians in the American Southwest. The clay bricks enabled people to build huge communities with bigger, more durable and restorable buildings. Pecos, Puyé, Pueblo Bonito and Chaco Canyon, which, at their peak, were home to thousands of people, still stand today as proof of the strength, adaptability and environmental soundness of adobe and show the people's close ties with this extraordinary building material.

The word for clay in Tewa, the language of some Northern Pueblo people who live in the Upper Rio Grande Valley, is *nung*; a word for people is also *nung*. To Pueblo people, humans are clay, mud and earth. People needed clay for shelter and for storage and cooking vessels.

The adobe structures flowed out of the earth and it was often difficult to see where the ground stopped and the structures began…. As we are synonymous with and born of the earth, so we are made of the same stuff as our houses.
Rina Swentzell, Santa Clara Pueblo landscape historian

Africans, African-Americans and Indians

Africans have been in the Americas since Europeans arrived in the late 15th century. One of the first recorded encounters between Native people and Africans was in 1540. It was between the A:*shiwi* or **Zuni** and a North African Spaniard or 'Moor' called Estevanico or Esteban, who represented the Spanish in their explorations into the Southwest. They met and fought at a village called Hawikuh, where the Zuni killed Estevanico and others who had threatened them and demanded tributes for the Spanish King. Other Natives first met Africans and people of African descent in the Caribbean, where Spanish and Portuguese brought them as slaves.

Early colonists in the Caribbean and on the American Continent tried to enslave Indians, forcing them to work the sugar and maize plantations alongside Africans. Many free blacks worked on the whaling ships operating from the New England Coast and they worked alongside Native **Algonquian** peoples from the area. They intermixed with those peoples, creating the mixed-blood, tri-racial **populations** of coastal Indian peoples in the Northeast, such as Narragansetts, Pequots and Shinnecocks.

Slaves often ran away from their masters, fleeing to friendly Indian towns. Several Northern tribes, such as the Tuscaroras who had moved from the South in the 18th century, helped runaway slaves escape to Canada. Some of these escaped slaves stayed, intermarrying with tribal men and women. **Intermarriage** and interbreeding occurred regularly between runaway and freed Africans and Indians, as it did between whites, Indians and blacks. Some **Northwest Coastal** peoples held slaves who never rose beyond slavery. Other tribes in the Southwest had forms of slavery – more like an agreed contract over a number of years – that would absorb slaves (Indian, white or African) into the community when their period of slavery was over. For some tribal peoples, such as **Creeks**, **Seminoles** and Choctaws, interrelationships were common and there were even recognized groups of African-Indians, such as the Black Seminoles.

For **Cherokees**, however, slavery remained of the kind familiar in the American South. The Cherokee Constitution of 1835 forbade intermarriage between Cherokees and Africans. In 1835, over 1,500 slaves lived in the Cherokee Nation, the property of a few wealthy Cherokees. Planters, such as the Vanns who owned over 100 slaves according to the 1835 Cherokee Census, used slave labour to cultivate crops and work as servants. Cherokees took slaves with them to the West during **Removal**. After the **Civil War**, the Cherokees extended 'all the rights of Native Cherokees' to some 2,500 former slaves (thereafter called 'Freedmen'). Cherokees established separate schools for Freedmen, who could also claim 160 acres of Cherokee land. Some tribes never did grant full tribal membership to Freedmen, unlike the Seminoles, who even made elected slots for them in its tribal government.

Before the **Civil War** (1861–65), many blacks moved west, some as traders in the Rocky Mountains, others as members of the US Army, sent to pacify the Indians and ensure that tribal lands were taken, often at gunpoint. These men became known as 'Buffalo Soldiers'. The opening of Indian Territory to settlers, some of them blacks, created greater divisions because some of the land **allotted** to blacks was land removed from Indians. At **schools** such as Hampton Institute, founded in order to educate blacks and Indians, their education was separate. The founding fathers feared the 'race mixing' that inevitably would and did happen when they were put together.[2]

Agriculture and farming

One of the great misunderstandings about American Indians is that they were all hunters and gatherers before European **contact**. By 2,000 BC, Indians in the Andes, Mexico and the American Southwest domesticated at least four major Native **food** plants. For over 10,000 years, indigenous women in the Northeast, the Southeast and the Central Plains and men in the Southwest had been developing plant breeding. They had selected and refined useful plants, such as **maize**, **beans** and **squash**, and had domesticated some wild varieties. Using a mixture of communal and individual land ownership and use, Natives had adapted farming techniques to the environment and climate.[3] Many tribes cultivated and farmed the majority of their foods and readily shared this knowledge with the European newcomers. Indians of North and South America domesticated six of the world's 13 major food plants (maize, brown beans, peanuts, potatoes, cassava and sweet potatoes).

The Plant People were put here for us. The sky is the one who does the planting…. He moves clouds… male rain… female rain and dark mists over the plants, and they grow…. They are our food and our medicine and the medicine for our livestock. From the Plant People we have Iináájí Azeé – the medicines of the Life Way….
George Blueeyes, Navajo storyteller and teacher

For centuries most Native people lived well on some combination of farming, gathering, hunting and fishing. Their agricultural systems – both in terms of production and the distribution of goods – were deeply connected with their spiritual belief, **ceremony** and with social relationships. For example, among the **Iroquois**, the tribes of the Southeast and the Mandan, Hidatsa and Arikara of the Northern Plains, the products of agricultural labour were the women's to trade and distribute.

The European systems of agriculture were introduced into a world where many Native peoples had been farmers for centuries. When the US and Canadian governments tried to 'civilize' the Indians they saw as 'Savage' hunters by converting them to farmers, they disrupted Native systems and ideas and changed forever those spiritual, social and economic relationships so carefully constructed over thousands of years.

On the often unarable, water-starved **reservation** lands, men who could not and did not know how to farm were encouraged or forced to do so, while women (who had been the farmers and distributors of agricultural goods) were supposed to learn the 'domestic arts' of European women and leave the land. However, many could not meet their needs for food and cash income on these lands. They were dependent on the rations given by the government in **treaty** payments that were often inadequate or even denied.

You ask me to plough the ground! Shall I take a knife and tear my mother's bosom? Then when I die she will not take me to her bosom to rest. You ask me to dig for stone! Shall I dig under her skin for her bones. Then when I die I cannot enter her body to be born again. You ask me to make hay and sell it, and be rich like white men! But dare I cut off my mother's hair?
Smohalla, the Wanapum prophet, c. 1880

I was now seventeen years old… and got very much interested in farming…. Gradually I forgot my earnest promise to my father, that I would some day suffer in a Sun Dance, and became quite reconciled to the government's orders.
Goodbird, Hidatsa, 1913

4 Below Dakota (**Sioux**) schoolboys with watermelons they grew at Lower Cut Meat Creek Indian Day School, Rosebud Reservation, South Dakota, c. 1895–99. The Indian **schools** taught European-style agriculture and students grew unfamiliar crops using unfamiliar farming methods.

As time went by… Pueblos began to gradually move away from farming the land, and as a result many of the lands became fallow, as one generation succeeded the next. There was less and less emphasis on farming, and more and more emphasis on arts and crafts.
Gregory Cajete, Santa Clara Pueblo educator

Later, when Europeans had introduced new animals and plants into the Americas, women once again became the centre of the new plant and animal **economies**. Women were responsible for sheep in the Southwest, pigs and fruit orchards in the Southeast and Southwest, and cattle in the Northeast. Some Indian men, such as Crows and Shoshone, took more to cattle and **horse** ranching than to farming. A few tribal people have, in the last 10 years, revitalized Native agricultural methods, attempting once again to raise Native varieties of maize, beans, squash and **tobacco**. They are also bringing back **buffalo** to the grasslands.

Alaska Native Claims Settlement Act (ANCSA) of 1971

This land settlement awarded $962.5 million in compensation and ownership of 44 million acres of land to Natives of Alaska (United States). Although most settlements of land claims made the point that it was land, not monetary compensation, that mattered, many did involve financial payments and a system of settling such compensations that can now only be regarded, like **treaties**, as insufficient in comparison to what was given up.

The effect of the ANCSA, which established 13 Native corporations in place of tribal membership, will be the end of Native **status**. The ANCSA, in effect, extinguished aboriginal title to the land. Native children born after the ANCSA, unlike their parents and grandparents, were not granted automatic membership and shares in the corporations. People afraid of losing ancestral lands started a tribal movement to have changes made to the ANCSA and to re-establish the languages, **ceremonies**, traditional forms of government and the **subsistence economies** based on **hunting** and **fishing**.

Native land is now a corporate asset.
Justice Thomas Berger, 1985

Alaska Purchase

In 1867, the United States bought the rights to Alaska from Russia. The Russians had first begun colonizing in the **Aleutian** Islands via **fur traders** and **hunters** in the mid 18th century. They had **Christianized** many Yup'ik, Tlingit and Aleut peoples from the Aleutian Islands to the area known as Prince William Sound. Nevertheless, the Alaska Purchase from Russia brought an entirely new set of colonial values and efforts into an already devastated world.

He said… he's here to talk about ANCSA (the Alaskan Native Claims Settlement Act) … . They might not like what he has to say but what he says comes from the heart… . He said that the Russians did not live here… because the Russians were not born here, and they did not own this land, that it was illegal for them to sell it… . The Russians sold it like they owned it and ignored the real owners… the ancestors who originally owned it, way before recorded time.
Peter Waska, Yup'ik, at a land conference

Alcohol, alcohol abuse

Very few indigenous communities – and none in the Eastern Americas – made any fermented substance at all before the arrival of the Europeans, but Indian alcohol use and abuse became a serious problem in the 17th century. The enormous American alcohol **trade** developed on the back of the slave trade and sugar cultivation in the Caribbean. It was as important an economic factor in the Americas as the **fur trade** and the **maize** and **tobacco** trade in the 17th and 18th centuries. At a time when most North Americans drank daily amounts of alcohol unthinkable today, alcohol was used as enticement, as pay and as a weapon against Indians whose goods, lands and rights were wanted by the government and private business alike. The short- and long-term disastrous effects of alcohol abuse were clear to both Indians and non-Indians and led to a never-ending debate on the supply of alcohol to Indian areas. The alcohol trade brought a direct and forceful response from many Indians and from whites associated with them. Others supported the trade, seeing the benefits it brought them in obtaining land, goods and the utter demoralization of Indian communities.

5 Above This buckskin banner, made *c.* 1900 by the women of the Women's **Christian** Temperance Union from the Warm Springs Indian **Reservation** in Oregon, is white to signify 'social purity'. On the banner, the women raise the Indian tomahawk and the hatchet of the temperance reformer, Carry Nation, against the enemy alcohol. They use the symbol of the pipe (well-known to whites) to show the alliance of their cause with that of others. The 'Don't Tread on Me' snake of the American Revolutionary motto may represent the healing snake of **Salish creation stories**. The beaded flowers – the most common symbol on Plateau and Great Basin **beadwork** – probably represent the flowers of the camas root, one of the most important ceremonial and food plants of the Wasco and Salish peoples.

6 Above Susan LaFlesche and some members of her family, c. 1880.

There has been much speculation on why Indians abused alcohol, including ideas about genetic susceptibilities, Indians' belief in the power of alcohol to produce **dreams** and visions, and the Europeans' part in the social and mental degradation that came with alcohol and its abuse.

Handsome Lake declared alcohol the greatest source of sin…. Alcohol was the biggest force of sin in changing the lives of the Native people.
Reg Henry, Cayuga faithkeeper, Six Nations Reserve

Although statistics on modern alcohol abuse by Indians do not differ much from those of other people in their areas, the stigma and consequences of alcohol abuse still deeply affects Indian communities more negatively than others. A substantial movement in Indian Country – a new temperance movement – has recommended and achieved sobriety. Associated with women's suffrage, the 19th-century temperance movement was a part of the reform movement in America that demanded justice for American Indians.

By the turn of the century, many Indian women had joined the temperance movement. Susan LaFlesche (1865–1915), an Omaha and the first Native woman to become a doctor, was a notable activist for Indian rights. With her sister Susette (1854–1903) and other relatives, she lobbied for the banning of alcohol on **reservations** and for health reforms. Realizing that alcohol was a means of making Indians sign over their lands and goods, she fought against the corruption of the government and its laws that tried to make Indian people dependent and demoralized.[4]

Aleut/Alutiit/Alutiiq

The Russians called the Native residents of the Aleutian Islands, Kodiak Island, the Alaska and Kenai peninsulas and Prince William Sound Aleut or Aliut. These peoples were Sasignan/Unangan and Suqpiaq/Alutiiq peoples, related to Yup'ik of Western Alaska and Inupiaq of **Arctic** Alaska. By 1900, **disease**, environmental disasters (such as earthquakes, tsunami and later oil spills) and political upheaval as a result of the Russian colonization reduced the once large population of sea-going, **hunting** and **fishing** people. The presence of the Russian Orthodox Church and Russian customs and language is still felt in these areas. The United States re-colonized this area and its people after the **Alaska Purchase**, forcing them to adapt to a new culture for a second time. Many still speak Russian, English and the Alutiiq or Suk language, although that language may be more endangered than the other two. Although the Alutiiq way of life has suffered greatly from the environmental and cultural changes forced upon it, there have been recent attempts to revitalize its culture and its **subsistence economy**.[5]

Algonquin/Algonquian

With the exception of the **Iroquois**, Algonquian-speaking groups populate Northeastern America. These communities in Canada are dominated by two language groups (**Ojibwa** and **Cree**) and one dialect referred to as Oji-Cree. They occupy a large area known as the Eastern Woodlands. This diverse environment has forests, lakes and rivers, cold winters and short summers and an abundance of game, **fish**, berries and **wild rice**. The Northern communities live in small independent groups, such as the Saulteaux, Ottawa, Mississauga, Algonquin and Nipissing. The Cree, Montagnais and Naskapi are also from the same linguistic groups, but see themselves as separate political groups.

Allotment, General Allotment Act/Dawes Act

The period of allotment, under the General Allotment Act or Dawes Act of 1887, brought economic and cultural disaster. With **Removal**, many Indians, such as the Choctaw, had been given the chance of choosing allotment within the lands they had given up. They would then become citizens where they were instead of moving west. Under the Dawes Act, Indians received certificates entitling them to a land allotment. They had a period of 25 years to learn how to run a business and how to **farm**, after which time the land was to be given to them. Allotment was part of the assimilation policy (see **acculturation**), and it was assumed that all Indians would take to farming. Indian agents denied rations and other payments set out in the **treaties** to Indians who did not work their allotments. Much land could not be farmed and many more acres were lost through the then-legal sale of individual lands. Indian landholdings were reduced to one-third of their former size (from 138 million acres in 1887 to 48 million by 1934).

The US government mixed the issue of **citizenship** with allotment – issuing patents-in-fee (deeds of ownership) and American citizenship to Indians (usually mixed bloods) who they believed were 'competent' and holding lands in trust for those they considered 'incompetent'. In this way, the **Cherokees** received only 110 acres each in 1902 and so were no longer able to hold land in common as they traditionally did or to

continue as an independent nation. Although many wanted to oppose allotment and keep their own government and identity, wealthy Cherokees, railways and mining companies and homesteaders (who went west to settle) argued for it. The Cherokee Republic and its institutions formally ended when Oklahoma became a state in 1907. The state fell under the control of white homesteaders, who outnumbered the Indians seven to one. Two-thirds of the Indians lost the small allotments given to them within 20 years, due to an inability to pay taxes, the pressures to sell to whites or outright fraud. Cherokees could obtain homesteads as well as their allotments. They could not sell their allotted land without permission. Many traditional Cherokees, such as those of the Keetoowah Society, refused to have anything to do with allotment or the soon-to-be-formed state of Oklahoma. Redbird Smith, the Keetoowah leader at that time, and Eufaula Harjo, a **Creek**, founded the Four Mothers Society to resist allotment and to support continued communal ownership of property and the preservation of traditional ways.

American Indian Religious Freedom Act of 1978

This Act was meant to counteract the long history of official and unofficial hostilities against American Indian religions and religious practice. It was intended to protect the religious rights of American Indians and remove 'unnecessary impediments to Indian access to sacred sites'. However, the Act was intentionally vague and had no provisions on how to enforce it, and so has achieved little.

The first colonists in North America regarded Native religious beliefs and practices as barbarous. **Missionaries** and government leaders adopted policies that would change what they saw as the Indians' 'savage' ways through schooling, conversion to **Christianity**, and the banning of Native **ceremony**, dress, medical practices and language. There was even violence toward Native religious ceremonies and expression. Indian religious and ceremonial objects were taken to museums and Indians were forced from their lands of origin and sacred places.

The government, missionaries, industries and **tourists** have intruded on **sacred sites**

7 Right A sign posted on one of the *kivas* (ceremonial dwellings) at San Ildefonso Pueblo warns visitors not to intrude into sacred space.

can go to practise their sacred ceremonies without disruption.

From the beginning of time the Pueblo of Taos and its people and the elders before them, they were using this place known as Blue Lake area. And for a religious purpose. Man should have a privacy… to do their own talking to the Great Spirit.
Paul Bernal, Taos religious leader, 1990

Pueblo people believe it is their obligation to share their **food**, their prayers and their **dances** with all those who come to the pueblos (towns). Yet so many interested non-Indians visit pueblos on ceremonial days that they trample villages. In many places, such as Taos Pueblo, tourists have invaded sacred places, such as the *kivas*, essentially contaminating holy space. In 1990, the Zuni Council closed Shalako, one of their winter ceremonies, to all outsiders, as tourists had continued to violate its sanctity with photography, film and tape recording. The pueblos have special procedures to restrain people during feast days, for example parking rules and restricted access to old or fragile structures. Tribal police and, during ceremonial times, sacred **clowns** keep people from disrupting ceremonies and from being disrespectful to the private lives of residents and to religious sites.

Apache
Apaches, all Athapaskan-speaking peoples, are composed of several quite diverse groups who live in the Southwestern United States. Plains Apaches encountered the Spanish in the 16th century. They adapted to **horses** immediately and expanded over the Southern Plains. By the mid 18th century, Plains Apaches formed in three groups (Jicarillas, Lipans and Mescaleros), who traded with Mexicans and spoke Spanish. Most Mescaleros were imprisoned with **Navajos** by the US Army at Bosque Redondo (see **Long Walk of the Navajo**) in 1868, but escaped in 1873. The US Army imprisoned Kiowa-Apaches with **Geronimo** and the Chiricahuas at Fort Sill, Oklahoma. Jicarillas and Mescaleros were separated when sent to **reservations**. Following their imprisonment, most Chiricahuas joined the Lipans and Mescaleros in their New Mexico reservation, but some stayed at Fort Sill in Oklahoma

8 Above During feast days, Santa Clara Pueblo posts regulations suggesting appropriate conduct for visitors. Tribal police and members of the *kivas* enforce good behaviour. In charge of them is the War Captain, who traditionally used to deal with enemies and who now deals with the world outside the Pueblo.

and religious rites of Native peoples. Tribes try to restrain people and organizations from violating traditional ceremonial grounds, such as **stomp dance** grounds or ancient places for prayer or rituals. For example, in 1906, the US Forest Service took over Taos Blue Lake, the sacred waterspring of the Taos Pueblo people, and made it a part of the newly developed Kit Carson National Forest. For 65 years, the people of Taos tried to regain their sacred site. In 1971, they succeeded and now manage it as a preservation site where they where they remain today. Eventually, both Jicarilla and Mescalero reorganized themselves and tried to restore their culture. They became ranchers and now operate a successful tourism business.

Western Apaches lived for a long time in Arizona before the Spanish occupation in 16th century. The White Mountain and San Carlos Apache belong to the **Athabaskan**-speaking family related to **Navajo**. They are **agricultural** peoples from the uplands, and their main spiritual connections are with mountain spirits or Crown **dancers** (*gaan*) who return from the mountains during puberty **ceremonies** for the purpose of healing. Although heavily **missionized**, much of Apache traditional spiritual practice – centred on women's puberty ceremonies in this **matrilineal** group – persists. White Mountain has many natural resources, while the high desert San Carlos has a long history of hostile relations with the US government and heavy environmental exploitation with logging, **dams** and mineral extraction.

Architecture

Chickee (**Seminole**), hogan (**Navajo**), wickiup (**Apache**), roundhouse, tipi (Plains tribes), longhouse (**Iroquois** and **Northwest Coastal** peoples), arbor/ramada (many Southwestern, Southern Plains people), plank house (California people), pit house (California), **adobe** (Pueblos), earth lodge (Pawnee, Mandan/Hidatsa), igloo (**Inuit**), wigwam (**Ojibwa**), sweathouse/sweatlodge (many Native people).

North American Indians developed hundreds of types of permanent and temporary, domestic, communal, ceremonial and public buildings. Climate, technologies and materials influenced the way they built. Seminoles in the hot, wet areas of Florida made chickees open to the air on all sides. Inuit igloos, made of snow blocks, offer maximum insulation from the cold and wind.

In addition, Indians' social, religious and political structure as a people, together with their beliefs about their origins and their philosophy on life, affected the kinds of structures they built and used. The Pawnees' beliefs about their relationship with the celestial universe caused them to build homes that opened out and were directed at the skies for observation. An understanding of the importance of human relationships led

the **Iroquois** and **Tlingit** to build structures that could contain an entire **clan**. Long-held religious and social traditions of where people lived and whose family controlled property caused some peoples (for example Navajos, Apaches and Crows) to have women build and control the use of a house. Hidatsa/Mandan women built the earth lodges and their daughters inherited them. The lodge was home to all these women, their children, husbands and brothers.

W e thought an earth lodge was alive and had a spirit like a human body, and that its front was like a face, with the door for a mouth.
Maxiwidiac/Buffalo Bird Woman, Hidatsa, 1921

Many forces altered traditional forms of architecture, including **Removal** from traditional lands and the assault on religious and cultural lifestyles. **Traders**, white farmers and persons new to Indian lands constructed new buildings such as churches, schools, military and government buildings. People often combined traditional forms of architecture with the new forms. **Cherokees** and **Senecas**, for example, who had always built structures for the storage of **maize**, began to build maize cribs that were more like those of their Scots-Irish neighbours.[6]

9 Above This engraving shows a **Creek** house in 1791, by this stage essentially a log cabin much like those of white neighbours.

10 Above The **Tlingit** Whale House of Kluckwan Village (built in 1835) was an enormous structure for the time. Fifteen metres wide and deep, built of cedar and spruce planks, the simple external structure with its deeply pitched and peaked roof housed elaborate and beautifully carved house poles (see **house posts**), a cedar plank ceremonial screen and carvings of the Tlingit religious universe. This winter house, built to represent the title and crests of a particular family, was home to that family's ceremonies and **potlatches** and could accommodate its own **clan** and others during those formal events.

11 Right These Inuit ivory snow knives are for carving snow to make it into structures such as igloos. They are simple but versatile tools for such complex architectural ideas.

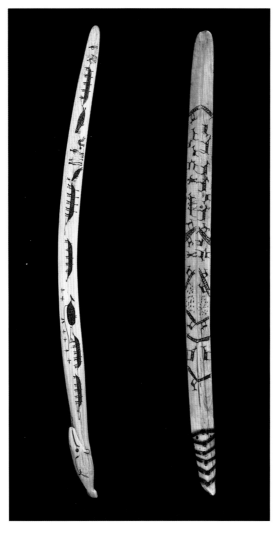

There are new buildings in Indian Country. Some repeat old forms and are used ceremonially, ritually and in remembrance, including tipis put up for special annual gatherings (such as the Crow Fair and the Anadarko Fair for Kiowas and Comanches). Mass public housing was built on **reservations** by the US Office of Housing and Urban Development, the **Bureau of Indian Affairs**, and the Department of Indian Affairs (Canada). Other structures are by an entirely new generation of Indian architects who use traditional forms, materials, processes and ideas to inspire new architecture in the building of Native schools, museums and other public buildings.

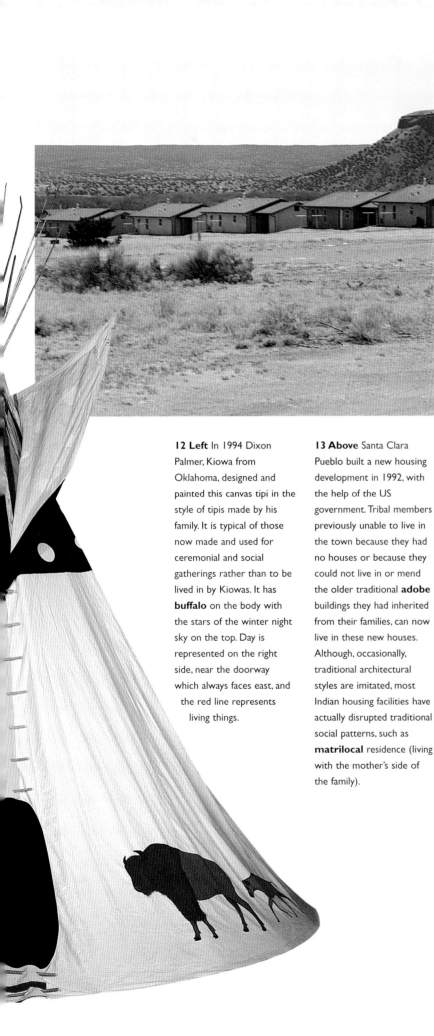

14 Above The Canadian Museum of Civilization, designed by Douglas Cardinal, **Blackfeet/Métis** architect. Douglas Cardinal was born in Calgary, Alberta and grew up in the prairie town of Red Deer. He opened his own firm in 1964, and his first contract, an Indian church, won him national recognition. He explored his native heritage, asking the council of elders for advice on his projects. Cardinal has developed a powerful and distinctive style, influenced by the curving, natural forms in the geography of his Alberta homeland. This museum was his first major commission and the first major building in Canada designed completely on computer.

12 Left In 1994 Dixon Palmer, Kiowa from Oklahoma, designed and painted this canvas tipi in the style of tipis made by his family. It is typical of those now made and used for ceremonial and social gatherings rather than to be lived in by Kiowas. It has **buffalo** on the body with the stars of the winter night sky on the top. Day is represented on the right side, near the doorway which always faces east, and the red line represents living things.

13 Above Santa Clara Pueblo built a new housing development in 1992, with the help of the US government. Tribal members previously unable to live in the town because they had no houses or because they could not live in or mend the older traditional **adobe** buildings they had inherited from their families, can now live in these new houses. Although, occasionally, traditional architectural styles are imitated, most Indian housing facilities have actually disrupted traditional social patterns, such as **matrilocal** residence (living with the mother's side of the family).

Arctic

Above latitude line 66° 30′ North, millions of square miles of land and sea make up the Arctic Circle. In this vast area, the sun does not appear in mid winter or set in mid summer. In the Arctic there are hundreds of species of animals such as caribou, **whale**, moose, seal, polar **bear** and a wide variety of birds. Average winter temperatures are -24 to -26 °C. In this environment, north of the tree line, the **Inuit** live in the Arctic tundra. They have adapted to life in this inhospitable climate by using the environment well. Inuit in the Arctic Circle have linguistic and cultural similarities with other circumpolar groups, such as the Inupiaq of Northern Alaska and Inuit of Greenland. In the Eastern and Southern sub-Arctic live the **Cree**, Naskapi and Montagnais, called Innu in Labrador. In the Western sub-Arctic, the Yukon and the Northwest Territories live the Dené.

Art

Most traditional Native art forms had an established function in cultural life. No-one hung a painting on a wall or mounted a **sculpture** on a pedestal just to admire, instead almost everything that was made for daily life was decorated in some way. Art was part of daily life – in **food** preparation, spirituality, language, teaching, philosophy, **agriculture** and much more.

Indian people have no word for art. Art is a part of life, like hunting, fishing, growing food, marrying and having children. This is an art in the broadest sense... an object of daily usefulness, to be admired, respected, appreciated and used, the expression thereby nurturing the needs of both body and soul, thereby giving meaning to everything.
Mary Lou Fox Radulovitch, Ojibwe Cultural Foundation

Where the environment allowed more leisure time, as in the case of the **Northwest Coast** and Eastern Woodlands, objects were more highly decorated. In the mid 1800s, when European art materials became available and Native artists began to copy European painting techniques, much changed. Some of the old 'craft' disappeared entirely. Some arts failed, then returned; others never went away.

Indian people still make 'traditional' craft objects for **dances** and for **ceremonies** (including ribbon shirts, Gourd Dance **blankets**, dance sticks, **flutes**, bone breastplates, **beaded** hair ties and buckskin dresses). Some of the old **basket** and **pottery** styles have been revived and the new painting and **sculpture** has evolved into a living, breathing art.

When some Kiowa, Comanche, Cheyenne and Arapaho warriors were taken to Fort Marion in Florida from jails in Oklahoma, after the terrible wars that would bring the end of the world as they once knew it, the last thing they might have imagined from their own and tribal tragedy was the beginning of contemporary American Indian art. From the ledger drawings that, like Bear's Heart's, mourned the past life, to the new **dream** vision paintings produced by Kiowas, new art forms were born. Awa Tsireh's remembrances translated into canvas, paper and chalk, recalled old stories. Out of old rocks and the paintings on them, from the landscape itself, Bob Haozous' sculptural forms took life. Horace Poolaw's **photographs** documented the Kiowa world of the 1930s that no-one else was interested in.

By the time he was a young man, my father had got enough of farming. He wanted to be an artist, a painter.... At some point he moved out of that old world of the Kiowas.
Scott Momaday, Kiowa writer

Shelley Niro's photographs of an unexpectedly comic and crazy **Iroquois** country insist that we pay attention to its heartless history. Nora Naranjo Morse's clay sculptures transport old clay pottery to a new world, while Lil Pitt in the state of Oregon gives us Africa and Japan out of clay masks that remember the **Salish** past.

The 20th century saw the emergence of a lively contemporary Native art movement. Internationally renowned artists in visual arts, **literature**, dance, theatre, **music** and crafts have combined traditional and contemporary influences in a new creative voice which is informed by Native issues, histories and stories. Art schools, such as the Centre for Indigenous Theatre in Toronto and the Institute of American Indian Art in Santa Fe, specialize in teaching skills and creating work with Native skills and ideas. Communities rich with artisans working in beadwork, quilting, carving, dance and storytelling keep communities culturally alive.[7]

It is this blessing of being able to make things that reconstruct my life, that gives me the knowledge to restore myself. The things I saw – the collaborative living structures, the places of worship and feasts, the outfits of antiquity, the buckskin garments, the beaded objects, the woven baskets for subsistence, the cradleboards for protection, the feathers of prayer, the couriers to a higher thought. They were made, traded and collected by great-grandparents and by living relatives, and I saw that they loved deeply. These messages – the beaded birds, horses, trees, stars and geometric abstractions – are like prayer, a prayer for our present worlds to know again the root connection to our existence.
Elizabeth Woody, Navajo, Wasco, and Warm Springs artist and writer

Athabaskan/Athapaskan

The Athabaskan-speaking peoples in Alaska include the Tanaina (Dena'ina), Kutchin (Gwitch'in), Holikachuck, Koyukon, Tanana, Upper Tanana, Tanacross, Upper Kuskokwim, Han and Ingalik (Deg Het'an). Most live in remote villages where people alternate a few mainstream jobs in the community with seasonal **hunting** and **fishing**. They have traditional forms of government along with new government under the **Alaska Native**

Awl

An awl might represent the work of women in Indian Country, just as a **bow and arrow** might the work of men. Indians gladly accepted the **metal** awl tips, fixed into wood, bone, antler or horn handles, that came with the **traders** from Europe. Native women everywhere used awls to punch holes in hides, wood and **bark**, so that they could join or decorate those hides and utensils with **beads** and quills. They used them to tighten a **basket** weave. Men usually made the handles for them. A young girl might receive her first awl at the time of her first menstruation and she could then practice her **quillwork**. Women on the Northern Plains carried their awls, their most treasured tool, in small rawhide or beautifully beaded and decorated cases, usually on their belts.

Men, too, used awls, to make and repair some of the things for which they were responsible. Jim Northrup, an Anishinabe writer and humorist, calls the awl an Indian cordless drill.[8]

Claims Settlement Act and elected governments administered through the **Bureau of Indian Affairs**. The **Alaska Purchase**, the Yukon River Gold Rush (*c.* 1890), the intrusions of Russian traders and missionaries into Athabaskan territories in the 19th century and the building of the Alaska pipeline in the 20th century had far-reaching consequences for these and other peoples in Alaska. Some land and cultural revitalization has occurred through the Alaska Native Claims Settlement Act and through strong campaigning for Native **subsistence**.

Navajos, Apaches and Beaver, Chipewyan and Dogrib people in Canada share an Athabaskan language with the Alaskan peoples.

B

Baby carrier

Many Native peoples used baby carriers or cradleboards. They were made of wood, reed and hide, and some had hide or cloth covers. Some people carried babies for the entire first year of their lives, so baby carriers had to be strong and comfortable for the carrier and the baby. The carriers held the babies securely, perhaps strapped to a woman's back while she worked, leaving her hands free. Some could be leaned up against trees or supports, and others could be strapped to **horses**. **Inuit** women carried their babies in the hoods of special **parkas** called *amauti*.

Baby carrier decorations of carvings, **beads** and embroidery symbolized protection as well as being entertaining for the child. Today, decorated traditional baby carriers and carrier covers are made for show pieces and for special **gifts** to the parents and child, although they no longer have the widespread practical uses they once had. Modern manufactured baby carriers used worldwide by non-Indians are similar to the ideas and designs of Indian baby carriers.

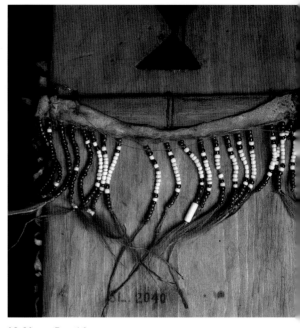

18 Above Detail from an early Cree cradleboard from Hudson Bay, decorated with beads and quills.

17 Right This 19th-century wooden Mohawk cradleboard, with an elaborately carved back and simple head piece and footrest, is from the St Regis area, on the border between Canada and the United States. The baby was bound to the board by a cover (missing) and a tumpline or burden strap.

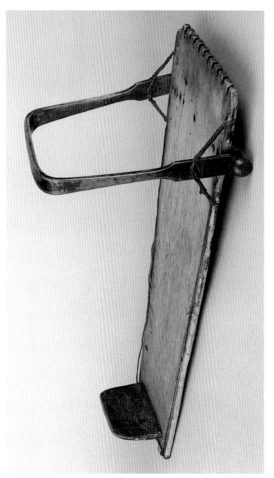

19 Right Horace Poolaw, a Kiowa **photographer**, took this picture of Lizzie Little Joe in Oklahoma in 1955. Wearing high-heeled shoes along with her traditional dress and the **elk** tooth decorated baby carrier, Mrs Little Joe embodied the ways in which Indian people merged the new Western ideas with traditional Indian ways.

My mother used to tell me that when I was still a baby in the cradle, she would strap my cradle to her saddle and drive a herd of ponies across the prairies, sometimes all day long.
Arapaho woman, c. 1930

Bandolier bag

Native peoples made all sorts of strapped bags, pouches and purses to carry tools, personal effects, cosmetics, plants, hunting and gathering tools and shot for rifles. Originally, they made bags from hide and decorated them with quills, shells, **feathers**, bone and animal hair. Following **contact** with European **traders**, bags were also made from trade cloth, trade **beads** and woven cloth. Some people developed very elaborate bandolier bags, so called because the straps went across the chest like a band. Most Southeastern bandolier bags hung from fingerwoven sashes, but the Choctaws, Alibamu and Koasati (Coushatta) often used belts from red trade cloth with the older white seed bead designs. Some men wore two belts or sashes, crossed over each side.

These bags often held ammunition and military and hunting equipment. Men later valued these bags as ceremonial or formal wear, even when they had no practical use anymore, and they can be seen today as part of **dance** costumes.

20 Above That the Choctaw men were wearing these bandoliers (minus the bags that usually accompanied them) with **feathered** hats in 1908, along with their Western-style, rural American clothing, shows how much the Choctaws had resisted the assimilation efforts directed toward them and their fellow Southeastern Native peoples (see **acculturation**). Note the **stickball** sticks in the hands of the man to the right. The Mississippi Choctaws, having resisted **Removal**, retained their language, traditional **foods** and **agricultural** lifestyle as well as the **music**, **dance** and **games** of their ceremonial life, even though they appeared to be 'Christianized' on the surface.[10]

21 and **22 Above** Ken Taylor, **Creek** and **Cherokee**, in 1992 making the 19th-century Southeastern-style bandolier bag (**top**). Ken reproduces old clothing styles that he studies in museum collections. The bag he is making won a prize for traditional costume at the prestigious annual Indian Market in New Mexico. It has white seed **beadwork** in Mississippian-period designs on flannel or red **trade** cloth.

Bark

Bark was one of the main materials used by Indians to make clothes, utensils, **transport** and housing. The skills involved in transforming tree bark into fibre that could be woven into cloaks or bent into a waterproof frame are complex. On the **Northwest Coast**, Native peoples made cedar bark into clothing and, in the area of the Great Lakes and the **Algonquin** Northeast, birchbark was used to make house walls, cooking vessels, **baskets** and **boats**. Birchbark was an invaluable material because it was thin, tough and waterproof, and Indians learned to manipulate it with steam, sap and ingenuity. Perhaps the most skilful use of bark was the birchbark canoe, an engineering innovation so perfect that it remains unchanged from its original design.

They always respect the birchbark… when you go you respect the trees because they make big canoes out of it …. It's based on respect for the birch, because you can make sutures out of it, sleds and lots of good out of it.

Belle Deacon, Athabaskan basketmaker

23 Left A 1940s replica of an 18th-century Mohawk-style birchbark pail used for collecting maple sap. For centuries, Indians in the Northeast exploited the maple tree each year, drawing sap and making sugar from it.

24 Above A very early **Beothuk** *Guin-ya-butt*, which means 'water **basket**' or bucket, made from birchbark and sewn roots.

Basket, basketmaking

Native peoples have woven baskets from plant materials such as vine, tree **bark**, branches, wood strips and grasses for more than 10,000 years. Basketry is one of the oldest and most widespread forms of work done by Native peoples and shows the most diverse use of materials, tools, shapes and forms of any craft. Ancient people used baskets, along with **pottery**, as their main utensils. Basket-weaving techniques were used to make **food** containers, storage containers for plants for **medicines**, mats, **fish** traps, clothes (such as **footwear**, **headgear** and cloaks), small water **dams**, animal pens and housing. Some baskets are so finely made that they are watertight; others so strong that they can be used for cooking. Even when made for the most basic of uses, Indians decorated their baskets. The three

25 Above This Nuu-chah-nulth/ Nootka cedar bark, nettle fibre and goat hair cloak was brought back to England by Captain James Cook from his third voyage in 1776–80 to the **Northwest Coast** of America.

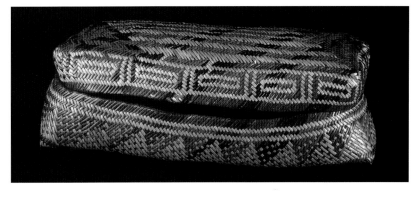

26 Below Nuu-chah-nulth/ Nootka people used this walrus bone or ivory tool to beat the cedar bark so that it could be spun and woven into material for clothing.

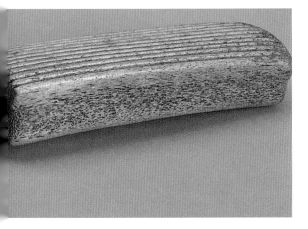

27 Above This 18th-century **Cherokee** lidded basket (*talusa*) is from South Carolina. It is plaited from river cane and dyed in natural dyes, which were probably made from pokeberries (*tsayatika*) or mulberries (for red/blue/purple), sumac (*kalogwa*) or walnut (*sedi*) (for black) and bloodroot (*gigage unastetsi*) or coreopsis flowers (for yellow). It is one of the two oldest known surviving Cherokee doubleweave baskets, brought to Sir Hans Sloane in 1725 by the colonial **British** Governor, Sir Francis Nicholson of South Carolina.

major techniques used in Native basketry are plaiting (**Cherokee**), coiling and sewing (Hopi) and twining (Hupa/**Yurok**/Karok).

Basketmaking – like weaving and pottery – is deeply connected to ceremonial and ritual life. It is taken very seriously because ancient stories associated it with the very origins of life. The way the materials are gathered and how the baskets are given and used are also very important. The techniques for gathering and preparing materials followed the seasons. The construction and design of the baskets were often accompanied by ritual, song and prayer. The **Inuit**, for instance, have many songs associated with gathering grasses. Yuroks credit rattlesnakes with being the first basketweavers, so they pray before they go into woods, hoping rattlesnakes will leave the fields. If a snake is seen leaving the fields, it is a sign that it has given permission to use the materials.[11] The **Navajo** have ceremonial

wedding baskets, and the religious rules about making these baskets are so strict that many Navajos have stopped making them, leaving the business of wedding basket manufacture to Paiutes, Utes and Hopis.

S ometimes I get sad because today we do not have very many old weavers left…. I get… upset when I hear people say that weaving is a dying art… that nobody is doing it… I'm doing it… I know… there are others… going to carry on that wisdom and that knowledge.
Susan Billy, Pomo basket weaver, in 1994

Basketmaking had economic significance for every Native group, whether or not they made them. Indians who made baskets always used them as a desirable trading item with other tribes and, eventually, in the Northeast, Great Lakes, the Great Basin and the Southwest as a trading item with Europeans. Indian baskets, made by men and women, also became a major part of the tourist trade. At Niagara Falls, Wisconsin Dells and the along the coast of Maine, **Mohawks**, **Senecas**, **Abenakis** and **Ojibwas** sold baskets to visitors. Some of those – such as the Adirondack pack basket, fish creels, Victorian sewing baskets and egg baskets – became the standard forms by which other baskets were known and judged.

Museums and private collectors acquired Indian baskets during the 19th century, particularly the complex and refined baskets of California, the Great Basin and Southwestern peoples.

T he earth is shaking
From our beating the basket drums.
A Tewa song from the Basket Dance

Now, where some Indians rarely make and need practical baskets for use in their communities, they make them for an external **art** market. Basketmaking materials, from often non-renewable resources, are threatened everywhere, and some suffer from pollution and environmental damage. Competition from low-cost baskets from Asia and Africa makes basket production for a commercial market unattractive. However, for as long as people need and want ceremonial baskets, basketmaking will continue in Native communities.

Most Southeastern Native peoples used river cane and rush, found in and near the waterways of the South, to make mats for ceremonial uses, and to make bedding, flooring, seating, lining walls, ceilings and containers. They stopped making many of the mats when they changed their houses to the log cabins and frame structures of white men. Their uses of baskets also changed. Baskets for gathering medicinal plants became egg or sewing baskets, also used by their white neighbours.

After **Removal**, Oklahoma **Cherokees** no longer had river cane (*ihya*) available to them and used oak (*tala*), hickory (*sohi*) and honeysuckle. For the Cherokees, then in North Carolina, river cane became scarce, threatened by extensive roadbuilding along old waterways and damage caused by carbon monoxide from cars. Both Eastern and Western Cherokee women have revived basketmaking, more for the tourist market and art market than for their own use, but also because basketmaking reflects a pride in maintaining ancient traditions. Where they can find river cane, Cherokee weavers still make doubleweave baskets.

My grandmother made baskets. When I was a little girl, I would go with her down in Southeastern Oklahoma to gather dye plants and buckbrush and honeysuckle…. I hated gathering black walnuts because they would stain my hands and clothes with a sticky black substance, and because they were hard to crack and eat. But… the pokeberries were juicy and fat and I loved the purple stain they made on everything. If we were gathering honeysuckle, I would help strip it of leaves and twigs, coil it in a circle for storing and carrying, then later strip off the bark after it was soaked and boiled…. My grandmother later in her life took the Baptist church very seriously and she stopped making medicines because the preachers told her it was heathen nonsense. So she didn't make medicine for her arthritis, which made her hands hurt, and she stopped making baskets.
Rayna Green, Cherokee folklorist

Beads, beadwork

Before **contact** with Europeans, Indians used beads made of clay, **quills**, **shells**, horn, **feathers**, ivory, bone and some **metal** (copper or lead) for ornamentation and design. When Europeans brought glass beads to the Americas, Native peoples adopted them immediately and they became a major part of the **trade** between Indians and Europeans. Indians used beads on clothing, implements, household goods and **horse** equipment. Beading societies replaced and supplemented the old women's quilling societies as women's trade networks elaborated on the beadwork traditions. Women of the Plains and the Plateau tribes specialized in beadwork. They used their skills to create elaborate and complex floral and geometric designs or beaded designs on cylindrical objects using the so-called 'peyote' stitch. Indians have used traditional techniques and designs to transform commercially manufactured objects and Western objects.

Ant was a very clever young man who wished to marry the daughter of a great chief. The latter told Ant he could not marry his daughter until he performed a difficult task. At that time, beads were scattered all over the earth, and the chief asked Ant to gather them all up, heaping each colour in a pile by itself. This seemed impossible to Ant, and he went to his Grandmother, Short-Tailed Mouse, for advice. She told him how to do it; so he accomplished his task, and won the girl. He heaped the beads in seven piles – red ones in the first, then blue, white, black, yellow, green, and bone beads in the seventh. After this, his father-in-law used beads on his clothes, and other people began to do the same.
A Salish story

Old One gave four bundles to a man who had treated him kindly. He gave the man a bundle each of porcupine quills, red headed woodpecker scalps, eagle tail feather and dentalium shells, telling the man that people had not valued these things before, but would value and use them from that time forward.
A Salish story

Since Indians started using European glass and ceramic beads (mostly from Italy and Czechoslovakia), they have been beading items of clothing and tools. In the 19th and 20th centuries, Plains Indians beaded doctor's bags and stethoscope ear pieces, ladies' shoes and evening bags as gift or

29 Above Nettie Watt (**Seneca**) made this early 20th-century style of shopping basket in 1985. She could make many of the older style baskets, such as a basket for washing hominy (hulled **maize**), rarely used nowadays. Most baskets like this one are made for a different market. The old shapes and forms have changed to fit more modern uses and decorative ideas.

presentation pieces for special friends. Nowadays, Indians bead everyday items of clothing (such as denim jackets) and presentation pieces (such as academic/graduation gowns). In some instances, expert beadworkers choose difficult objects, such as a mayonnaise jar or a pair of athletic shoes, to demonstrate their skills.

30 Below A 19th-century Dakota **Sioux** beaded vest. The beaded images, almost like ledger drawings, show an Indian warrior battling another Indian warrior and a Cavalry soldier.

31 Right A Plateau beaded vase, c. 1987. Great beadworkers attempt beaded objects like this one to show off their skills in an extremely difficult piece.

Beans

Native peoples developed many varieties of beans. They provide humans with one of the major sources of vegetable-based protein and amino acids. Like other legumes, beans return more nitrogen to the soil than they take out. Thus, they replenish the soil with nutrients removed by other crops, such as **maize**. Many can withstand heat, drought and disease, and can be grown in conditions that would starve other similarly nutritious and high yielding **food** crops. Throughout the Indian Country, they are intercropped (grown together) with maize and **squash** to meet most of the nutritional needs of the people who grow them. Along with maize and squash, they are sacred food for Indians and form the 'Three Sisters' of **Iroquois** religious belief.

Taken from wild seeds, beans have been cultivated for 8,000–10,000 years by Native Americans. By 1,000 AD maize, beans and squash were among the most important food plants in North America. Bean seeds were also traded from the Southwest to Mexico. Many Indians annually cultivated at least five varieties. Some villages may have held more than 15 different varieties in their seed stocks, planting them and replenishing them each year. The **Iroquois** once grew over 60 varieties of beans. Indians have continued to grow some of the varieties most important to them. Native farmers and environmental biologists interested in the preservation of old species and varieties, have cultivated some of the beans, once gathered wild, such as the tepary (*phaseolus acutifolius*).

The tepary is well suited to its native high desert where the growing conditions are hard. Tepary beans need less water and attract fewer pests than other types of beans. Until recently, teparies were used as a staple food by many Southwestern tribes, such as the Yuma, Tohono O'odham and **Zuni**. They are high in fibre and protein, and are rich in iron and calcium. They become even more nutritious when grown under desert conditions, because the amount of protein they contain increases in dry climates. Although extensive cultivation of tepary beans ceased among most Southwestern tribes at the beginning of the 20th century, current research indicates that by returning to a more traditional diet of high fibre and slowly digested tepary beans (as opposed to rapidly digested pinto beans) Southwestern Indians may be able to reverse the rise in diabetes.

So that is why the white tepary bean is the child of the Desert People. It was born here and endures dryness. When it doesn't rain enough, the white bean still comes up. The Desert People will always eat it and live here. The Milky Way is said to be the white bean. He lives clear across the sky. Beans grow in abundance and we see them scattered across the sky.

Sand Papago story

Bear

The bear – polar, brown, black, Kodiak and grizzly – is one of the most revered animals among Native peoples, along with salmon, **eagle**, **coyote**, **raven** and **buffalo**. For many Native peoples, the bear was a symbol and a source of power, wisdom and **medicine**, often taking human form. Sometimes the bear can have dangerous powers. At such times bears and bear power are to be avoided. The bear was often a **clan** animal, so there are many stories of bears in their human and bear form, and pictures of bears and bear paws (as well as actual fur and claws) are common on clothing and pots. **Navajos** believe that Changing Woman gave them the bear for protection, and bear imagery appears in their songs and **art**. On the Northern Plains, a special affinity for the bear existed among the **Blackfeet** and Assiniboine, giving men a special power to heal and the medicine power for war. Men of this group wore bear claw necklaces, carried bear shields and used knives set in bear jaw handles.

32 Below Marjorie Bear Don't Walk, a **Salish**-Chippewa designer, made this beaded bear claw necklace for her friend Rayna Green in 1994, telling her of the need for the ancient power and protection associated with the bear. Marjorie's brother obtained the bear claws and she did the **beadwork** onto them, stringing them onto old brass **trade** beads.

33 Left A bear-headed rattle from the **Northwest Coast**.

34 Below A bear paw is a common symbol on Santa Clara **pottery**. It is used on this blackware water jar (c. 1920) by the famous potter Margaret Tafoya. The bear represents good fortune to Santa Clara people; an old story tells of how the bear helped them find water during a drought.

23

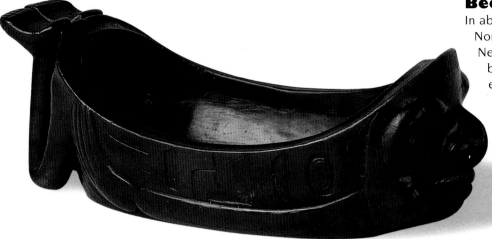

35 Above A **Haida** carved wooden **food** bowl inlaid with mother of pearl and haliotes **shell**. The bowl is in the form of an animal with some features of a beaver and its tail, but with an **eagle** and human face that forms the handle. It is highly polished from the oils of **fish** (eulachon) and sea mammals served in it. Bowls like this were greatly valued and used for feasts and ceremonial occasions that required the lavish hospitality of chiefs and their clans. The greater the carving on the food bowls, the higher the status of the chief giving the feast.

Beaver

In many tribes there are **clans** associated with beavers. The beaver was, for many peoples, a major source of food, fur and **medicine**. Beaver and deer were the main animals in the Eastern **fur trade**. Beaver hides were sent to make the **headgear** fashionable in Europe at the time. Those hides were certainly the most important currency in the 18th-century **Iroquois**-European trade. The **British** and French fought fiercely all over northeastern North America for the beaver trade, securing Indian allies and **hunters** in a competitive war that almost wiped out the beaver, as well as the deer, in the Southeast.

> Too great is what you are doing our chief.
> Who equals our chief?
> He is giving feasts to the whole world.
> *Tlingit potlatch song*

Beothuk

In about 1,000 BC, the Beothuks of the Northeastern Coast of North America (now Newfoundland and Labrador) may have been among the first Natives to encounter Viking sailors. When Europeans arrived, the Beothuks, weakened by **disease** and famine, battled with the French **fishermen** and settlers over resources. They are among the first groups to have had bounties placed on their scalps by governments. French and **British** settlers and fishermen drove the Beothuks into further starvation and isolation, ultimately into virtual extinction. Although some Beothuk descendants may have joined with traditional friends, such as the Montagnais in Labrador, the last identifiable Beothuk, a woman named Nancy Shanawdithit, died in 1829. They are thought to have been the first to be known by Europeans as 'Red Indians', because they used red ochre on their bodies and clothing, although the term was later generalized to other Indians.

36 Right A Beothuk bone/antler comb, possibly an amulet.

37 Below This fringe may have been part of the rectangular cloak, sometimes with a deep collar, worn by Beothuk men and women. Little of Beothuk culture survived their disappearance; a few pieces exist in the British Museum in London.

Bering Strait Theory

Since the mid 19th century, scholars have believed that the peoples called 'Indians' came to the Americas 12,000–60,000 years ago, over a land bridge formed during periods of glaciation. That land bridge (called the 'Bering Strait') stretched between the continents of America and Russia, in Siberia (or Beringia). Animals of the last Ice Age and then humans travelled across it over many thousands of years, coming in small groups to settle in the northern reaches of the Americas. According to the theory, they then travelled south, and many thousands of years later, around 300 BC, a new migration crossed the Bering Sea in **boats**. The different migrations might explain the many different **language** families and patterns of settlement of the highly diverse Native population of North America.

Although there is very little scientific evidence to dispute this theory, there is also very little to prove it, only the genetic and skeletal similarities of the Natives of Siberia, Asia and Native North America. Although continuing evidence suggests that Indians have been in North America for more than 20,000 years, most Native people would challenge the Bering Strait Theory. Each Native group has its own theory and origin/**creation story** about its beginnings, attached to the places which it finds sacred and significant.

Blackfoot, Blackfeet

The powerful Blackfoot Confederacy (Blackfoot in Canada, Blackfeet in the United States) was composed of the Blackfoot, Blood, Piegan and allied Sarcees and Gros Ventre. At the height of their power, the Blackfoot held vast areas from the Battle River to the Missouri River, covering much of the modern province of Alberta and the state of Montana. This area was short-grass high plains and they hunted in the foothills of the Rocky Mountains. Pressure from the **Cree** pushed them south until the Blackfoot were on the Bow River and the Blood and Piegan/Pikunni in southernmost Alberta and later Montana.

Originally, the Plains **Cree**, **Ojibwa** and Assiniboine were on friendly terms with the Blackfoot Confederacy, joining together to drive the Kutenai, who were trying to encroach on **buffalo** hunting, out of Southern Alberta. Disputes over **horses** caused the Gros Ventre to break with the Confederacy. At the beginning of the 19th century, the Cree and Assiniboine moved onto Blackfoot land and hostilities began. This warfare continued until the **reservation** period in 1870.

The Blackfoot were nomadic people, who travelled over great distances to hunt, trade and fight. After the decline of the buffalo due to overhunting by Europeans, the Blackfoot were obliged to sign **Treaty** Number 7 in 1877 and eventually to move onto reservations. Today, the Blackfoot occupy a reservation along the Bow River, the Blood south on a reservation near the Belly River, and the northern Piegan have a small reservation near the Blood. The Southern Piegan occupy the Blackfeet Reservation in Northern Montana, bordering the massive Glacier National Park. The Sarcee took land near Calgary.

Modern Blackfeet in Montana have lost millions of acres of land due to **allotment**, land leasing and government mismanagement, although stockraising and small enterprise, along with tribally controlled education, have given them back some measure of control over their lives.

Blankets

Until **contact**, Indians wore robes of animal fur, hide and **feathers** for warmth and cover. A few peoples in the Northwest and Southwest had woven materials. When the Europeans arrived, especially in the 18th century, woven wool and cloth blankets became the major item for the Indian trade. The Hudson's Bay Company blankets, for example, set the standards for the trade **economy**. A blanket which had four or five woven marks on it indicated that it was worth four or five **beaver** or deer skins. Particular blankets, associated with particular companies, were sought after at different times.

The private Pendleton Company made other types of blankets that, like some Hudson's Bay blankets, are still in use and still immensely popular with Indians. Some Pendleton patterns were heavily influenced by Spanish designs; others adopted **Navajo**, then Great Basin and Plains designs. One of the most important patterns is the 'Chief Joseph Pattern' – named after Chief Joseph (1840–1904), the Nez Percé leader who led his people into exile escaping the US Army.

Indian women developed uses for blankets other than just as cloaks and

38 Below Rayna Green wears a modern capote coat, made in 1992 from a new Hudson's Bay blanket by Marjorie Bear Don't Walk, a **Salish**/Chippewa designer. This red blanket coat is typical of the coats that **hunters**, trappers and **traders** wore in the 19th-century Canadian West during the **fur trade**.

padding. They cut them up to make baby blankets, bags, pouches and leggings. Blankets (mostly Pendletons and Hudson's Bays), shawls (adapted from the Spanish) and quilts were used for **dance** and for **diplomatic** and ceremonial **gifts**.

We welcome our children with a handmade quilt or small Pendleton blankets as we wrap them in our prayers... . For a couple's marriage, we share wisdom and a feast that includes cornmeal mush. To honour the occasion, the woman's body is draped with a Pendleton shawl, the man's with a Pendleton robe. As we move into old age, we pay tribute to the spirit world with ceremony, prayers and gifts. Often we bury our people with their special possessions and beautiful Pendleton blankets.
Rain Parrish, Navajo artist, 1997

A blanket is an extension of an Indian man's status and feelings. In the past, an Indian man judged wealth and status in numbers of horses. Today, trade blankets are like horses were in past times... if a man's daughter is chosen to be a princess for a gathering... he shows his appreciation by giving blankets to the people who bestowed this honour on his daughter... . When a man receives a blanket as a gift from a special person... he will consider this blanket above all other blankets... . A blanket is the most prized gift and it is given for special reasons... to express appreciation to someone who has come from afar to attend the dances... to a person or a family who has shown kindness in hard times or in times of sorrow over a lost loved one... to acknowledge someone for their |work|... giving the gift is important... receiving a blanket is another show of acceptance.
Bob Block, Osage, 1997

Boats

Three basic types of canoes were used by Indians. The first was the elm, birch**bark** or animal hide covered wooden frame used in the Northeast and Great Lakes. The second was the whole log dugout used on the Northwest Coast, where people hunted large mammals on the open sea. The third was the plank canoe from Northern California. Some **Northwest Coastal** peoples recently brought back the construction of plank and dugout canoes in order to restore the ceremonial life connected with the boats, hunting and seagoing.

Canoes, dugouts and kayaks (and their larger relative, the *umiak*) were associated with war and hunting, and so with survival and danger. This meant that building and navigating them were processes filled with ritual, **ceremony**, songs, prayers and charms. Those who made these vehicles were highly skilled, and able to follow the rituals needed to complete the work to make a boat both technically and spiritually good.[12]

Native people developed types of boats other than the canoe. Typical in the Northern Plains was a kind of skin boat called the bullboat. Mandan and Hidatsa people used these to navigate rivers and streams. Animal (including **buffalo** bull) hide covered a rounded frame, made of bent wood like the top of their earth lodges. Although these bullboats were not as easy to manoeuvre as the kayak or canoe, they did provide basic water-going transport for land-based people who needed to **transport** small loads.

My family made these travels in sealskin boats, which were wooden frames covered with sealskins. They used to be called the women's boats because they were sewn by the women.
Pitseolak, an Inuit artist

39 Above A model of an *umiak*, an **Inuit** boat for several people.

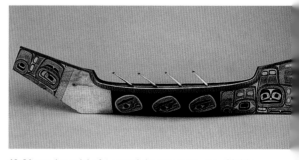

40 Above A model of a carved dugout ocean-going **Haida** canoe, used for hunting, trade and ceremonial purposes. These excellent, sculptured canoes hold from two to twenty people.

Boudinot, Elias

Elias Boudinot (c. 1804–39) was the first American Indian editor and publisher. He was originally called Buck Watie (born *Galagina*), and was the brother of the famed **Cherokee** Confederate General Stand Watie. He began his literary career as a Bible translator for the **missionary**, Samuel Worcester. Sent to a Moravian mission **school** by his family when he was a small boy and tutored by a white minister, Reverend Boudinot, Watie took the name Boudinot in the man's honour. When he entered theological college in the East, he fell in love with a white woman, and in marrying her, caused protest even from the **Christian** whites who supported Indian causes. He went home to Georgia, and from 1828 to 1832, he published the *Cherokee Phoenix*, the first Indian newspaper. The newspaper – devoted to Cherokee culture, history and politics – was printed in New Echota, Georgia in the Cherokee syllabary (a set of characters representing syllables), developed by **Sequoyah**, and in English. The *Phoenix* printed the laws of the Cherokee Nation, local, national and international news, scripture, editorials and advertisements. It inspired generations of tribal and Indian newspapers and magazines. After **Removal** and Boudinot's death, the *Phoenix* ceased to operate. The newspaper, revived as the *Cherokee Advocate*, was published again in Indian Territory by the Cherokees in 1844–1906 and again today by the Cherokee Nation of Oklahoma.

To obtain a correct and complete knowledge of these people, there must first exist a vehicle of Indian intelligence… . Will not a paper published in Indian Country… have the desired effect? I do not say Indians… may exhibit specimens of their intellectual efforts, of their eloquence, of their moral, civil and physical advancement, which will do quite as much to remove prejudice and to give profitable information.
Elias Boudinot, 1826

Boudinot, his brother Watie, his uncle (The Ridge) and others who were involved in the Removal Party insisted that Cherokees' safety lay in a move to Indian Territory. This was a feeling not shared by others in the Cherokee Nation. The **Treaty** Party was in favour of negotiation with government on Removal, but the elected government of John Ross forbade any debate on the topic. In 1828 Boudinot and others illegally signed the Treaty of New Echota with the US government, agreeing to Removal and the confiscation of Cherokee lands in Georgia. Cherokees exacted the law of blood revenge on Boudinot and the other Treaty signers, such as Boudinot's uncle, assassinating them in Indian Territory after Removal.

You must not remain longer in your contact with the Whites. Sure safety lies in isolation. Fly – fly for your lives.
Elias Boudinot on the subject of Removal

41 Above The front page of the Cherokee *Phoenix* on 4 June 1828.

Bow and arrow

A highly efficient tool for hunting and self-defence, the bow and arrow epitomizes the skills of the Indian male. Bows and arrows are some of humankind's oldest tools (the oldest bow in North America is at least 5,500 years old). Unlike arrowheads, they show very little variation in form, although much variation in material, decoration and accompanying carrying cases. Indian bows and arrows are forms of bent and straightened hardwoods, and whether small (for birds) or large (for animals and humans), they are ingenious devices. Like the 'atlatl' (the ancient object used to propel spears), they increase the force of the projectile. Making and using these devices was an essential and highly valued skill among men. As early colonists discovered to their surprise, a man using a bow and arrow could easily outfire a man using the awkward, heavy, long rifles first brought by Europeans to the Americas.

42 Below This Omaha bow and arrows with quiver is made of Osage orange or bois'd'arc wood, and the quiver is made of mountain lion skin. It was probably collected by Duke Friederich Paul Wilhelm of Wurtemburg on his voyage to North America in 1823.

Box of treasures

Northwest Coastal peoples often carved and painted boxes which represented the **clan** histories, maps, laws, genealogies, symbols, **name**, origins, social ranks and duties (*ada'ox*). These boxes were brought out at important occasions when the history and laws of the people were recited. In 1997 in a ruling for the clan houses of the Gitksan and Wet'suwet'en nations, the Supreme Court of Canada decreed that the laws and testimonies described in such ways had standing in courts when considering the settlements of aboriginal titles. When, in the court, the hereditary chiefs 'opened their bent-cedar boxes', according to their tradition, their 'box was full'.

43 Right The making of both a straight-sided and bentwood box is one of the most difficult tasks for a woodworker. That challenge was more than met by the skilled woodcarvers on the **Northwest Coast**. This grooved, steamed, bent and carved **Tlingit** bentwood 'box of treasures' stored crest hats and clan regalia that kept and told the history of the clan.[13]

44 Right On the Northwest Coast, high-ranking Tlingit men, the hereditary chiefs of their clans, wore these crest hats (*at.oow*) at feasts and **potlatches**. The hats are skilfully made with intricate twining of spruce roots and are painted in the traditional colours of red, black and blue. Some believed that each of the cylinders on top of the hat represented a potlatch given by the owner. Others believe that the number of cylinders is associated with a particular crest fixed long ago. Similar hats were worn by and made for Pacific Eskimo, Chugatch and Koniaq men, probably received in trade with Tlingit.[14]

Brant, Joseph

Joseph Brant (*Thayendanega*) (*c.* 1742–1807) was, like **Red Jacket**, a powerful non-hereditary chief of the **Iroquois** Confederacy. He favoured alliances with Europeans instead of war. His grandfather was among the four Indian 'kings' who visited Queen Anne's Court in London in 1710. Joseph and his sister, **Mary (Molly) Brant**, were among the most influential Iroquois of the 18th century. They were comfortable in both **Mohawk** and English societies. Yet to some Iroquois, they were traitors because of their affiliations with the **British**. His sister was the common-law wife of Sir William Johnson, the Commander of British Colonial Indian Affairs in the North (New York and Canada). Brant was generally able to negotiate favourable agreements for his people. After the American War of Independence, the British offered him land in Canada as compensation for losing his territory to the Americans during the war, and he led a group of Mohawks, **Senecas** and **Cayugas** to settle there in 1784. The descendants of those people now live on the Six Nations Reserve in Canada.

45 Above A 1786 painting, *Joseph Brant, Mohawk Indian*, by Gilbert Stuart, who was known for his portraits of men such as George Washington. Notice Brant's silver gorget given to him by his **British** allies, and the **trade** silver brooches worn on his very Iroquoian headpiece and European-style collar. Brooches like these and, later, Iroquois-made brooches, had symbols of **clans** and European church and social groups, such as the masons.

Brant, Mary/Molly

Mary Brant, or Molly as she was called, was the sister of **Joseph Brant**. She was highly placed politically in the **Iroquois** nations because she was a **clan** mother. As the common-law wife of Sir William Johnson, Commander of **British** Colonial Indian Affairs, she had a powerful influence on Iroquois affairs. Nevertheless, although several portraits and mementoes of Joseph Brant have been preserved, no object commemorating Molly Brant's place in history has surfaced.

In 1762, *Kanadiohora*, a **Seneca**, told Sir William Johnson that he was to come and speak to the Council, at the request of the women. However, Johnson was opposed to both men and women attending the Council meetings with the British. He insisted that only the chiefs should come, as with British practice. *Kanadiohora* said, 'It was always the Custom for them to be present at Such Occasions (being of Much Estimation Amongst Us, in that we proceed from them and they provide our Warriors with Provisions when they go abroad), they were therefore Resolved to come down.'[15] It is ironic that Johnson should have been the one to disrupt the traditional power of the women, as, by marrying Molly Brant, he had benefited greatly from the relationship and access to influence brought by his own wife.

Our Ancestors considered it a great Transgression to reject the Council of their Women, particularly the female Governesses. Our Ancestors considered them Mistresses of the soil. Our Ancestors said who bring us forth, who cultivate our Lands, who Kindles our Fires and boils our Pots, but the Women, they are the Life of the Nation.
Domine Pater or Good Peter, a Seneca-Cayuga orator, 1788

British, The

When the British founded what became the first permanent settlement in North America at Jamestown, Virginia, in 1607, they were one of the first groups of colonists to encounter and displace Indians in the Americas. They engaged in **wars** and battles with the other settlers, and with the support of various Indian groups, they gained or kept **land** and power in the former Indian territories. However, in general, like the French and

Dutch, they tried to play one Native alliance off another in cycles of **treaty** making, mutual aid, **trade** and peacemaking. Most tribes supported the British in the American War of Independence of 1775 (the Revolutionary War), as the American rebels clearly represented the interests of encroaching settlers. After the American defeat of the British, such support resulted in no **status** for Indian allies of the British in the Treaty of Paris of 1783.

The Crown had official Indian policies administered through the colonial government, such as that run by Sir William Johnson in the 18th century. In New England, the Southeast and the Mid Atlantic, British military, religious and commercial interests had different relationships with various Indian groups and with other

European groups, depending on their negotiations over Indian lands with commercial potential (such as for **tobacco** and **maize**). Through the Hudson's Bay Company, the British (English, Scots and Irish) established trading posts and trading relationships with Indians who brought **furs**.

The **Royal Proclamation** of 1763 and the Indian Act of 1876 established in Canada the equivalent of the US **Bureau of Indian Affairs**, called the Department of Indian Affairs, creating an administrative office for the Crown's relationships with Indians. These Acts also created boundaries for colonies, establishing the incongruities typical of the US relationships with Indians, pushing Indians onto lands then taken by whites. In Canada, the British government (like its US cousin) had decided in 1830 to set aside lands where Indians could be 'Christianized' and 'civilized', and had entered into **treaties** with tribes in exchange for the hand-over of lands. In return, the tribes were guaranteed reserve lands, annual payments, education and other services.

47 Left Different kinds of **gift**s were exchanged between allies or those hoping to make **diplomatic** and military alliances. The British, Dutch and, later, 'Americans' liked the presentation tomahawks and silver gorgets (the tomahawk being emblematic of the Indian **wars** in North America). This 18th-century pipe tomahawk, made for **Joseph Brant**, but never given to him after he escaped to Canada, is engraved with a typical scene in which an Indian is tomahawking an enemy, with the other side showing the common engraving of two hands shaking in peace and friendship.

Buffalo

The animal ancestors of the buffalo (called *bison bison* or the 'American bison') have lived since the second Ice Age. These huge mammals lived on the vast grasslands of the American Plains and Midwestern Prairies, although some smaller types inhabited the Appalachian hills, the grasslands in the Southwest and the desert of the Sonora. Indians from these areas always had a special relationship with the buffalo which, before the arrivals of Europeans and their **horses** and guns, formed a major part of their spiritual and day-to-day life.

Buffalo were hunted by Indians. Their meat was used as **food**, their hides were

46 Above The **Iroquois** valued silver as a symbol of spiritual purity, strength and prestige. They adopted the art of silversmithing and the giving of silver **gifts** from the Europeans. Settlers and diplomats presented gorgets like this one to Indians as a sign of respect, as evidence of the wealth of white colonists and to encourage **trade** and friendship. This gorget is engraved with a British coat of arms and bears the mark of Dutch silversmith Barent Ten Eyck of Albany, New York. It is inscribed with the name 'Daniel Cryn' and dated 1755. It is possibly related to the family 'Kryn', Mohawks of Caughnawaga, a **mission** at Sault-Ste Marie.

used as clothing and housing, and their bones were made into tools. The hides were also used as canvases on which the Indians painted their personal and tribal histories. Some paintings on the hides, called Winter Counts, were an attempt to record the events and significant moments of each calendar. Others, made by individuals, painted a history symbolic of significant events in their lives.

The near extinction of the buffalo on the Plains of North America, slaughtered by American and Canadian hide hunters at the end of the 19th century, came to symbolize the probable disappearance of Indians. By 1880, the Canadian Prairies were empty of buffalo. The **Sioux wars** came as a direct result of hunters and the military separating Indians from, and starving them of, their major resource. The United States and Canada enacted laws and regulations that further separated Indians from the buffalo. The military protected the **traders**, **hunters** and cattle ranchers. Hunters who formerly only took winter long-haired buffalo for their hides, throwing the meat away, developed a

48 Above In the late 19th century, imprisoned Indians and Indians sent to boarding **schools** began drawing pictures of their lives and histories on paper given them by their captors. A Cheyenne named Bear's Heart made this 'ledger' drawing of men hunting buffalo and men and women in tipis.

method of processing short-haired animals. The resulting slaughter was immense. Then hunters bought buffalo guns, rifles that could kill the animals at some distance. The buffalo all but disappeared. Once the Indians had been placed on **reservations**, the new cattle industry grew, with its profits coming from cheap or free Indian lands and sales of new range-bred cattle to the government to feed then-starving tribes.

However, cattle could not replace the buffalo in the ceremonial life of the people. The Sioux continued to tell the story of White Buffalo Calf Woman who brought the 'Way of the **Pipe**' and Truth to the people. They believed she would return when the tribes drove out the whites and returned to their old ways. *Wovoka*, the Paiute prophet, said that the buffalo would return if the people performed the **Ghost Dance**. The buffalo spirit was the source of warrior bravery and even the **Cherokees** and the Pueblos, who lost access to buffalo long before their brothers on the Plains, kept songs, **dances** and masks of this important animal.

Although the tribes were never able to restore life on the Plains and although they shifted their attentions to beef for everyday **food** and to deer or **elk** meat and their skins when they could get them, they never forgot the buffalo. Buffalo remains the ceremonial food and buffalo imagery continues to dominate **art**. Recently, Indian people, environmentalists and ranchers have revived buffalo raising. Tribes have worked together to bring buffalo to Indian Country and to restore grasslands and prairies devastated by drought and huge agricultural development.

49 Below This watercolour, *Buffalo Dancers, c.* 1925, is by Awa Tsireh (Alphonse Roybal), a Pueblo artist. Pueblos still perform annual Buffalo Dances, symbolic of the times when buffalo were important to them, and they would exchange valued goods with buffalo hunting Comanche **traders**.

50 Below Dennis Fox, Jr. (Mandan, Hidatsa and **Sioux**) painted this hide of a young buffalo in 1992. On it, he tells his version of Hidatsa history. Fox shows the changes with the coming of the railroads, **missionaries** and cavalry, the change from the buffalo to cattle, and the change from growing **maize** to a dependency on goods bought from stores and **traders**.

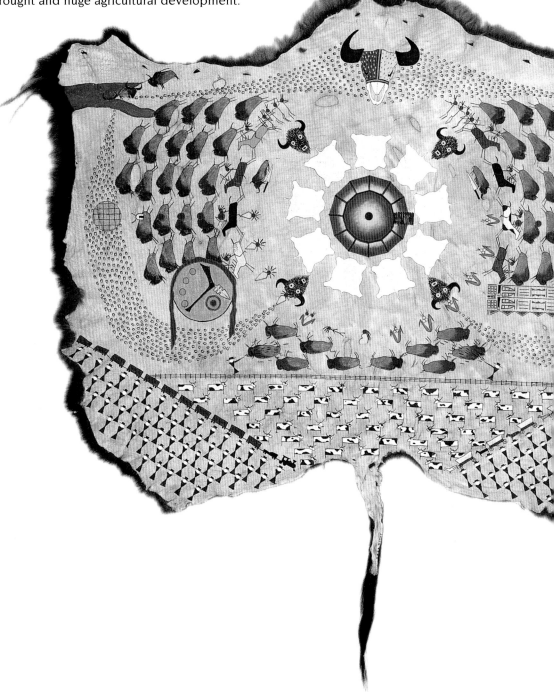

51 Right Anna Old Elk, a young Crow and **Sioux** Indian, wears Dennis Fox's painted buffalo hide to show the way such hides – painted and perhaps **quilled** – would have been worn by Plains Indians in the 19th century.

Bureau of Indian Affairs

The US War Department created the Office of Indian Trade in 1806 to manage the relationships between the government and the Indians. The Office had dealt particularly with **land**, **treaties** and the 'Indian trade'. The Bureau of Indian Affairs (BIA) was created in 1824, primarily to manage treaty-making and trade; it was moved in 1849 from the War Department to the Department of Interior. After the **Civil War**, the BIA handed over much of its authority to Indian agents and, sometimes, to **missions** and churches. The Indian agents distributed rations and goods, managed **schools** and supervised lands under treaty agreements. They also supervised **allotment** from the 1880s until the early 1900s. Essentially, they stripped any remaining power from the **tribal governments** and leaders.

In 1934, a new Commissioner of the BIA, an anthropologist called John Collier, helped halt the government's official policy of **Christianization** and 'assimilation' (see **acculturation**) and initiated reforms in tribal government that still remain controversial. Despite Collier's reforms, however, the BIA managed to supervise the **termination** of 100 tribes during the 1950s.

Today, the BIA has four main functions: education, services to **reservations** (such as housing, roadbuilding and the management of natural resources), economic development and BIA operations. The BIA operates tribal schools, hospitals and clinics, and is meant to protect Native American land and resources. Increasingly, it is supposed to support tribes in taking responsibility for the administration of the government's programmes and services of benefit to Indians.

Indians have a complex relationship with the BIA and, indeed, with the US government. Indians in the 1960s used to say that BIA meant 'Bosses Indians Around'. Indians accuse the BIA and the Department of Interior of corruption, inefficiency, wastefulness and bureaucracy. However, the BIA represents the carrying out of the government's promises to Indians through treaties, the so-called 'trust relationship'; so, for many Indians, the BIA and reservations may be the only visible symbol left of that continued relationship.

So far, the self-determination policy can only be judged a limited success. BIA administration and budget control continue to severely constrain tribal governments and Indian reservation communities. Despite continuing tribal efforts to decentralize BIA administrative and budgetary powers, the BIA will most likely remain a major force in Indian affairs… well into the next century.

Duane Champagne, Turtle Mountain Chippewa scholar

Calendars and time

In the Americas before the coming of Europeans, each group kept their own calendar with their own systems for marking the passage of time and the seasons. The Maya and Aztec referred to years simply as specific annual periods based on their complex calendric system. Most calendric systems in Native North America were based on solar (sun) or lunar (moon) and stellar (star-based) observation and systems to predict their seasonal round of **hunting**, **farming** and **ceremonial** life. Calendars and astronomical observation are linked. Indian people took note of and recorded (by word of mouth or in pictures) happenings on Earth and in the skies. Pictorial stories, called Winter Counts, were painted on animal hide or paper by tribal historians on the Plains. These were historical records of important events and changes in the lives of groups and individuals. These included astronomical and celestial events (such as eclipses, meteor showers, earthquakes and floods), the battles and deeds of warriors, events such as the time when the Pawnees stole many Lakota **horses**, the deaths of important people, the coming of smallpox and measles epidemics, and even important mythological events (such as the bringing of the **buffalo** and the **pipe** by White Buffalo Calf Woman).

Indians had many ways of keeping and telling time, and marking events. Calendar sticks of all sorts were common. Before the Pueblo Revolt, runners took a deerskin strap with knots tied in it to each of the pueblos (towns), telling them to untie one knot each day, and the last knot would be the day to begin the resistance to the Spanish.[16]

52 Above In this photograph of 1921, Joseph Head (Pima) holds a calendar stick made from the ribs of a saguaro cactus. The stick's markings begin with 'the night the stars fell', noting an 1833 meteor shower visible in the Southwestern desert.

January was *Wicogandu*, Centre Moon (also Big Moon)... February was *Amhanska*, Long Dry Moon... March was *Wicinstayazan*, Sore Eye Moon... (snow blindness was common)... April, *Tabehatawi*, Frog's Moon... May, *Induwiga*, Idle Moon... June, *Waweqosmewi*, Full Leaf Moon... July, *Wasasa*, Red Berries Moon... August, *Capsapsaba*, Black Cherries Moon (Chokecherries)... September, *Wahpegiwi*, Yellow Leaf Moon... October, *Anukope*, Joins Both Sides (the middle)... November, *Cuhotgawi*, Frost Moon... December, *Wicogandu-sungagu*, Centre Moon's Younger Brother.... Old men kept account of the days in a moon by notching on their pipe cleaners, one notch for a day. These pipe cleaners were made from a small willow branch the size of a pencil and about a foot long. A row of notches the length of a pipe cleaner would constitute a moon period, or a month.... One of these sticks notched down four sides counted four months, and three fully notched sticks made a full year.
James Larpenteur Long, Assiniboine

Ultimately, Indians were forced to work and live to the Western clock. The **school** bell, the **mission** bell, the **Christian** calendar, the watch and the train schedule all altered the way in which Indians had measured time and the periods of their lives.

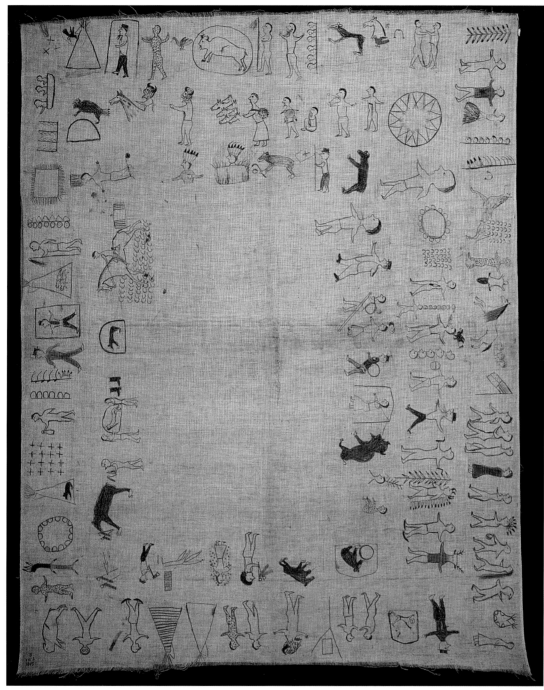

53 Above A Winter Count, painted onto hide.

Many **treaties** were negotiated in Canada after the **Royal Proclamation** in 1763. Native groups worked hard to obtain fair agreements for their lands and to retain certain basic rights. The government saw its role as to protect, **civilize** and gradually move Native people into the mainstream society. The **British** North America Act (now known as the Constitution Act of 1867), which formed Canada, gave the Canadian government responsibility for Indians. The Indian Act of 1876 put them in a different legal category from all other Canadians. This division was meant to further the federal assimilation policy (see **acculturation**), but instead restricted Native people and isolated them.

Women who married non-Native men were removed from Indian **status** (recognition as Indians by the government). Men who did the same did not lose their status and the non-Native wives of Native men automatically became Native. Anyone who obtained a university degree or a profession could be removed from status and Native men and women could give up their status for lump sum payments of money. The Act banned any festival, dance or other ceremony that involved giving or paying money or goods, and gave the

The train was called the Chili Line... people kept time by the whistle because... the one that came from the North always came by about the same time. So when people were out in the fields working, they went by the whistle... well, people didn't have wristwatches and they went by the line of the sun and their shadows, just knowing that it's noontime and time to go home. But anyway, they changed from the shadow to the sound of the whistle.
Esther/Estefanita Martinez, San Juan Pueblo

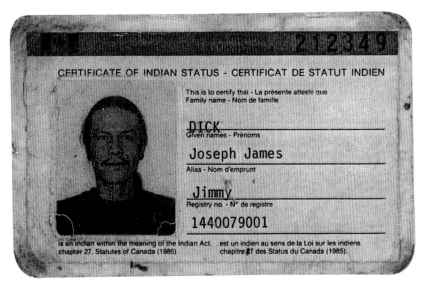

54 Above This Canadian Indian **status** or band card identifies a person from the Moose Factory Reserve. Unlike Certificates of Degree of Indian Blood (CDIB's) or tribal enrolment cards in the United States, Canadian Indian status cards do not show blood quantum (see page 40).

Indian agents complete control over **reservations**. In 1951 revisions to the Act reduced government powers and dropped the ban on ceremonies. In 1960, voting rights were granted to Native people and it was possible for them to obtain Canadian **citizenship**.

In 1969, the Canadian government proposed sweeping changes to the Indian Act and the way in which Native relationships with the government were structured. The Indian Act continues to prohibit First Nations from ownership of the reservations, rights to resources and personal property. People who live on reservations do not pay any personal property or land taxes, although on-reserve employment can be taxed. Some recent negotiations have allowed for transfer of some responsibilities to First Nations communities and some bands now have control over their own finances, education and social programmes. A few bands have also recently negotiated self-government (**self-determination** in the United States) agreements which give them more control over their lands and resources.

> L et no-one forget it… we are a people with special rights guaranteed to us by promises and treaties. We do not beg for these rights, nor do we thank you… because we paid for them… and God help us the price we paid was exorbitant.
>
> *Chief Dan George, Squamish Nation*

Following changes to the Act in 1985, any

woman who lost status through the Act's original provisions can now regain it without marrying another Native. In the future, two Native parents will be able to pass on their status. A child with one Native parent will be considered Native, but will not be able to pass on status to his or her children. By late 1994, approximately 93,000 people had obtained status under this Act.

Cayuga

This Nation of the **Iroquois** Confederacy originally lived on the shores of Cayuga Lake in Western New York State. Their name means, 'the place where locusts were taken out'. The community has four **clans** and ten delegates in the Grand Council of the Haudenosaunee. After the American Revolution, large parts of the tribe were removed to Canada and scattered to Ohio, Oklahoma and Wisconsin. Cayugas also joined with **Senecas** on the Cattaraugus and Allegany **reservations**. They began official land claims for their original homelands in the late 1970s and are still negotiating them in the late 1990s. Today, gaming provides huge revenue to a number of Cayuga communities.

Ceremony

All Native people, indeed all peoples everywhere in the world, engage in some forms of ceremonial life. Whether based in an organized, written and 'official' religious philosophy (such as Judaism, Islam, **Christianity** or Buddhism) or in less organized spiritual beliefs, every culture has means of religious observation structured in a ceremonial way.

Ceremonies are characterized by the participation of special people and/or special roles played by people who otherwise lead ordinary lives. These people wear special clothing, offer special prayers and perform **dances**, songs and acts (rites or rituals) as part of the ceremony. For most Native people, ceremony was a part of daily life – from the daily prayers and songs at dawn or sunset to the elaborate rituals surrounding healing, **hunting** or **war**. Ceremonies ensured that things would go well, by restoring balance and harmony in relationships. Some ceremonies or rituals were given to the people in their origin stories (or myths). These important stories about their past

55 Above A common Pueblo way to store ceremonial or **dance** clothing was on a pine pole. This one – provided by a Santa Clara Pueblo man – hung in the house from the ceiling. The evergreen pine is important, and evergreens are used as part of a dancer's ceremonial costumes. On the pole hangs a Pendleton **blanket** shawl, a woman's back shawl (*aahi*); **turtle-shell** rattles (*oku*); a man's **rain** sash/belt (*se'yen*); a **Navajo**-style woven belt (*se'yen*); a girl's black *manta* (dress) from San Ildefonso Pueblo; a woman's embroidered *sega* (dress) made by Janice Baca, Santa Clara Pueblo; a man's shell **bandolier** (*ove*), worn across the chest; a boy's kilt (*waage*) made by Janice Baca; a man's fox skin (Dee Khowaa), and a man's skunk fur anklets (*saa*). The year-round presence of ceremonial clothing reminds family members of their ceremonial responsibilities.

described certain songs, clothes or objects (often thought to be prayers in a material form). The sandpaintings made by **Navajo** singers (*hataali*), the Hopi **Bean** Dance, Longhouse singings and sitting at the **drum** were all given to people by specific characters or figures (human, animal or spirit) in their stories.

Some **games** and dances once served important ceremonial functions, often built around the calendar, as prayers to the gods. They expressed the hope for fertility, for **rain**, for giving and prolonging life or for healing. They also provided entertainment and a chance for people to display physical powers. **Iroquois, Ojibwa, Cherokee** and Muskogean peoples (**Creeks** and **Seminoles**) played lacrosse and **stickball**, not only as a form of mock war, but also as a healing ritual.

Come and be blessed, come to the people of the village and let them give you thanks. They will feed your spirits with corn meal and sing their songs of love for you.
The people will wear the costumes of ceremonial, and their women will shower blessings upon you.
San Juan Pueblo song

The Holy People gave us this earth to live on. That is Hozhoni, or beauty, which the Diné are required to live by. When something goes wrong… the effort to achieve beauty is destroyed. We… have a… Ceremony to make things right.
Jesse Biakeddy, Big Mountain Navajo

Cherokee

The Cherokee (*Tsalagi*), who also called themselves The Real People (*Aniyunwiya*), had been living in the Southern Appalachian region for centuries when they began to have frequent **contact** with **explorers** from other continents in the early 1700s. The arrival of outsiders, particularly Anglo-Americans, brought dramatic changes to their way of life. Early in the 1700s, the Cherokee started using guns rather than **bows and arrows** to **hunt** large animals. As the men became skilled with guns and traps and killed more deer, they traded in deerskins for European goods, such as **metal** hoes, knives, axes, copper kettles, cloth and **blankets** and more guns and ammunition. This brought more European goods into Cherokee daily life and depleted the hunting grounds. Now hunters had to travel farther and stay away longer in search of deer. Women, the **farmers** in Cherokee life, took time away from the fields to prepare hides for the **trade**. Like the men, their traditional areas of power, authority and skill were undermined. However, with the goods came the newcomers' greed for **land**, and Cherokees took up arms in defence of their homelands.

By the 1790s, the Cherokees were plagued by **war** with frontier Anglo-Americans, extreme poverty and severe **food** shortages. They realized that they could not preserve their Nation by war and decided instead to make peace. The US government encouraged Cherokees to farm in the Anglo-American style, with its unfamiliar values of individual effort and profit. In return, the government promised full and equal **citizenship** to Cherokees and other American Indians.

In the face of cultural and political war, some Cherokees clung to their ancient traditions. Others adopted **Christianity**, European-style **farming** and other aspects of white culture. To drive the Cherokees from their Southeastern homeland, the majority of US policymakers and most citizens ignored the Cherokees' rights, guaranteed in **treaties**, US law and court decisions, to remain on their land. Cherokees and other Southeastern Indians became a main target of **Removal**. In 1838, the Administration run by Andrew Jackson brutally tore most of them from their homelands and sent them to Indian Territory.

God is dissatisfied that you are receiving the white people in your land without any distinction. You yourselves see that your hunting is gone – you are planting the corn |maize| of the white people – go and sell that back to them and plant Indian corn and pound it in the manner of your forefathers; do away with the mills. The Mother of the Nation has forsaken you because all her bones are being broken through the grinding |of the mills|. She will return to you, however, if you put the white people out of the land and return to your former manner of life. You yourselves can see that the white people are entirely different beings from us; we are made of red clay; they out of white sand. You may keep good neighbourly relations with them.
Vision experienced by three Cherokees, 1811

The lands in question belong to Georgia. She must and will have them.
Resolution of the Georgia Legislature, December 1827

The Cherokees have been stripped of every attribute of freedom and eligibility for legal self-defence… . We are denationalized! We are disenfranchised! … . We are deprived of membership in the human family! We have neither land, nor home, nor resting-place, that can be called our own.
John Ross in a letter to the US Congress, 1835

The Cherokee's Removal became known as the Trail of Tears. The Cherokee, Choctaw, Chickasaw, **Creek**, **Seminole** and numbers of other Midwestern and Eastern tribes (such as the Delaware, Sac and Fox, Miami and Cayuga) were promised protection in their own Indian Territory once removed from their traditional homelands, but they did not receive it. Further attacks by the US Army, **missionaries**, agents and **traders** made Indian separation impossible. The **Civil War**, **allotment** and the disbanding of Indian Territory in 1906 further damaged Cherokee **sovereignty**.

About 1,100 Cherokees managed to avoid Removal, and most settled in North Carolina. As they lived on non-tribal lands outside the main Cherokee Nation, they were not taken by the US Army. Few wanted to assimilate into Anglo-American society, and their remote mountainous locations limited contact with outsiders. Change came gradually to the Eastern Band of Cherokee Indians, but traditional beliefs, pastimes and lifestyles endured. Some Eastern Cherokees had to develop new skills for living near non-Indian groups.

After the **Civil War**, the government forced the state to acknowledge them as permanent citizens and they were brought under the laws of the state of North Carolina in 1889. Most moved to the officially recognized area of Qualla Boundary. The land there is held in trust by the US government and cannot be transferred out to anyone other than tribal members. Today, most of their **economy** has been based on **tourism** to this beautiful Appalachian mountain area.

The 175,000 member Cherokee Nation of Oklahoma (Tsalagi Ayili), the second largest Indian tribe in the United States, resides not on a reservation, but in a legal service area in the former Indian Territory. Membership is composed of the surviving original enrolees of the tribe under the Dawes Act (see **allotment**) Census of 1906 and their descendants. Its members occupy a considerable portion of land in Northeastern Oklahoma, spread over 14 counties. The Nation runs a successful business, and is one of the most financially secure and growing economies in Indian Country. It is one of the tribes which has self-government (see **self-determination**) under the new structures approved by the United States, and the tribe controls and administers its own health, education, social and legal services, as well as its own courts and tax systems.

Christianity

Converting the Natives of North America to Christianity was a major goal of the European colonists. **Missionaries**, soldiers and colonists all targeted Natives. In a different way to the political and military pacification, which inevitably involved brutality and physical extermination, Christian pacification (Catholic and Protestant) was meant to exterminate Native values, and social and religious systems.

For many Native people, the conquest was so devastating that they accepted the strength of their conquerors. Perhaps they thought they could achieve some of that power if they followed the strangers' ways.

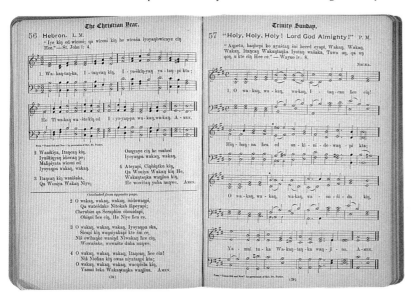

discarding their previous ways of worship and belief. Others, such as the Pueblo people, managed to absorb aspects of Christianity into their traditional and ancient religious beliefs and practices. Many others took their traditional lifestyles underground, into the *kivas* and into their houses where the priests and ministers would not see them.

57 Above Mose Sanders, Joanne McLemore, Joanne Fourkiller, Louise Dreadfulwater and Georgia Glass, members of a Cherokee Baptist choir, sing Christian hymns in the **Cherokee language**. Many of their songs are Cherokee in origin, such as 'One Drop of Blood' and 'Orphan Child', both said to be written on the Trail of Tears. Others, such as 'Amazing Grace', are Protestant songs. Ironically, Cherokee Christian churches helped maintain Cherokee culture by preserving the language, in the Bibles, sermons, prayers, songs and lessons written and given in the Cherokee language.

56 Above Hymns in the Lakota **language** from *Okodakiciye-Wakan Odowan Qa Okna Ahiyayapi Kta Ho Kin* (Hymnal With Tunes and Chants According to the Use of the Protestant Episcopal Church in the Missions Among the Dakotas), 1931.

In addition, Native religious belief was often incredibly flexible and open, allowing for many different ways of being and thinking. Native people could not conceive that a religion would demand that they cast aside their previous gods, spirits, beliefs and practices. Yet, little by little, Native beliefs and practices were eroded. **Schools** were established to teach Indians to read English (in order to read the Bible). Missionaries often made their first task the translation of the Bible into Native **languages**. However, many did not accept early attempts to Christianize them. 'Well, it seems to be a good book', Cherokee Chief Yonaguska is said to have remarked after hearing a reading of the Gospel of Matthew. 'Strange that the white people are not better, after having had it so long.'

Some Native people adopted Christianity,

58 Right This cope made in 1985 for the priest at St Joseph's **Apache** Mission Church in New Mexico, pictures a *gaan* or Mountain Spirit, a Mescalero Apache masked **dancer** with traditional symbols of magic, authority and power. The swords and crosses are symbolic of the healing powers of traditional Apache religion combined with Christianity. The crowns represent mescal, the cactus, from which the Mescalero Apaches derived their Spanish name.

59 Right The title page of an 1860 **Cherokee** Bible. The Reverend Samuel Worcester, a minister to the Cherokees and **Elias Boudinot**, translated the Old and New Testaments into Cherokee in 1825.

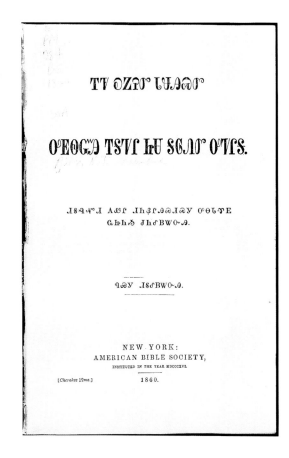

TᏝ ᎤᏃᎭᏍᎬ ᏩᎭᎣᏍᎬ

ᎤᏕᎣᎦᎫ ᏔᏍᏯᎢ ᏞᎤ ᏚᏣᎠᏍᎬ ᎤᏙᏍᎦᏍ.

ᎫᎥᏴ .ᏞᏍᏫᏴᎠ.

NEW-YORK:
AMERICAN BIBLE SOCIETY,
INSTITUTED IN THE YEAR MDCCCXVI.

[*Cherokee 12mo.*]   1 8 6 0.

60 Right This model of a common Pueblo Catholic household shrine reflects the mix of ancient Pueblo and Christian practices. On the shrine stands a *retablo* or painted wood panel of saints, an ear of corn and a clay-covered gourd, taken from the last feast day **dances**. These rest on a Hopi style woman's dress (*sega*), made by Jessie Overstreet of Isleta Pueblo, along with a commercial statue of Santa Clara, their patron saint, a cross, a rosary, votive candles and another *retablo* of El Santo Niño de Atocha. In addition, there is a statue of **Kateri Tekakwitha**, a **Mohawk** woman, one of the first North Americans declared Blessed by the Catholic Church.

Citizenship, tribal

Indians in the United States and Canada dispute issues of tribal citizenship more than issues of US or Canadian citizenship. Citizenship, in the case of Natives, is almost the same as identity. Long-standing ideas about gender, marriage, race, blood and ethnicity govern ideas about tribal identity.

Canadians have endured massive disputes over who can and cannot be identified as **status** Indians. In the last 20 years there have been strong debates over the means of determining status through the provisions of the **Canadian Indian Act**. In the United States, the Supreme Court has upheld the notion that tribes are free to determine their own membership. Much of the dispute over tribal membership or status came about because of forced changes in attitude to and treatment of women, marriage and race.

Since the Indian censuses of the 19th century, taken in order to make **Removal** easier, the US government classified Indians according to their blood quantum (degree of Indian blood), rather than by general lines of ancestral descent. After Removal, tribal citizenship or enrolment was carefully documented to establish the right of individuals to remain on tribal lands and to share in payments and other benefits guaranteed by **treaties**. The first blood quantum standards were set under the Dawes Act (see **allotment**), to determine who was eligible to receive land. Tribes, forced to list their members, designated those of 'one-half or more Indian blood'. During the **allotment** period, so many did not qualify for enrolment under the blood quantum standards accepted by the tribes that the lands eventually passed out of Indian hands. Since then, the government has raised and occasionally lowered blood quantum standards to control who is eligible for land, housing, healthcare, education and all those benefits guaranteed by treaty.

Today, tribes can set standards for enrolment into the tribe that are governed by lines of ancestral descent along with blood quantum. Multi-tribal intermarriage for over a century has virtually ensured the birth of people who cannot meet minimum blood quantum standards. A person can be a 'full-blooded Indian', that is have eight-eighths Indian blood, but still not be enrollable in X tribe if the tribe's and the government's standard holds enrolment to those with one-quarter and over blood quantum. If a man who is one-quarter Potowatomie and enrolled there, one-quarter Pawnee, one-quarter Shawnee and one-quarter Otoe marries a woman one-quarter Choctaw, one-quarter **Creek** and one-half **Cherokee** (but not descended from someone on the Dawes Act Rolls), their child would be 'full-blooded', but not enrollable in any of the seven tribes.

In the Cherokee Nation of Oklahoma, for example, only those who can trace their descendency to Dawes Act Enrolees of 1906 can be enrolled, regardless of their blood quantum. In other tribes, enrolees can come only from persons who have one-quarter or more blood descended from someone living on the **reservation**. In others, someone who can prove one-quarter blood descended from an enrolled father or enrolled mother (*Onondaga*) may be enrolled.

Set the blood quantum (standard); hold it to a rigid definition of Indians, let intermarriage proceed as it had for centuries, and eventually, Indians will be defined out of existence. When that happens, the federal government will be freed of its persistent 'Indian problem'.
Patricia Limerick, historian, 1987

Citizenship, US and Canadian

The right to vote in public elections, to hold public office and to participate in some public welfare programmes is restricted to those who hold US citizenship, although most other political and legal rights are guaranteed to all. American Indians were not citizens of the United States until after the Indian Citizenship Act was passed in 1924. A few had previously become citizens by joining the military in the First World War or by applying to the federal courts for citizenship (if they were living in one of the territories that were not yet states). Many Indians who signed treaties and gave up their lands became state citizens, but they lost their tribal citizenship in the process. Some tribal and very traditional peoples regarded US and state citizenship as negative, unnecessary or secondary to their tribal citizenship. The 1924 Act guaranteed citizenship to all born within US territory, without affecting tribal citizenship. Today then, Indians may hold both tribal and US citizenship.

Canadian Indians in tribes that had negotiated treaties with the United States could hold joint US/Canadian citizenship and/or cross the border without a passport (according to the **Jay Treaty**). Canadian Indians, however, were not granted voting rights and Canadian citizenship until 1960.

'Civilization' policy

In the latter part of the 18th century, the US government introduced its 'civilization' policy for Indians. This was followed in the 19th century by an assimilation policy (see **acculturation**). The thought was that the so-called 'Indian problem' would go away when Indians ceased to act like Indians.

Missionaries, often working with the government, urged Natives to give up their 'savage' practices. After many Indians were **reservationized**, the government banned **ceremonies**, songs and **dances** and forced them to wear 'citizen clothes'.[17] Often they put traditional and ceremonial dress in **museums**.

Children were taken away to boarding **schools**, splitting families up even further. Young **Sioux** girls married white men and never came home or returned as white women, no longer Sioux in behaviour or **language**. Old people, once respected for their wisdom and guidance in traditional Sioux culture, were rejected, and the **medicines** and skills they had known so well were condemned as savage silliness.

Many **Cherokee** families adopted almost the entire way of life of white Southerners around them. Some joined the plantation **economy** of the American South and became wealthy. Many more accepted some things such as log houses and **metal** tools, but rejected **Christianity** and the English language. Others reacted to change by returning to traditional practices. Most Cherokees were **farmers**, supplementing their meagre livelihood by **hunting**, **fishing** and gathering. Like their ancestors, they cultivated Native **maize**, **beans** and pumpkins (see **squash**) on small garden plots. Now, with the aid of shallow draft ploughs and steel hoes introduced by Europeans, they were encouraged to farm. Many adopted new plants (such as wheat and potatoes) and used **horses** for ploughing, hauling and riding. They earned a small cash income from the sale of surplus livestock and forest products to American markets, and their household implements included some Anglo-American goods alongside traditional Cherokee items.

Civil War, American

Many tribes were drawn into the American Civil War (1861–65). The Civil War, or the War Between the States, affected issues over **Removal** and slavery among Southeastern tribal members. Though Eastern tribes generally fought for the Union, many of the tribes in Indian Territory signed alliance **treaties** with the Confederacy. The Confederacy promised to follow former treaty obligations, protect tribes from invasion and invite Indian representatives to the Confederate Congress. In return, tribes would defend themselves. Many favoured neutrality, but they were caught between the Confederacy and nations who were not neutral.

During the war, **Cherokee** lands, for example, were ravaged both by Union troops and pro-Union Indians. The Cherokees in Indian Territory had just recovered from Removal and the Trail of Tears when the Civil War struck and tore them apart once more. As the war in the East escalated, the federal government abandoned its promise to protect Indians in Indian Territory. Guerrilla bands on both sides stalked the area and raided communities. Old divisions among the Cherokees were once again inflamed. Many Cherokees were forced into Confederate regiments. Thousands of Cherokee civilians fled to Kansas and Missouri, and others to Texas. By the end of the Civil War, more than 7,000 Cherokees had died, many had been made homeless, one-third of the women had been widowed and one-quarter of the children had been orphaned.

> **M**y father was neutral and did not want to go away; he did not believe in fighting [but] father was forced into the Southern Army. At the time they took father away, there were no other families left in the country. [We tried] to stay as near to father as we could… but in a short time the war became so fierce that mother realized that we must get out of the country or be killed.
> *Betsy Thornton, Cherokee*

After the end of the war and the defeat of the Confederacy, there was turmoil in the former Union and Confederate areas in Indian Territory, with great destruction of Indian property and economic disaster. The Union government punished those who had joined the Confederacy with new treaties that forced them to give up more land.[18]

Clans

Although not all Indians organize themselves into clans, for those who do, clans describe a system of relationships, government and behaviour that teaches humans their place among plants, animals and fellow human beings. In the Anishinabe world view, for example, the clans have certain responsibilities. Some may be responsible for the water, for the earth and the places under the earth. For other peoples, the clans have responsibilities for human experiences, such as healing, singing and **ceremonial** life.

> **M**y clan is Bitter Water [Tó dich'ii'nii]. I am Bitter Water…. My connection to the land, to creation, to religion, is directly connected with the beginning: Bitter Water Clan created through the Holy People by Changing Woman.
> *Luci Tapahonso, Navajo poet*

Organization by clan – by family relationships either through the maternal or paternal line of the family and clan outmarriage (between members of different clans) – had a practical origin and nature. Ancient peoples appear to have understood how marriage and relationships out of one's own group can be politically and economically useful. Furthermore, early people must have begun to recognize the problems associated with **intermarriage** within a family, and cross-clan marriage helped to prevent genetically transmitted **diseases**.

Indians followed their clan relationships in many ways. For the female-centred **Iroquois** and **Cherokee**, every clan had a clan mother. These clan mothers 'raised up' or deposed the men who carried out the day-to-day government. They traced inheritance of personal common property and the right to hold office through the female line. Women joined men in Council and represented children as well. Mothers of those killed in battle and the clan mothers had control over the fate of prisoners, and could intervene in the path of **war** and peace itself. They also had authority over how the products of their work and the work of the men (including **food**

many cases, these symbols, such as the carved heads of birds, animals or fish, are not only clan animals, but the animals to be hunted or those with spiritual power.

Ah-ji-jawk (Crane), *Mahng* (Loon), *Gi-goon* (Fish), *Muk'wa* (Bear), *Wa-bi-zha-shi* (Martin), *Wa-wa-shesh-she* (Deer), *Be-nays'* (Bird). The seven original clans *o-do-i-daym'-i-wug* (clans) of the Anishinabe.
Eddie Benton-Banai, Anishinabe teacher

The Seven Cherokee (*Ani Yunwiya*) clans: Deer (*Ani Awi*), Long Hair Clan (*Ani Gilohi*), Paint Clan (*Ani Asuwisga* or *Disuhwisdi*), Wolf Clan (*Ani Waya*), Wild Potato Clan (*Ani Nunaanisaquali*), Bird Clan (*Ani Jisgwa*), Blue Clan (*Ani Sagonige*). *From oral tradition*

Clowns

A considerable number of Native peoples have a role in their **ceremonies** for characters that might be called clowns.

In some pueblos, clown societies are attached to *kivas*, with clowns initiated very young and committed to the role of sacred clown for life. In Hopiland, sacred clowns (*tsuskut*) arrive during the **katsina** dances. Initiates are often made members of the Clown Society just a few days before a dance by the sponsor of a dance or by a *katsina* group. Clowning is religious duty. Clowns teach people to laugh, look and learn. They perform satirical and disrespectful songs. They are instructed to sing, and warrior *katsinas* torture them, drench them with water, whip them, then give them **gifts** of **food**.

The clowns at Zuni perform in the plaza during the season. Wearing Clown University sweatshirts, they play basketball and imitate a Plains Indian **pow wow** dance. They also mimic popular political figures. The clowns in Zuni, called mudheads (*koyemshi*), have conflicting qualities – they are both serious and comic, respectful and disrespectful. They represent the chaos that can come to life if prayer, ritual and respect are not observed by everyone.

Western **Apaches** at White Mountain, for example, practice their spiritual connections to the mountains through the Clown or *gaan* (mountain spirit) Dance. Those spirits drive away evil. During the times of the dance, clowns enter the community with a wand that represents **rain**, thunder and lightning, and a

61 Above A painting, *The Iroquois Tree of Peace*, by Oren Lyons (**Onondaga**), *c.* 1970. The Great Law of Peace was proclaimed by *Deganawida*, the Peacemaker. The law established the **Iroquois** Confederacy and set out the principles by which the five nations were to co-operate and live. The Law and the religious authority bound in it are symbolized by the white pine growing in the earth on Grandmother Turtle's back. Animals that represent most of the maternal family clans are grouped around the tree. The clans shown here are Heron, **Eagle**, Eel, **Beaver**, Wolf, **Bear**, **Turtle**, Snipe, Hawk and Deer. With its four white roots of peace extending north, south, east and west, the pine draws the people together at its base.

and other resources) were distributed.

As cross-clan marriage was needed, and in order to recognize the clan relationships in political, social and ceremonial contexts, Native peoples made images of clan symbols on ceremonial objects (such as **headdresses**), instruments (such as **rattles** and **drums**) and in **architecture** and **sculpture** (such as the totem or house poles of Northwest peoples). Many everyday tools and utensils (such as spoons, combs, weapons and **fishing** and **hunting** lures) also show clan symbols. In

62 Right Lois Gutierrez de la Cruz and her sisters (Gloria Garcia and Thelma Talachy from Santa Clara and Pojoaque Pueblos) make **pottery**. Lois and her sisters' work explores common themes in Pueblo philosophy and ritual practice. Here, the traditional clowns, called *kossa* in the Tewa language, gamble, read upside down, wear cowboy hats and sunglasses and eat their traditional **food** of watermelon. On the water jar itself, the world is upside down, even though the jar's steps to heaven are the right way up.

63 Below A photograph by Owen Seumptewa, a Hopi photographer, of a young clown from Hopiland, who is painted in traditional white and black stripes of clay and wearing his cap of **maize** husks.

noise instrument (bullroarer) that represents the winds. The clowns and *gaans* appear at sunrise and during ceremonies, including girls' puberty ceremonies.

Clowning can be fun, but it is sacred too. Clowns and *gaans* are sacred. They have the power to cure.

Edgar Perry, White Mountain Apache

Contact

In 1492, an Italian **explorer** called Christoforo Columbo (Christopher Columbus), who was working for the government of Spain and looking for a route to Asia and the 'Indies', came across a small island in the Caribbean he called 'San Salvador'. That voyage and his two subsequent trips to this 'New World' began the encounter between Native peoples and Europeans that reshaped the history of the world. The residents of what Columbus thought were the Indies became 'Indians' or 'Indios' (which means 'In God' or 'Of God' in Spanish). A wave of exploration and conquest began in the newly found 'Americas'. In the 10th–15th centuries, the Norse from Iceland arrived in what became Newfoundland and met the **Beothuks**. Later they travelled to Greenland, encountering **Inuit**/Eskimo. In the 15th century, they became involved in **trade** disputes which led to violence and to their departure. People in the far **Arctic** and Northeast, then those of the Southwest and Southeast, were the first to experience contact with Europeans. Then from 1540 in the Southwest and 1607 in the Northeast, the strangers from Europe once again entered Indian land.

The European invasion of North and South America started enormous biological and cultural change, sometimes referred to as the 'Columbian exchange'. Plants, animals and **diseases** were passed back and forth between the Americas and Europe, and on to Africa and Asia, altering life on all the continents. Religion went only one way, from Europe to the Americas. This exchange deeply affected the indigenous population, the 'Indians' 'discovered' by Columbus. Many of the first Native peoples experienced contact with Europeans before they ever encountered an actual European person. Diseases such as smallpox and tuberculosis travelled north from South America and the Caribbean and killed many thousands. Whole communities were devastated by these new diseases to which Native peoples had no resistance. Many tribal groups were entirely wiped out. In the first 200 years of the European occupation of North America, it is estimated that between 8 and 20 million Native people died.

Suddenly, peoples new to the Native world appeared, demanding **land**, demanding that they abandon their traditional religions, demanding their **food** and goods, even demanding their labour and their loyalty. Although Indians resisted these demands, the effect on the people and communities was devastating. Native people must have felt that their own gods and spirits were weak against the extraordinary powers of these people with weapons (guns and germs) that killed at a distance.

Columbus made three voyages to the Americas, confining his explorations to the Caribbean. He died a bankrupt and bitter man. During the anniversary 500th year of his voyages in 1992, the man and the results of his explorations were criticized by Indian, **African**-American and Hispanic artists, scholars, **political activists** and writers.

Corn, see **Maize**

64 Right A jacket or shirt patch, issued by the American Indian Movement in 1992 on the anniversary of the Columbian 'discovery' of America. The picture is of one of Columbus' ships from his first voyage (the *Niña*, the *Pinta* or the *Santa Maria*) with the international symbol for 'No' or 'Off' through it.

65 Right This Zuni pot, *c.* 1700, is from Hawikuh, a town occupied by Zuni at the time of the Spanish invasion. It was the site of a struggle in July 1540 between Spanish soldiers under Francisco Vasquez de Coronado and the Zuni. The Spanish, seeking Cibolá, the 'Seven Cities of Gold' (which did not exist), interrupted religious **ceremonies** and a battle followed. The town was abandoned after the **Pueblo Revolt** of 1680. Zunis **traded** with many people at this time and, when the area was later excavated by archaeologists, much **pottery** was found there.

JAUNE QUICK-TO-SEE SMITH
OCTOBER 10 – NOVEMBER 14, 1992
RECEPTION: 5:00 – 7:30 P.M., SATURDAY, OCTOBER 10
B E R N I C E   S T E I N B A U M   G A L L E R Y
132 GREENE STREET   NEW YORK CITY 10012   (212) 431-4224

66 Above Jaune Quick-to-See Smith, a **Salish** artist, offered her 1992 version of 1492 in this pastel. Modelled on sets of paper **dolls** for children combined with references to the 'Barbie' doll, the costumes of Smith's Ken and Barbie Plenty Horses portray the history introduced by **schools**, priests, **disease** and economic powerlessness.

45

BUFFALO BILL'S WILD WEST
AND CONGRESS OF ROUGH RIDERS OF THE WORLD.

WILD RIVALRIES of SAVAGE, BARBAROUS and CIVILIZED RACES.

67 Above The poster for the 1890 Buffalo Bill's Wild West Show, portraying the 'Wild Rivalries of Savage, Barbarous and Civilized Races'.

'Cowboys and Indians'

The 1890 Buffalo Bill's Wild West Show set the stage for the powerful image of 'cowboys' and 'Indians' which was then played out in films, television and folk mythology throughout the next century. Bill Cody was a cattle herder, wagon driver, fur trapper, miner and Pony Express Rider before he became an Indian Scout for the US Army. He developed the Wild West Show 'to give a realistic entertainment of wild life on the Plains' and to earn money in the show business he had come to enjoy. **Reservationized** Indians defeated in the Plains Wars joined in the fantasy of the Wild West Show. They included Pawnees such as Knife Chief and Young Chief and Lakota such as **Sitting Bull**, American Horse and Long Wolf (who died in England and whose body was returned to his family in

1997). Cody, Indians, cowboys and *vaqueros* (Mexican cowboys) toured the United States and Europe, appeared in England and met the Queen. In the show, Indians rode, shot and attacked wagon trains, the Mail Riders and the cowboys.

This fantasy continued in the children's game of 'cowboys and Indians', which is still played by millions of children in the Americas and in Europe. It requires a toy tomahawk and **feathered** headband for the 'Indians' and a hat and toy gun for the 'cowboys'. Rather than the existing vocabulary for Indians' roles (brave, squaw, etc.), there are gestures and pidgin-English words. In the game, the 'Indians' 'walk Indian file', they howl and yell, putting their flattened palm repeatedly against their pursed mouths in an imitation of the shrill, ritual 'lu-lu' of Plains women or the battle cry of men. They greet each other with the upraised right forearm, saying 'how' in a misunderstanding of the Lakota greeting *'hau kola'* or 'greetings, brother'.

The 'Indians' 'creep up' on the 'cowboys', who do not use such sly behaviour. This part of the game is left over from the shock that the **British** and French troops suffered when Indians would attack from the shadows rather than lining up and marching straight towards the enemy in one line, as 17th- and 18th-century European warfare demanded. In the game, the 'Indians' are allowed to 'run wild' and shout, whereas the 'cowboys' must behave scrupulously, staying silent and calm.

Cowboys, Indian

Despite the images from the Wild West Shows and films, Indians have always been 'cowboys'. Plains and Great Basin Indians were the ultimate 'cowboys'. They were noted for their horsemanship from the moment the **horse** came to Indian Country, . Many, such as the Nez Percé, bred and trained horses. The agile and intelligent Appaloosa (or 'paint pony') became highly favoured as 'cow ponies' by cattlemen and Indians alike. Indians were often hired as cowhands by stock and cattle companies, and, after **reservationization** they were given cattle as part of the **treaty** payments and raised cattle themselves.

Ranching, although difficult on their small **allotted** lands, allowed many of the former **buffalo** people to continue their traditional collective practices of getting and using meat. Today, many tribal peoples on the Plains and in the West have remained cattlemen and some are raising buffalo again. In addition, Indians have taken to the American rodeo, demonstrating their continued excellence in horsemanship and cowboying skills. Indian rodeo, particularly among **Navajos** and other Western tribes, is a big business as well as a pastime.

68 Above Champion rodeo bull rider J.P. Paddock, a **Navajo** from Winslow, Arizona.

69 Left A watercolour of 1940, *Bronco Busting*, by Ma Pe Wi (Velinos Herrera), a Pueblo artist.

47

Coyote

Known to non-Indian ranchers and **farmers** as a nuisance and a predator that steals eggs, lambs and calves, Coyote is something quite different to Indians. He is a creator in the lives and legends of many Native peoples, including the **Navajo**, Karuk, Spokane (*Spilyé*) and Tohono O'odham. Navajo elders, for example, say that *Ma'ii*, the trickster Coyote, hastily tossed the stars into the heavens. He has many names, according to the different people, and is bumbling, clever, foolish, greedy and lustful. He is a creator, but he is also destructive – a type of reverse role model for good behaviour. He has powers of transformation and is like other 'tricksters', such as Spider (**Sioux**/*Iktomi*), **Raven**, Crow and **Rabbit**, who lie and steal their way through life. Stories about him make people laugh, as do the actions of ceremonial **clowns**, but they also make them take note about how to behave in relationships with others.

70 Above Harry Fonseca, a Maidu artist, produced a series of paintings in the 1980s built around the exploits of a very modern Coyote. In the best known of this series, called *Portrait of the Artist As A Young Coyote*, Coyote is a very American Uncle Sam, 'shuffling off to Buffalo' (an old vaudeville dance routine).

Coyote was given some good corn [maize] seed after the fall [autumn] harvest, but instead of saving it for the next planting, he ate nearly all of it. When the summer rains finally came, he had forgotten to prepare some good land. He finally just threw the seeds along the bad ground around a wash. Then Coyote slept through the growing season. He didn't learn the right songs to sing to the corn when it did come up. Knowing that he had to sing something to make it grow, he just made up a song. It was terrible. The corn grew anyway. But it didn't grow up to be corn, because it never heard the corn's songs. In a poor place like the rough edge of a wash, only another kind of plant would grow. The plant grew up to be *Ban Wiw-ga*, Coyote's Tobacco (wild tobacco).
Story recorded by Juan Delores, Papago, c. 1911

Creation stories/origin tales

Every cultural group in the world has origin or creation stories about how the world came into being and about how people were created.

Some of those stories are made 'official' in written texts – the Book of Genesis in the Old Testament, the Ramayana and the Koran tell Jews and **Christians**, Hindus and Muslims how they, their world and their religion came to be. Other creation stories were passed by word of mouth, only written down at the end of the 19th century or even unwritten to the present day.

Such stories appear in song, **dance**, **art** and **ceremonial** drama.

Lizard said, 'I'm going to make human beings.' Coyote told Lizard, 'Oh, don't do that. [They will just fall to arguing and cause trouble.]' But Lizard said, 'I'm going to do that.'
Lizard, His Song, sung by Nancy Richardson, Karuk teacher

These stories not only tell *how* things came to be the way they are (why women are priests and why the possum's tail is bare), but *why* things are the way they are (because *Iyetiko* was angry with the men for their drunkenness and **gambling** and because **Coyote** was angry with the village when they would not let him marry a beautiful woman). These tales often tell how people came to live in a certain place, making them important in establishing their ownership of the land. They describe many kinds of creators (spirits, ancient animal and human ancestors) and the relationships between people, animals, plants and spirits in the natural universe.

We do not like our stories referred to as myths; this is because our sense of who we are and our world view are wrapped up in these stories. Even clothing, tools, baskets… so important in everyday life have direct links to the stories of the people.
Dale Curtis Miles, San Carlos Apache

The way in which people see the roles of men and women in their culture can come from the roles that men and women had in the origin stories of their people. For many Indian people, the origin of their people stems from a woman or a female spirit. Unlike the Judeo-Christian tradition in which there is one God and he is male, many Native peoples insist that the spirit or process of their creation comes from the female and from more than one being.

Many people believe that female spirits are central to everyday life and to ceremonial life. **Cherokees**, for example, say they came from the breast of Corn Mother (*Selu*), who died so that **maize** would spring from her body and give life to the people. The **Iroquois** believe they were born from the mud on the back of the Earth, known as Grandmother **Turtle**. Apaches believe that they are descendants of Child of the Water, a male child of White-Painted Woman, who kept the child safe to slay all the monsters and make the world safe for The People. For the **Sioux**, White-Buffalo Calf Woman gave the people the 'Gift of the **Pipe** and Truth'. The first mothers of all the Tewa Pueblo people were called Blue Corn Woman, Summer Mother, White Corn Maiden and the Winter Mother.

Once all living things were in the womb of Mother Earth. Corn Mother caused all things to have life and start to move toward the surface of the Earth. With Corn Mother's help, the people were born onto the surface of the Earth, but because the people did not know how to care for themselves, they started to wander… . Finally the Arikara came to a beautiful land where they found everything they needed to live. A woman of great beauty came to them and the Arikara recognized her as Corn Mother. She stayed with them for many years and taught them how to live and work on the Earth and how to pray. When she died, Corn Mother left the people a corn plant as a reminder that her spirit would always guide and care for them. The Arikara say that the beautiful place where they learned to live was the valley of the Loup River in Kansas.
An Arikara story

Cree
The Cree originally occupied lands surrounding James Bay and the western shores of Hudson Bay north almost to Churchill River, where they bordered the **Inuit**. Their territory extended as far west as Lake Winnipeg and as far south as Lake Nipigon. Profits from the **fur trade** lured them to expand far west, eventually occupying the south of the western sub-Arctic as far as the Peace River in Alberta. Many groups pushed out onto the Plains, allying with the Assiniboine against their enemies.

By the 19th century, Cree speakers with nine different dialects occupied the largest area of any Canadian Native group, stretching from Labrador to the Rockies. The Cree hunted moose, caribou, **buffalo**, **bear**, **beaver** and waterfowl. Birch**bark** canoes, sleds, snowshoes and toboggans were used for travel. The Woodland Cree lived in conical wigwams, often covered with caribou or moose hides, while the Plains Cree lived in buffalo-skin tipis. They wore tanned hides with **quills** and later **beads** and colourful threads in floral designs.

In the woodlands, three to five families travelled together as a hunting group and larger groups gathered at one location during the summer months, generally near water. Men were the hunters, while women trapped smaller game and **fish**. Women collected firewood, cooked, prepared hides and made and mended clothing. To the Woodland Cree, hunting was religious activity and they believed that animals could only be killed by following the proper ceremonies. Plains Cree followed the typical northern plains lifestyle that centred on the buffalo.

Woodland Cree culture was similar to that of the **Ojibwa** to the near south and, as the fur trade expanded, many Cree and Ojibwa communities joined in hunting and trapping groups. More isolated communities to the north are often located at the sites of former trading posts. Plains Cree bands in Alberta, Saskatchewan and Montana have taken reservations in their traditional areas. The northern communities are mostly Native, but many have Euro-Canadian administrators, teachers, **missionaries**, merchants and medical personnel. The government of the communities or 'bands' shifted from the traditional informal methods to an elected chief and councillors. On many northern reserves, the band government is the major employer of those working in construction, logging, **tourism**, guiding and commercial fishing. Rather than having to attend residential **schools** in the South, many communities are now taking control of their own education through distance learning, technology or the construction of local schools. Trading posts have remained central to the communities and are now retail stores. Unemployment is high and bands are always exploring economic development projects.

The introduction of Euro-Canadian culture changed Native life in the North. Rifles and steel traps replaced traditional methods. Like the Inuit, the Cree use motor **boats**, snowmobiles and aeroplanes for travel. Many communities are accessible only by air travel. However, some families still go to the bush to hunt, trap and fish for part of the year. In areas such as James Bay, parents often withdraw their children from school in order to teach them the 'bush skills' they need to survive as a Cree.

Throughout Western Canada, Cree have surrendered most of their land through **treaties**. In Québec and Labrador, Natives did not sign away their lands. Finally in 1975, the governments of Canada and Québec and the Cree and Inuit of James Bay signed the first **land claims** agreement in modern Canadian history (after the 1867 Canadian Confederation). In return for the surrender of lands, the Cree and Inuit received $225 million, as well as ownership of the lands around their communities and exclusive hunting, fishing and trapping rights over a much larger area.

Creek/Muscogee

More widely known as Creeks, the Muscogee people, Natives of the Southeast, had no single name for themselves and no single political organization at the time of **contact** with the Europeans. They held 50–80 towns, with at least 20 ethnic groups speaking different **languages**. After settling in Alabama and Georgia, the villages banded together in a loose Confederacy based on a common language. The prospect of war with Europeans and the need to protect their boundaries brought Creeks into a tighter group. However, individual towns could reject the decisions of the regional Confederacies. During the American Revolution, the groups made the decision to remain neutral, but a number of Creek towns allied themselves with the **British**. The Treaty of Paris in 1763 put the Confederacy within the boundaries of the newly created United States. The Muscogee worked to protect their territory and culture. The **Red Stick Wars** evolved out of their attempts to protect themselves against constant invasions.

Alexander McGillivray, son of a Scots trader and a Native and French mother, was probably the best-known Creek leader of the 18th century. He was called Great Beloved Man (*Isti atcagagi thlucco*) by his fellow Koasati Creeks. This educated man from the Wind Clan focused on forging alliances between various Creek groups and the British, and later the Spanish. He pushed for towns to develop a unified foreign policy. His leadership helped to form a Council, culminating in the 1790 Treaty of New York in which the United States pledged to protect the Confederacy from outside settlement and compensated the Creek for their loyalty. The loyalty did not last for long when the Creek realized that the government was allowing settlers into the state of Georgia.

During the 1820s, the leaders reluctantly realized that absolute resistance was impossible. In 1832, they signed a **treaty** outlining the terms for **Removal**. Most Creek emigrated west, but a few remained in Alabama. A new Council was created to act on behalf of all towns and a new entity, called the Muskogee Nation, was created. The unity was short lived as the **Civil War** erupted and old loyalties and tensions surfaced. After the War, rival groups were able to bridge their differences and to unite again. Some Creeks remained in Alabama, where their **land** was turned over to sharecroppers (who didn't own the land, but who worked for farmers for a share of the income from the crops). In 1963 the remnant of these groups organized themselves as a tribe once more, and in 1980 the United States accepted them as the Poarch Creek.

In 1899, the Dawes Commission began to allot to individuals land that was once communal. Resigned, most Creeks accepted it. In 1934, the Indian Reorganization Act halted the allotment policy and the tribe was able to gain more recognition. In 1972, the tribe gained full control again and became a **sovereign** nation even though it didn't have a communal land base. The present capital of the Muskogee Nation is Okmulgee in Oklahoma. Businesses there include casinos as well as services for the local community. Despite 300 years of conquest, many customs remain and district representatives still meet in Council to handle tribal affairs. Creek still attend ceremonial stomp **dances**, hold the **Green Corn Ceremony** and identify themselves by town affiliations. Families gather, fast and play **stickball** and speak the Muskogee **language**.

D

Dams

Issues concerning Indian lands – of **water**, **fishing** and **hunting rights**, mineral exploitation and land-based economic development – have always been at the forefront of any debate involving Indians. Colonization, **disease**, **Removal** and urban **relocation** programmes have caused many Indian peoples to move.

Much Indian **land** was redistributed due to **reservationization** and **allotment** and this caused much cultural loss. The building of dams and reservoirs on Indian lands in North and South America – usually in order to provide water and electrical power for non-Indians – had a similar effect.

There is no tribal area unaffected by dams. Virtually all areas have seen the relocation of thousands of people and the destruction of traditional fishing, hunting and plant-gathering grounds. Even the dead have undergone Removal. For example, the grave of Cornplanter (the great **Seneca** leader and brother of the prophet **Handsome Lake**) was moved when Kinzua Dam covered the traditional land of the Seneca in the states of Pennsylvania and New York. George Gillette, the Chairman of the Mandan-Hidatsa-Arikara tribe at Fort Berthold, North Dakota, wept as an agreement negotiated by the **Bureau of Indian Affairs** was signed which would move his people off their land to make way for Garrison Dam. The people of Fort Berthold are still struggling for compensation from the US government for what was promised them 55 years ago when they allowed the dam to be sited in their territories.

Cochiti Dam was built by the US Army Corps of Engineers in the 1960s in order to provide water for recreation and **maize farming** in the dry New Mexico highlands. However, the dam has leaked, causing the area to become wetlands, and the proposed income from tourism has never materialized.

Cochitis want the dam removed so that the lands can be converted back to farming. They achieved a partial legal solution in 1990 by having Congress forbid the construction of hydro projects using the Cochiti Dam.

Cree land claims and unresolved treaty issues came to a head in 1971, when Québec launched a massive hydro-electric project, which blocked and diverted the rivers flowing to James Bay. The **Cree** temporarily halted the project, which threatened to flood their traditional hunting and fishing areas and relocate several villages. More recently, the Cree of James Bay, under the leadership of Grand Chief Matthew Coon-Come, have been fighting a new hydro-electric project by Hydro Québec. The Cree wouldn't allow a repeat of the environmental damage caused by the first hydro project in the 1970s. Through local, national and international pressure, they gained support from powerful environmental groups. After New York State and a number of other large consumers said that they would not buy power from the new hydro site on Cree lands, Hydro Québec cancelled the project.

71 Above Seferina Ortiz made figures in the style of 19th-century humorous Cochiti **pottery** 'Monos' or 'Men' (sheriffs, priests and **cowboys**). She started making these 'bathing beauties' in the early 1970s, after thousands of outsiders came to the recreational lake formed from Cochiti Dam. 'We never saw these things before', she said, when she saw the tourists in their bathing suits.

VOICE FROM THE WISE:
THE LAND IS, AND HAS BEEN FOR THOUSANDS OF YEARS, THE ECONOMIC BASE OF MY PEOPLE.
LEFT ALONE FOR ANOTHER THOUSAND YEARS, WE WOULD STILL SURVIVE!
-JOHN PETAGUMSKUM
CREE ELDER OF WHAPMAGOOSTUI

72 Above A Canadian Indian sweatshirt, c. 1995, which tells people to 'Stop James Bay', the hydro-electric project sponsored by the Québecois government and opposed by the **Cree** and **Inuit** peoples of the Northwest Territories.

51

Dance

In Native cultures, the art of dance, like song, is connected to **ceremony**, ritual and prayer. Dance is usually an expression of the relationships between people, animals and the spirits of the world. Particular dances (and dance clothing) came to people in **dreams** and visions (for example the Kiowa **Ghost Dance** and the jingle dress). Most North American Indian dancing has a religious and seasonal meaning (for example the Crow Sun Dance, the Pueblo Corn Dances and **Cherokee** and **Creek stomp dances**). In the traditional Plains 'straight' dance, men wear undyed **feathers** and animal parts and imitate the movements of animals and birds.

Some dance is social, rather than religious. 'Good time' dances and songs, mostly expressed in round dance in North America, were used in courting or celebrating the company of other Indian people. Although much Native dancing was originally specific to particular tribes, it has developed into intertribal, social or **pow wow** dancing that is often for display and competition (for example 'fancy' dancing and hoop dances).

> The Creator again sent someone from his heavenly domain to restore peace and love amongst his Native people… . This was the second religious reform among us Iroquois… . To restore peace he made the Natives more aware of our Creator; he taught them to appreciate most everything that was created for us… through ceremonies that mostly consisted of dancing… . These ceremonies were continuous from when the air is warmed in the spring until the air grew cold in the fall from frost. It was a continuous event of thanksgiving dancing.
> *Reg Henry, Cayuga faithkeeper, Six Nations Reserve*

Department of Indian Affairs, Canada

Amendments to the Indian Act in 1880 formally established the Department of Indian Affairs (DIA) as the Canadian government agency responsible for all recognized '**status**' or registered Indians. The DIA was to carry out the Indian Act's policy of assimilation (see **acculturation**). It controlled all aspects of Native life, including **agriculture**, government, education, religion and travel on and off the reserves.

Over the years, there have been many amendments to the Indian Act and the DIA.

Today the DIA works towards handing over the responsibilities of education and social services to the communities themselves. Some think that the Canadian government is off-loading responsibility for Natives without formally recognizing their aboriginal rights or methods of **self-government**. The Canadian government set up a Royal Commission in 1992 to study aboriginal issues. One of its recommendations was for major changes to the role of DIA.

Diplomacy

Indian tribes have been sending specially appointed persons to represent them and their interests to government officials in England, France and the United States for four centuries. In turn, they have received political delegations representing those countries. Diplomatic **gifts**, such as pipe tomahawks and presentation tomahawks, trade medals, **blankets**, strings and belts of **wampum** and silver gorgets are evidence of diplomatic efforts between Indians and whites.

When Thomas Jefferson was President of the United States, he sent a number of Peace Medals to be presented to Indian 'chiefs' by the members of the Lewis and Clark expedition to the West. M. Lewis and W. Clark told the tribes that 'a great chief of the 17 great nations of America' had replaced the French and Spanish in the West and that he had adopted them all as his children. They said, 'When you accept his **flag** and medal, you accept therewith his hand of friendship, which will never be withdrawn from your nation as long as you continue to follow the councils which he may command his chiefs to give to you.'

Indians who have Peace Medals passed down to them continue to wear them on ceremonial occasions because they represent the government's promises of peace and friendship.

From the period of **Removal** to the present day, tribal delegations have travelled to Washington, D.C., to take their concerns, pleas, questions and gifts to the Great Father. The National Archives and the White House collections are rich with objects presented by Indians to officials. Similarly, tribal peoples still display and wear items given in diplomatic meetings between their ancestors and government officials.

74 Above A pair of 19th-century moccasins, made of hide and cloth, with glass and **metal beads,** made as presentation pieces for Queen Victoria by a Cape Breton, Newfoundland **Mi'kmaq** woman, *Whycocomaughh*.

73 Above Four members of a **Mohawk** delegation were painted by John Verelst in portraits commissioned by Queen Anne during their diplomatic visit in 1710. In one painting, Brant (*Sa Ga Yeath Qua Pieth Tow*), the grandfather of **Joseph Brant**, wears a scarlet cloak, white cloth shirt, quill-decorated black-dyed moccasins, a powder horn and a burden strap belt. He has a series of blue tattoos over his face and body. The **bear** in the background indicates Brant's **clan**.

75 Above Lewis and Clark presented this medal to an Osage chief. It has the bust of Jefferson on one side and the clasped hands of friendship beneath the crossed **pipe** and tomahawk. It was passed down through the generations to Chief Henry Lookout, and loaned to and then sold to the Smithsonian Institution by his heirs.

76 Left These moccasins are in the British Museum's collections, and are believed to have been given by one of the four **Mohawks** who went on a diplomatic mission to England in 1710.

77 Above A delegation of Southern Cheyenne and Arapaho men in Washington, D.C., Smithsonian Institution, 1899. Left to right, front row: Lame Man, Yellow Eyes, Henry Roman Nose, Turkey Legs, He Bear, Little Chief or White Spoon, Yellow Bear and Little Man (all Cheyenne). Left to right, middle row: Black Coyote (Arapaho), Andrew John (**Seneca**), Leonard Tyler (Cheyenne) and Phillip Cook (Cheyenne). Left to right, back row: Cleaver Warden Victory (Arapaho), Bird Chief, Sr. (Arapaho), Grant Left Hand (Arapaho), Jesse Bent (Arapaho) and Robert Burns (Cheyenne).

Disease

The introduction of diseases such as smallpox and cholera after European contact in the 16th and 17th centuries caused a massive decline in the Indian **population**. These diseases spread widely and from 1500 to 1800 the death toll was close to 10 million. Wars, **Removal**, migration, loss of **hunting** and **fishing** lands, and a complete change of diet caused further illness. Loss of traditional **food** resources and increasing environmental and industrial pollution caused yet more hazards. By 1900, the 'Myth of the Vanishing Indian' was a near reality. Infectious diseases that came under control for other Americans by 1900 were still common in Indian populations by the mid century. Even in 1980, Indians were still three times more likely to die or be ill with diseases such as tuberculosis and adult-onset diabetes than the majority of the population.

Dog

Dogs were the earliest domesticated animals and have lived in relationship to Indians (like their relatives **wolves** and **coyotes**) for centuries. Some Natives (**Apaches**, for example) used large dogs as pack animals, before there were **horses**, donkeys and mules in Indian Country. Many Plains women (such as Hidatsas and Mandans) used dogs, hitched to travois, to haul wood and smaller loads. The most well-known use of dogs is the Eskimo sled dogs. These dogs are specially bred and trained to travel long distances and pull sleds or toboggans heavy with **fishing** and **hunting** equipment, **food** and clothing. The Inuit development of work dogs is so much admired that Alaskans have developed dog sled racing and breeding into a competitive **sport**.

Many Indians considered dogs close relatives and involved them in ceremonies or

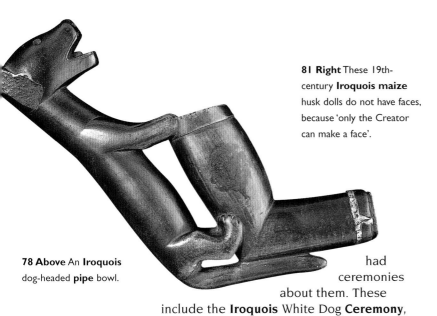

81 Right These 19th-century **Iroquois maize** husk dolls do not have faces, because 'only the Creator can make a face'.

78 Above An **Iroquois** dog-headed **pipe** bowl.

had ceremonies about them. These include the **Iroquois** White Dog **Ceremony**, the San Juan Pueblo Dog **Dance** and the Grass Dance (a dance with many meanings shared by several Northern Plains peoples). The **Sioux** still eat dog after the ceremonies associated with vision-seeking and healing.

79 Below A 'mother' *katsina* doll, *Hahay'i*.

Dolls

For most Native peoples dolls are made mainly for children's play. Yet the dolls' dress was also important because dolls were meant to teach children their roles in society and ceremonies. Some were used by adults and children in ceremonial and ritual ways. *Katsinas* at the Bean **Dance** (*Powamu*) or at the Home Dance (*Niman*), give *katsina* dolls. *Katsina* dolls, which are made from

80 Below Rovena Abrams (**Seneca**) made these **maize** husk dolls in 1985, dressing them in the style of late 18th-century Senecas. From the dolls' necklaces, we can tell that they belong to the **Turtle Clan**, and so are probably related, perhaps brother and sister. Nowadays, presentation pieces can be very elaborate.

cottonwood roots painted and decorated with **feathers**, teach young girls about being Hopi. They are like prayers for water, as cottonwoods only root in wet areas and seek water. Although girls are still given dolls, today artists produce them for the commercial market as well for the traditional uses in the community.[19]

A female infant always receives a flat Ha'hay'i (*wuuti*) as her first *katsina* doll. A new bride is also presented one on the occasion of the Niman ritual. This doll she slides down her body... for the purpose of bearing many children.
Noq pu' manawya tihut susmooti makiwe', pam it hahay'it putsqatihut mooti makiwngwu. Pu' i' naat pu' löökökqa aapiy nimantikive piw put makiwe', pu'pam put naapa siroknangwu, pam hapi ti'o'oyniqey oovi.
Michael Lomatuway'ma, Hopi teacher

82 Left Owen Seumptewa, a Hopi photographer, took this picture of a Hopi girl with a *katsina* doll she had just received during a Home **Dance**.

Dreams

Many Indians value dreams greatly and believe that actions and behaviours can be accounted for by dreams. People may make certain designs on clothing, make objects a certain shape and paint them a certain colour, go hunting for particular animals, sing, **dance** or make **medicine** all because of dreams and visions.

In dreams we have learned how everything given to us is to be used; how the rice is harvested and the animals hunted. So that we would learn all the crafts, once a pair of humans was taken from the earth and brought to a place where they learned everything that the Indians know, even how you follow the [dictates] of dreams and honour the spirits.
Bill Johnson, Nett Lake Ojibwa, 1947

I am a medicine man because a dream told me to be one… you become a *pejuta wicasa*, a medicine man and a healer, because a dream tells you to do this.
John Fire Lame Deer, Lakota medicine man, 1972

Drums

Many Indians believe that drums are alive and have a body. The drum is a heart, a heartbeat. Drums breathe, as do **rattles**. Among the Anishinabe, for example, drums may be referred to as Grandfather or Little Boy. The drum speaks, and must be cared for by a drumkeeper, whose life is devoted to caring for that drum.[20]

About the Penobscot drum. They accompany their songs with drums. I asked the origin of this drum, and the old man told me that perhaps someone had dreamed that it was a good thing to have and thus it had come into use.
LeJeune, 1634

He says that drum… it's living. The drum, he said, is just like you… . That drum is a human being too… . Cause the Creator gave that to our people when the earth was new.
Tom Porter, Akwesasne Mohawk sub-chief and Longhouse speaker, 1980

Iroquois, Navajo, Cherokee, Creek and **Apache** people play small water drums, as do members of the Native American Church (or Peyote Way). A water drum is a small drum filled to various levels with water, which changes the tone. Navajos use water drums for social **dance** songs in the Enemy Way **Ceremony**. Cherokees use them for **stomp dances** and the Anishinabe for Midéwiwin ceremonies. It is common among **Inuit** and **Northwest Coastal** peoples and among peoples in the Great Basin and Plateau areas of the United States for both men and women to play hand drums in **gambling**, stick and bone or hand **games**.

Anishinabe/**Ojibwe** peoples used hand drums called **dream** drums, and the visions of men and women often determined the way that the drum was made or decorated. The colours, the types of hides and the way the drum is wrapped all have meaning.

Many say that the Grass or Omaha Dance came from the dream vision of a young Sioux woman, Wananikwe or an Anishinabe woman. A spirit came to her and said, 'Go at once to your people and tell them to stop their war and become friends with the white man. Do you see the sky, how it is round?… . Go then, and tell your friends to make a circle on the ground just like the round sky. Call that holy ground. Go there, and with a big drum in the centre, sing and dance and pray to me… . You will have one heart'.
Eddie Benton-Banai, Anishinabe, 1984

In the regions of the Plains and Great Lakes women generally have not sat at the 'big' drum or the medicine drum. Women, as Sissy Goodhouse (a Lakota singer) would say, are in the Third Circle (the *wiclagata*) behind the men. Their voices 'second' and join the men's. In the Southern Plains, women who stand behind the drum or 'sing behind' (second) are often called 'chorus girls'. Changes are underway, however, particularly in the Northern Plains, with more women 'sitting at the drum' or being 'called to the drum' in the way that men have been.

I have always looked after the drum; that is probably why they chose me to be drumkeeper. I felt the drum should not be alone. I felt that someone should look after it. I had to learn more about it… . The drum and I are not apart. We are one. When that drum beats, I beat, my heart goes the same way the drum goes… . It just draws you.
Margaret Paul, Maliseet drumkeeper

83 Below Thunderbirds fly on this early 19th-century Plains hand drum, perhaps because playing the drum calls the thunder and lightning. Many Native peoples feel that thunder is connected with the bringing and taking away of life. For Crows, the lightning flies out of the thunderbird's eyes and **rain** comes when it flaps its wings. On the Plains, thunderbirds are *wakinyan* or 'sacred flying ones'. For **Cherokees**, thunder is a friend, having warned them of and defended them against evil. **Ojibwe** and Kwakwaka'wakw people believe that the old and wise thunderbirds bring messages to humans.

84 Above In this photograph taken in Washington, D.C., in 1978, Matilda Mitchell, Nettie Showaway and Sylvia Wallulatum from the Warm Springs Reservation in Oregon sing and play the hand drums common in their region.

85 Above A group of **Navajo** singers from Chinle, Arizona, the 'Sweethearts of Navajoland', sing and play the water drum.

86 Right Chief Charles Shunatona (Pawnee), Leroy Two Hatchet (Kiowa), John Fitzpatrick (Crow), Jay Hill (**Seneca**), Dick Baker (Lakota **Sioux**) and Kirby Kimball (Ponca) sit at the big drum (**pow wow** or 'fun' drum) singing an intertribal round dance song in Washington, D.C., in 1989.

E

Eagle and eagle feathers

The eagle is a significant animal to Indians, who revere him as a messenger and an advisor. The eagle is the bravest of the birds, a living symbol of a warrior, that possesses special powers of sight. Eagles can transform into humans at will and bring their messages to humans. For **Iroquois**, he might be the Dew Eagle or thunderbird, always seen on top of the Tree of Peace. For the Maidu and Anishinabe, he is a messenger of the Creator. The Eagle **clans** in the Southwest are responsible for the sky.

87 Above In this watercolour by *Awa Tsireh* (Alphonse Roybal) of 1920, Eagle Dancers from San Ildefonso Pueblo perform one of the dances which, like the **Buffalo** and the Deer Dances of the Pueblos, honours and calls the spirit of the animal represented.

Eagle feathers are used in the most sacred and most important **ceremonies**. In the Southeast, eagle feather fans and wands were used in ceremonies. The **Cherokee** Eagle (*awoh'li*) **Dance**, which is no longer performed, had eagle feathers as its central symbol. Eagle feathers are worked into **headdresses** of all kinds, most notably the well-known Plains headdresses.

Eagle feathers are given to those who have brought honour to the people, for example in war, and bring with them much respect. In ceremonial dance, for example, only a warrior (or veteran) can retrieve a dropped feather; no-one else may touch it.

The United States adopted the eagle, probably derived from both Iroquoian and German ideas of him, as a symbol of democracy and union. The American eagle appears on **flags** and official symbols of the United States from the 18th century onward. Often he is holding the arrows representing unbroken unity in one talon – a symbol known to the Iroquois.

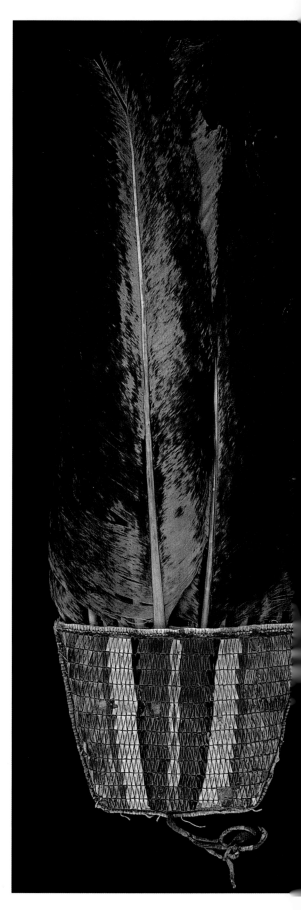

88 Right A 19th-century Plains **quillwork** and eagle feather fan. Fans can be made of an entire wing of a bird.

Economies and economic change

There were many types of aboriginal economies. Each was based on the tribe's cultural, political and religious understanding and use of land, water and other natural resources for obtaining **food**, clothing and shelter. There were simple resource-based economies which involved using local resources by **hunting** and gathering (**subsistence**). Some peoples had more elaborate and complex systems which involved the mutual and often disputed exchange of goods and use of territories between peoples. Groups such as the Pueblos, for example, exchanged goods in trade, sometimes across long distances. Other groups, such as the **Ojibwa**, exchanged agreements for the use of lands, animals and waters understood to be other's territories.

Many internal tribal economies had different systems of distributing goods within their own communities. For example, **Cherokee** and **Iroquois** women controlled the lands on which crops were grown and the distribution of cultivated plant foods.

Wealth has always been measured in different ways by different peoples. For some, the accumulation of goods and land measured wealth. For others (such as the Plains and **Northwest Coastal** peoples), wealth was measured by how much one accumulated in order to give it away. For some, it was the manner in which someone redistributed his wealth rather than in the way he accumulated it that mattered. For others, it was what kinds of goods he accumulated or what value was attached to those goods. A woman's worth might have been measured in how many **horses** it took to persuade her father to allow a suitor to marry his daughter. Status, too, may have been measured by another, less material standard. 'I have always been a poor man',

89 Above In Northern California, many tribal peoples used these carved and decorated 'purses' made of elkhorn (antler) for carrying the strings of dentalium **shells** that they referred to as 'Indian money'. Like **wampum**, abalone, conch and other shells, dentalia were highly valued in trade.

90 Right This beaded Indian chequebook cover symbolizes well the change from a barter to a cash and credit economy. It was made in the 1990s by an **Ojibwa beadworker** and sold through a tribal craft shop. It acknowledges the presence of a world of banks and paper money in Indian Country and shows their desire to remain Indian by Indianizing Western objects and Western ideas.

a **Navajo** man told an anthropologist. 'I do not know a single song.'

The coming of Europeans changed forever the internal economies of tribal peoples. The first changes came because of the different understandings held by Europeans and Indians about land ownership, the accumulation of wealth and the benefits of exchanging of goods. Then came the cash economy, which changed the lives of everyone, including the white men.

We know not what to think of the French. Why... did the French come into our country?.... They asked for land of us because their country was too little for all the men that were in it. We told them that they might take land where they pleased, there was enough for them and for us; that it was good the same sun should enlighten us both, and that we would give them our provisions, assist them to build, and to labour in their fields. We have done so, is this not true? What occasion then did we have for Frenchmen? Before they came, did we not live better than they do, seeing we deprive ourselves of a part of our corn [maize], our game and fish to give a part to them? In what respect, then, had we occasion for them? Was it for their guns? The bows and arrows which we used were sufficient to make us live well. Was it for their white, blue and red blankets? We can do well enough with buffalo skins, which are warmer; our women wrought feather blankets for the winter, and mulberry mantles for the summer; which were not so beautiful; but our women were more laborious and less vain than they are now. In fine, before the arrival of the French, we lived like men who can be satisfied with what they have; whereas that this day, we are like slaves, who are not suffered to do as they please.
Stung Serpent, Natchez, c. 1720

91 Above A Crow dress with elk tooth decoration.

Elk

For Indians, the elk was the symbol of fertility and long life. The elk provided **food** and highly valued and durable hide. In addition, the distinctive bugling songs of the spring courtships between male and female elk gave Plains peoples the rich gift of the societies of elk **dreamers** and elk dreamer songs. Elk tooth decoration on clothing was common on the Plains, such items being given as prestigious **gifts** to young women and girls in particular. The two elk teeth that came with each animal were highly valued as trade items, and were even swapped for **horses**. The dentalium **shell**, known as 'Indian money' in the Northwest was often substituted for the scarce elk teeth, and California Natives kept dentalium in elkhorn purses.

> Two teeth remain after everything else has crumbled to dust… and for that reason the elk tooth has become a symbol of long life… . When a child is born… an elk tooth is given to the child if the parent can afford the gift.
> *Okute, Lakota elk dreamer, early 20th century*

Explorers

From representatives of Spain, Italy and France in 1,500 AD to scouts for petrochemical companies in 1980, 'explorers' travelled to Indian Country in search of gold, goods, minerals, lands and souls. Columbus is perhaps the most famous of the explorers of the North American continent, but debates continue about who was the first to reach its shores. In the centuries after Columbus came a flood of soldiers, **hunters**, adventurers and scholars. Spanish, **British**, French, Portuguese, German and 'Americans' all sought something from the Indians.

Explorers – individuals and those representing governments and businesses – staked out the areas of New France, New Spain, New England, Nieuw Amsterdam, the Northwest Passage and the Pacific Coast. Captain John Smith, Sir Walter Raleigh, Jacques Cartier, Samuel de Champlain, Hernando de Soto, Captain James Cook, and Lewis and Clark were all explorers, as were lesser known men, such as Karl Bodmer (the painter), Prince Maximillian of Wied, Prince Paul of Wurtemburg, the Marquis of Lorne, Edward Curtis (the photographer), Herman Schweitzer of the Fred Harvey Company. There were also 19th-century anthropologists who travelled the North American continent and the South Pacific and the Caribbean making pictures of Indians, hunting animals and collecting Indian goods.

F

Feathers

Native peoples valued every usable part of indigenous plants and animals, but they always considered some parts more important and more symbolic than others. Indians used bird feathers of all kinds, and virtually every Native group of people recognized certain birds, even mythological birds such as thunderbirds that gave **food**, clothing, power, wisdom, **medicine** and spiritual protection. **Eagle** feathers have always been the most revered among Native peoples, but feathers of woodpecker, wild turkey, flamingo, macaw, parrot and prairie chicken have held special meaning for specific people.

People used feathers in prayer and ritual objects, for example in **headgear** and in ceremonial **dance** clothing. Particular feathers had significance for particular deeds, events or types of people. The kinds of feathers people held or wore, or the way in which they wore them, might define their status – social, political or religious. Thus, the number of feathers and the way in which they were worn on an **Iroquois** man's headdress (*gustoweh*) indicated whether he was **Mohawk**, **Seneca** or **Onondaga**.

Artists now replicate feathers in clay, paint and **metal**, because their presence still sends prayers up to the spirits and ancestors. Sculptors carve feathers into **masks**, wooden boxes and house poles (see **house posts**) in the **Northwest Coast** to represent important **clan** animals (such as the **Raven**).

Feathers, like some hides, remain part of wide-spread **trade** among Indians. The need for feathers was multiplied by the 19th- and 20th-century fashion for exotic feathers. They led to a number of bird species, such as flamingos and egrets, becoming endangered. Eventually, restrictions against bird hunting and feather gathering were introduced. In the latter part of the 20th century, Indian religious practices involving the use of feathers of endangered species caused renewed conflict between Indians and the government.

My children, my children,
The wind makes the head-feathers sing.
The wind makes the head-feathers sing.
Arapaho/Inuna-Ina Ghost Dance Song

92 Left A late 19th-century Crow feather bonnet.

61

Federally recognized tribes and status Indians

In the United States, certain groups of Native people (or 'nations' of tribes) negotiated their relationships with the US government, and thus their official existence, through **treaties**. These nations have what is referred to as 'federal recognition' by the US government and are guaranteed certain rights. However, numerous tribal peoples do not now have federal recognition. These are peoples who did not negotiate treaties with the United States, those who were in relationships with colonial powers (such as Russia or Mexico) before their lands were annexed or taken over by the United States, and those who were terminated as **tribal governments** by the United States (Modocs, for example). Some have been recognized by states as Indian tribes. Others have attempted and occasionally succeeded (Pequots, for example) in gaining recognition or in regaining it after termination by the United States (such as the Menominees). Issues surrounding who does and who does not have federal recognition (and the benefits that come to those who do via the **Bureau of Indian Affairs**) have caused an ongoing debate and continued test cases before the courts. The **Lumbee** of North Carolina, for example, recognized by their state of North Carolina, continue to seek recognition before the US government.

In Canada, tribal groups are said to have 'status', rather than 'recognition'. Others are 'non-status', that is they are not acknowledged by the **Department of Indian Affairs** in Canada for the purposes of government and rights. **Inuits**, for example, are recognized as Indians, and Canada has federal responsibility for them, but they do not have status under the **Canadian Indian Act** and do not have reserves. **Métis** are not status Indians, but are included as a political group in important discussions. Canada, unlike the United States, does not have an official category, other than state recognition, for non-status, unrecognized tribes or for individuals who are not or cannot be enrolled in a federally recognized/status tribe.

Fish and fishing

In the Northwest and in Southern Alaska, **salmon** and the other fish that swim in the big rivers are the source of life. Life revolves around fishing, whether in freshwater or saltwater. For **Arctic** peoples, the primary **food** sources are sea mammals and fish, for example the Arctic char, herring, lamprey eels, blackfish, tomcod, sculpin and salmon. The culture built around fish and fishing can be seen in the people's **dance**, ritual, song and **ceremony**. The fish and sea mammals feed them, and their **clan** and family spirits guide and define people's relationships.

In the Great Lakes, **hunting** and fishing, combined with the traditional gathering of **wild rice**, form the basis of social activity and **subsistence** living. The building of giant **dams**, the shifting of rivers, the pollution of streams and oceans and over-fishing brought great change to fish resources in the Northwest, Arctic and Great Lakes. Whereas some rivers were once alive with five varieties of fish (including salmon) in the Northwest, now just one variety is common. Sportfishing and **sport** fishermen, even Japanese industrial claims on fishing resources, have reduced the number of salmon available for Native peoples. Legal disputes challenging the Indians' rights to fish in once tribal waterways and to use traditional practices (such as gillnetting and spearfishing) have eroded Native spiritual and legal claims on those resources.

93 Below This **Inuit** ivory harpoon rest (usually lashed to the bow of an *umiak*) shows a **whale** being hunted. Inuit make other gear for fishing, such as hooks, lines, sinkers, gillnets, dip nets, netting needles, shuttles, floats, seines, fish traps, fish clubs, arrows, spears and lures, with the image or in the shape of the creature being hunted. The very representations of the hunted animals are a way of calling the animal to the hunter and display and celebrate the hunter's skill.

94 Below Sam Jones, a **Yurok** canoe-maker and traditional fisherman, made this cedar fish net needle in 1976. Used to catch freshwater **salmon** in Northern California, gillnets used by tribal peoples have caused enormous dispute and challenges in the courts to tribal **fishing rights** in the Northwest.

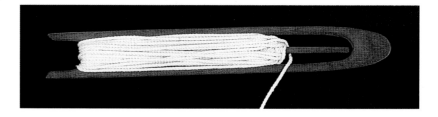

95 Left An ivory **Inuit** toggle, used to secure and mark the depth of line let out. It may have been used for hunting and/or fishing lines. The toggle, in the shape of a pair of breeches, has a human face carved on one side.

Fishing rights

In 1859, a treaty with the Yakama guaranteed the Northwestern tribes 50 percent of the catch from waters where they had traditionally fished. For years, they fished in off-reservation fishing grounds using gillnets in the **salmon**-rich streams, a practice forbidden to non-Indian fishermen. However, the enormous increase in the Pacific Northwest in commercial and **sport** fishing and the increased pressure on US fishing grounds from Japanese and Russians in the 1970s, was indirect competition for the Indian fishermen (who mostly fished for **subsistence**). Commercial fish wheels, which blocked rivers and funnelled fish to commercial **boats**, effectively stopped Indian fishermen from receiving any of the catch.

Despite the **treaty** provisions, hostilities increased during the late 1960s. Eventually, the government, acting on behalf of the tribes, took their case to the courts where, according the 'Boldt Decision', the tribes were found to have a greater and prior right to the catch than the non-Indian citizens of the territory. Indians have fought to protect the guarantees of resources – water, game and fish – laid down in the treaties. The fishing rights wars have provoked occasionally violent battles in Montana, Wisconsin, Minnesota and Michigan, between Indians and the white groups who protest against Indians' reserved rights.

A t this time our people are fighting to preserve their last treaty right – the right to fish…. Fishing is part of our art form and religion and diet, and the entire culture is based around it…. Our people have fought a legal battle for more than 49 years…. Our source (the salmon) is being depleted…. Finally, we said this is enough.
Ramona Bennett, chairwoman of Puyallup (Washington State) and Indian rights activist

T he privilege of hunting, fishing and gathering the wild rice, upon the lands, rivers and the lakes included in the territory ceded, is guaranteed to the Indians, during the pleasure of the President of the United States.
1837 Treaty with the Chippewa, Article 5

97 Below Lac Courte Oreilles tribal members spearing walleye on Round Lake in Sawyer Country, Wisconsin, in April 1998. Non-Indian sportfishermen oppose Indian **treaty** spearfishing. Some hold signs up at the lakefronts during the season that say 'Save a walleye, Spear an Indian.'

96 Below Traditional gillnet fishing in the Upper Skagit River, Washington, 1920.

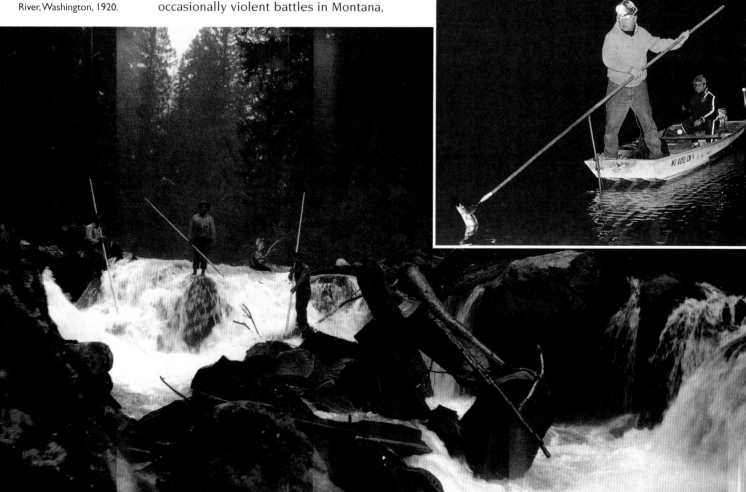

98 Above This **Navajo** weaving of 1920 was made by Nez Baza in honour of her son who served in the US Army during the First World War. It has 48 stars to represent the 48 states of the United States (Alaska and Hawaii were not states in 1920). When her son returned alive, she gave the rug in gratitude to the Indian school at Shiprock, New Mexico. The school raffled it off and the person who won it gave it to the Indian Commissioner, Cato Sells. Sells then passed it to the US National Museum (the Smithsonian Institution), where it remains in the flag collections of the National Museum of American History.

99 Right A Winnebago beaded **bandolier** bag.

Flag, American

Almost all Native peoples use the US flag, particularly on the Plains and in the Southwest, where the flag appears on clothing, in weavings and in representations of all kinds.

The Lakota were finally seduced, forced into and relegated to reservations in the late 1880s. During this time, the US flag started to appear in Lakota art and design in clothing and regalia… . History shows that a conquered people will adapt something, a symbol or some material representation, from their captors to maintain a sense of being or identity that helps them survive. I believe the Lakota people adopted the US flag as such a symbol because within the Lakota culture, the flag carries a far different meaning than that of patriotism… . In war times, flags captured by the Lakota were used as prizes of war. Some were donned as clothing to show off the prize, symbolic of bravery and glory. Many geometric configurations of the flag crept into the material culture and were expressed artistically in many mediums, especially in beadwork, quiltwork, porcupine quillwork, carvings, clothing and dance regalia… . The flag enjoys widespread utilization as a symbol to show beauty and attractiveness, to lend meaning to the warrior tradition, and more importantly, as a reminder of the relationship between the Lakota and American people… . Through the flag, the individual warrior is honoured, recognized and memorialized; it symbolizes the prowess of the individual warrior, not patriotism.

Howard Bad Hand, Lakota singer

100 Left A **British**-style police whistle, **bead**ed in a peyote stitch with a US flag design. 'Fancy' dancers often use modern whistles instead of those of bird bone or **eagle** bone used by veterans and 'straight' **dancers**. The flag design is often used to honour veterans.

Tunkasilayapi tawapaha kin oihanke sni naji ktelo, Iyohlate oyate kin wicicagin ktaca, lecamun
The flag of the United States will fly forever. Under it the people will grow and prosper. Therefore have I done this [fought for my country].
A Lakota flag song

Flute

Many Native peoples play some form of flute made of reeds or wood. The flute is one of the few non-percussive Native musical instruments. On the Plains, for **Sioux** and Anishinabe alike, the flute was a courting instrument played by a young man trying to impress a young woman. Birds and bird song were connected with flutes, and the courting 'dances' of birds were imitated by Indians in **dances** and songs.

Young Indian musicians have taken up the flute again as a performance instrument, and have developed both the flutes and the music played on them. Recordings of Native flute music have become very popular.

Some young women have taken up the Plains courting flute and others (including **Navajo**, **Apache** and Pueblo) compose new songs using the Indian flute (which has a different number of stops to the European flute, and is made of wood and played differently). One singer has even adapted flute songs for the voice, and others have transposed flute music for the piano and synthesizer.

101 Below A Plains-style cedar flute with six stops, decorated with hide ties.

In an **Ojibwa** love charm song, sung by Georgia Wettlin-Larsen (Assiniboine), a love-struck Ojibwa woman tries to get her beloved to take notice of her, but she tries and fails three times. Heartbroken, she asks her grandmother for advice: 'What do we have that equals the power of the flute?' Her grandmother tells her of the love charm songs, that, when sung, will cause the person you desire to fall in love with you. The song says, 'Truly, I am arrayed like the roses, and as beautiful as they.'[21]

Food

This man wanted to benefit his people, so he said, 'I am going to be a palm tree.' So he stood up very straight and very strong and very powerful, and soon the bark of the tree began to grow around him.... . The meat of the fruit was not very large, but it was sweet like honey, and was enjoyed by everybody – animals and birds too. The people carried the seed to their homes and palm trees grew from this seed in many places. The palm trees in every place came from the first palm tree, but, like the people who change in customs and language, the palms often were somewhat different... all, every one of them, came from this first palm tree, the man who wanted to benefit his people.
Francisco Patencio, Cahuilla

102 Right Charles Shunatona, a traditional (not elected) chief of the Pawnee, plays a Plains-style red cedar courting flute, c. 1990.

To talk of American Indian foods and cookery means, in one way, to talk of food and cooking traditions based solely in the natural universe. Things were gathered from the ground, trees and bushes, plants, fresh and salt waters, desert sands, mountain forests and animals. To talk of American Indian food and cooking is also to talk of dynamic and tragic change, of creative adaptation, like that of Indian people themselves. Long ago, there was **bear** and **buffalo**, seal, **salmon** and oyster, cactus fruit and **wild rice**, hickory nut and prairie turnip. There was **maize** from Corn Mother, which together with **beans** and **squash**, became what the **Iroquois** call the 'Three Sisters'. Now there is beef and pork, wheat flour and

65

sugar, cheese, watermelon, red peppers, lemons, coffee and gelatine. Once, there was food eaten raw, smoked, dried and boiled. Now foods are fried, baked and microwaved. The people still **hunt**, **farm** and gather, but they also get cheese and beans from the Indian agency. Like other Americans, they hunt and gather in supermarkets.

They also call us Sand Root Crushers. It must be true. We do dig the sweet potato-like plants with long roots. It is very good and sweet. We eat many different plants. The mesquite beans we pound and make a drink out of it. The desert asparagus [broomrape] that grows in the soft banks of the arroyo…. We eat fish from the ocean…. Sometimes we come [to the Picantes] to gather cactus fruit and deer.
Molly Jim Orozco, Sand Papago/Tohono O'odham

Ceremonial foods have remained important. Every morning in the Southwest, someone throws maize pollen into the wind and prays for the renewal of life. In the Northwest, someone fills the hole made when the camas root or bitterroot is dug with **tobacco**, and offers a prayer and thanks for its gift. Certain things are still eaten in certain seasons only by certain people. Everything is shared with

Before we eat whatever we grow, we feed the Spirit World… we have to feed the Spirit World first, and then we eat. Sometimes we forget, but then the old-timers remind us…. They take a little pinch of the food and throw it to the four winds – so that the Spirit World will have the same food that we are having here on Earth. And since the Spirits help to raise the food, it possesses great powers to heal the body and mind.
Pablita Velarde, Santa Clara Pueblo artist

For the Plains peoples, **buffalo**, deer and **elk** were their primary animal relatives and the source of life, supplemented in the Northwest by the abundance of gathered plants, such as berries, nuts and tubers. Buffalo and deer (meat and hides) were a major commodity for **trade** between Indian peoples and later with Europeans. Maize too became a cash crop for Indians, although it caused wars when Indian stores were taken or destroyed by the Europeans. Other crops and resources are used by Indians for cash income as well as for food, such as fish in the Great Lakes and Northwest, wild rice in the Great Lakes, ginseng in the Southeast, mutton in the Southwest, and sea mammals and fish in Alaska and Canada.

103 Right Made in the mid 19th century, in the 18th-century style, this bowl most probably was used to let dough rise. By the mid 18th century, Senecas were growing wheat and were already used to European-style leavened wheat breads.

family, with neighbours, with new friends. Now, as in the past, how much food there might be is less important than sharing whatever there is with, as the Lakota prayer says, 'all our relations'. Thus, food is central to being Indian and to life itself. For **subsistence**-based peoples, the animals they hunt and the things they find in the lands they inhabit provide food, clothing, tools, fuels and **medicines** – all that is needed for life to go on.

By the fires that night/we feasted… grease was beautiful/oozing/dripping and running down our chins/brown hands shining and running with grease./We talk of it when we see each other far from home./Remember the marrow/sweet in the bones/we grabbed for them like candy./Good/Gooooood/Good Grease.
Mary Tallmountain, Athabaskan poet

Some foods now closely linked with Indian peoples (for example frybread) and sometimes used in **ceremonies** come totally from European food sources. Wheat-based breadstuffs, such as bannock and scones, eaten by Canadian Indian peoples, are Scottish in origin. They were adapted by Native peoples who were colonized by Scots immigrants who came for the **fur trade**. On the Plains, a stew made from beef and Asian rice is a staple of everyday **Sioux** life. In the 16th century the Spanish introduced the pig to the Southeast and Northeast, and the sheep to the Southwest. These and other introductions into the diet, such as sugar and dairy products, have been welcomed and widely used, but they have not come without serious consequences for health and nutrition.

staple of the **Ojibwa** diet. Indians in rice-growing areas have turned some into cash crops. In the 1980s, some Pueblos turned to blue corn harvest and product manufacture. Northwest tribes process some fish for a gourmet market. Some tribes have brought back buffalo ranching. On the whole, however, tribal peoples have rarely been able to capitalize on those markets; inevitably, they are exploited by non-Indian interests.

In the Southwest, Northwest and Great Lakes, in particular, there are enormous efforts to prevent further economic, environmental and socio-cultural assaults on traditional foods and land where food is gathered or grown. Tribal peoples are buying back their **lands**, reintroducing traditional

104 **Above** Mary and George McGeshick (**Ojibwa**) parching wild rice in their rice camp on the Wisconsin-Michigan border in 1986. In the background, their canoe, in which they have gathered or 'knocked' rice, is filled with drying rice.

For the restoration and preservation of **ceremonial** foods and of the ways of life centred around traditional **agriculture** and subsistence, Native peoples everywhere are trying to save or support traditional foods, forms of gathering, preserving and growing. Some supplies have been considerably diminished and have had to be replaced by others. Other foods are so scarce that they have been reduced to occasional ceremonial or special use. Wild rice, however, remains a

animals and plants and teaching older and environmentally sound agricultural methods. Others are cleaning up contaminated land and water resources and attempting to halt development or further erosion of water and land resources. Tribes have, with the help of specialists such as plant ecologists, hydrologists, ethnobotanists, fisheries biologists, foresters and agronomists (some of whom are now Indian), started to protect their resources from further loss.

105 **Above** Agnes Vanderburg, a **Salish** elder, roasting camas root at her cultural camp on the Flathead reservation in Montana. The camas root is a sweet, starchy, nutritious tuber related to the lily. It is gathered in the regions of the Plateau and Northwest. Wheat **farming** diminished camas root fields in the Northwest, but elders help to restore camas fields by reintroducing traditional gathering, food preparation and food-related ritual practice to young people.

If it is not the roots, it is the berries, if not the berries,
then Medicine, something for the house,
sweet Cedar, Fir, Sage, or Juniper that beckons the industrious.
Gathering, the women are vessels holding vessels,
the roundness of our humanity.
Elizabeth Woody, Warms Springs/Navajo poet and artist, 1996

Footwear

Moccasin (*maskisina*) is an **Algonquin** word adopted into English and, since the 18th century, used to describe hide footgear for all tribes. Although most Natives used animal hides to make footwear similar to the **beaded**, **quilled** and embroidered moccasins used by Eastern Woodlands peoples, not all Native footgear was *maskisina*. In the Northwest and the **Arctic**, Natives made boots of seal fur or caribou hide to keep out ice, snow and water.

106 **Above** Beaded trainers made in 1990 by Cecelia Firethunder, a Lakota Sioux **beadworker**. Like the beaded baseball caps, lipstick holders and bingo markers that Indians all over North America have been making for the last 15 years or more, beaded athletic shoes tell a story of change and persistence in Indian Country.

Fur trade

Furs and hides were an important commodity for Indians – domestically and as trade items. When the Europeans arrived, they wanted to exploit the rich North American natural resources. The first demand was for **beaver** fur and deer hide. Later, fancy furs such as sable, otter and ermine became important too. These were exchanged for **metal** tools, cloth and other items. Initially, all furs were obtained from Native hunters through the long-established Native trade networks and alliances. However, Europeans eager to obtain furs started to by-pass this established system. This competition caused great disruptions in traditional alliances and damaged the traditional **economies** and cultures of Native groups. They were used to hunting for **subsistence**, and now had to compete for alliance with the European traders. Their economy was being transformed from one based on subsistence to one based on the need for European goods. Traditional territories and alliances were destroyed as groups warred among themselves for access to trading relationships.

As the fur trade expanded and pitted the French against the British in a search for more products, tribal rivalries became more intense as groups struggled to maintain dominance in the trade. Charles II of England granted the Hudson's Bay Company (HBC) Charter in 1670, opening a huge area of the sub-Arctic up to the fur trade, which it controlled until after the Canadian Confederation of 1867.

The French sent **explorers**, **missionaries** and **traders** into the Western lands and expansion continued in the 18th century. They built trading posts and intermarried with Native women. White trappers competed with Native ones, but did not respect the unwritten rules that stated what could not be killed (namely, pregnant and young animals). During the 19th century, over-hunting greatly reduced wildlife. By 1840, raccoons and **buffalo** had replaced the beaver trade in the West and many species (for example sea otters on the coast and deer

in the Southeast) were hunted to near extinction.

The fur trade with whites increased women's work, because they alone had the skill to tan the hides of deer, **elk** and buffalo. It might be true that the degradation which whites believed they saw among the Plains women was due to the increased burdens upon the women from the excessive demands of the fur trade. This was a disaster for both the women and the animals the trade slaughtered. It might even have been that some Indians' systems of multiple wives that so repelled whites may have increased as a result of the fur trade as so many more hands were required to prepare the food and hides when tribes entered a market economy.

Russians colonizing Alaska took **Aleut** slaves to work on **boats** hunting **whale**, walrus, otter and seal. Pacific Coast Native groups competed with the European trappers for goods. The Gold Rush of 1849 expanded settlements and forced local economies to change. Trading posts were closed and sold. The mid 19th century saw reductions in Native land holdings and the fur trade spread far north. By the 20th century **farming** had expanded, but the demand for fur continued and the railway now made **transportation** of goods easy. Many species were depleted, but Native groups continued to trap selectively which kept the populations viable.

Environmental groups, especially in Europe, kept up a strong anti-fur campaign through the 1980s and 1990s, which reduced the demand for fur products in Europe and prices dropped rapidly. In 1980, the HBC sold its stores in the North and in 1957 the New York factory of the American Fur Company closed. Generations of Native trappers found their economic bases severely threatened. Joined by non-Native trappers who harvest seals and the fur industry, Native trappers and political organizations mounted a major campaign of their own explaining humane trapping and the necessity of culling herds. In the mid 1990s, the Native fur industry seems to be making a slow come-back.

107 **Above** Moccasins from many tribal cultures. From left to right: **Inuit**, Nava, Kansa, Woods **Cree**, Tuscarora, **Sioux**, Alaskan (sic.), Chippewa, Shawnee, Cree, Kiowa, Arapaho, Kiowa, Sioux/Dakota, Slavey, Arapaho, Arapaho, Comanche, Montagnais/ Naskapi, Tohono O'odham, Oneida, Nez Perce, Chamula, Cree, Eastern Sioux/Dakota, Comanche, Eastern Sioux, Shoshone, **Algonquian**, Cheyenne, Arapaho and Blood.

G

Gambling

Gambling games or betting games have been common among Indians for centuries. Whether **games** of skill or chance, these competitive and often intertribal gambling games (called stick, hand or moccasin games) remain popular today, although rarely with the type of high stakes such as **horses** which used to be common in the 19th century. Plains Indians (Crows, Cheyennes and Kiowas for example), Great Basin Indians (Luiseños and Cahuillas for example) and Northwest peoples (at Warm Springs) still participate in gaming and gambling.

A rich song tradition accompanies most hand or **stickball** games. There were also magic songs associated with the games, as there were for **Cherokee**, **Creek** and Choctaw stickball. There are traditional gambling songs for the hand, stick or bone games. Among **Northwest Coastal** and Great Basin peoples, Ute, **Salish** and Kootenai, people sing in hand games as parts of a team, as lead singers. In Southern California, Natives sing for their gambling game *peon*. For Anishinabe, songs that came from **dreams**

and visions, accompanied by a **drum**, caused people to bet which of two moccasins a marked object had been hidden under.

The Osage play a traditional hand game with sticks. The object of the game is to guess who has a small item in their hand. Every time you guess correctly, you get a stick. You must win six sticks to win the game. In the old days, the singers sang hand-game songs while the game was played. At the end of each game, they would sing a Round Dance song. All the ladies would get up and put their shawls on and dance to the music. Then they would sit down and sing a giveaway song. They would pass out gourds to the people who would stand and shake the gourds. After that, people would put a donation up on the table. They still play hand games today at Gray Horse… . They raise funds with the money gathered at the games. Years ago, the winner would get a pig or a horse. Now, the players put money or groceries on each side of the game.
Abe Conklin, Ponca

Churches brought the game of bingo to Indians on the **reservations**, and it became so popular that many tribes used it as a money-making enterprise in the late 20th century. Small-stakes gambling came to be an important part of cash income on small reservations, just as it has for Catholic churches, volunteer firemen and social clubs such as the Masons.

I only have two dollars, but I'm going to bingo anyway.
eskanyeh songverse by Hubert Buck, Seneca, sung by his daughters Sadie and Betsy Buck

108 Below Osage handgame, with beaded tin can **rattle**.

109 Left A **beaded** bingo dauber.

110 Right A Pueblo needlepoint bingo bag. Some Indian people who gamble in small-stakes bingo have transferred many Native beliefs and behaviours to modern gambling and 'Indianize' gambling accessories.

However, the development of high-stakes Las Vegas style casinos as a form of economic development came to be a focus of the debate over Indian **sovereignty**. Over 100 tribes now have some form of gambling on reservation, and although practised by only 20 or so tribes, high-stakes gambling has increasingly proved to be both an economic boon and a hotly debated political and cultural issue for Native peoples. The tribes remain in constant battle with the US government and the states over attempts to control gambling on the reservations. They insisted that their ability to do what they wish on tribal lands is an issue of sovereignty.

Games and sports

Like all people, Indian adults and children played and still play many games and sports. Much sport was connected to ceremonial and ritual life, even to **war** in a symbolic way. Running was common to many tribal peoples. Although most Native running is ritual – as in the running that **Navajo** and **Apache** young women do during their puberty **ceremonies** – it has become a well-developed modern sport among Pueblos, Navajos and Apaches.

111 Above An aerial photo of the largest and most lucrative Indian casino, Foxwoods, at the Mashantucket Pequot Nation in Connecticut.

Y ou boys should go out and run. So you will
be swift in time of war. You girls, you should
grind the corn. So you will feed the men and
they will fight the enemy. And you should practice
running. So, in time of war, you may save your
lives.
Maria Chona, Tohono O'odham, 1934

Some games were not only tests of physical
skill or endurance, but also of mental agility.
Vi Hilbert, a Lushootseed linguist,
remembers that her family liked challenge or
competition singing.

112 Right Two Inuit
women – Madeline
Allagariuk and Phoebe
Atagotaaluk – throat singing.
They learnt this traditional
form of song from their
grandmother. Men and
women on the **Northwest
Coast, Inuit** and other
Arctic peoples engage in
competition singing. Inuit
think of throat singing as a
kind of game, the object
being to outlast the other
singer before giving way to
laughter.

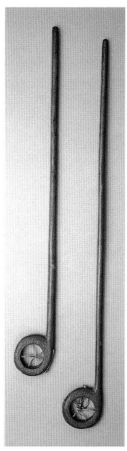

113 Above These sticks are
for the **Ojibwa** ball game,
which is similar to lacrosse.

114 Right Tohono
O'odham women play a
stickball game called *tóka*, a
game in which there
are two balls.

Many Natives (including the **Cherokee**,
Navajo, **Ojibwa** and Tohono O'odham) have
some form of **stickball**, that is a game
involving a ball hit with or thrown by
pouched or curved sticks. The stickball game
called lacrosse, played by **Iroquoian** and
Algonquin peoples across the Northeast, is
the most famous, having made its way into
the mainstream of international sport.

Although Native peoples still play
traditional sports and games, many also play
mainstream sports they have learnt at school,
such as basketball and American football.
American football had its major development
at Carlisle Indian School, by a coach named
Pop Warner whose best-known player was
the Sac and Fox athlete, Jim Thorpe.

115 Right In
many places in
the **Arctic, Inuit**
children and adults (here
probably Chukchi) play
kickball games. Sometimes
they used decorated and
moss-filled balls made of
hide. Some of these games
are similar to a modern
game called hackeysack, in
which the object is to keep a
small leather or cloth ball in
the air, solely by kicking it.[22]

116 Above Kahnawake Lacrosse Club in Montreal, in 1867.

117 Left New York and Canadian **Iroquois** still play an old winter competitive sport called snowsnake, in which players throw a long carved wooden pole down a long trough carved in the snow.

118 Below Inuit athletes compete in the neck pull. It is played competitively at the Eskimo Olympics. In the neck pull, competitors cannot use their hands and arms, and the object is to pull the other competitor off balance.

Geronimo (Goyathlay)

119 Right Most photographs of Geronimo show him as a fierce **Apache** warrior, armed and on horseback. Others, taken during his captivity, show him as a performer and a 'star', riding around in a Cadillac. Geronimo held authority over the Chiricahua band partly because of his status as a medicine man. In this photograph, he appears with the **headdress** that identifies him as a medicine man.

To non-Indians, there is perhaps no figure as famous (or infamous) as the Chiricahua **Apache** war chief Geronimo (*Goyathlay*). His raids on white settlers and his battles against the US Cavalry are legendary. Equally legendary are his refusal to accept **reservationization**, his final surrender in 1886 and his imprisonment. Less well-known are the roots of his and his people's hostility towards and resistance to Mexican and US troops who slaughtered, pursued, starved and dispossessed several groups of Apaches with which Geronimo was associated. Having been captured, arrested and imprisoned, Geronimo and his people (including a large number of Apache scouts who had worked for the US government for years) finally surrendered and were exiled to Florida, where many died. Another forced journey took the Apache prisoners, their wives and families to Alabama, then to Fort Sill, Oklahoma, with only 400 survivors.

He was, according to those who knew him at Fort Sill, proud of the watermelons he learned to grow and the cattle he raised. He loved attending the fairs at which he was paraded by government soldiers. He joined the Dutch Reform Church, later being expelled for **gambling**. He died in 1909, far from the territory and people that he had so vigorously defended. He remains a legend and a symbol to Indians and whites of the conflicts between them.

When they were released in 1913, some Apaches went to the Mescalero Reservation in New Mexico and others, Geronimo's Chiricahuas, stayed in Oklahoma where their descendants live today.

Ghost Dance

Tribal peoples across the Northern and Southern Plains adopted the Ghost Dance, a religious belief and practice based on prophecy by a Paiute man called *Wovoka* (Jack Wilson). He said that the people's belief could drive the white man from the West and cause the **buffalo** to return. He told how he had ascended to Heaven in a **dream** and had seen Indians living peacefully forever. He claimed that living Indians could have this paradise if they performed this dance and returned to their traditional ways. The **Sioux** changed this peaceful message to one that insisted that a messiah would make whites disappear and the buffalo return. That messiah assured the white bullets would not penetrate the special shirts (painted with figures of the moon, stars and buffalo) and dresses that the people wore when performing this dance and when fighting. The Sioux **Sitting Bull** (*Tatanka Yotanka*) became the leader for this new faith among his people.

Thus, the Ghost Dance was part of the battle to keep Indian lands and lifestyles, against the onslaught of **Christianity** and the extermination of Native religious belief. The government and the whites who saw such tribal religious behaviour were afraid of its consequences and fought back. This ended in the arrest and murder of Sitting Bull, and the massacres of Sioux men, women and children at **Wounded Knee**. The government outlawed the Ghost Dance in 1923, afraid that it would rejuvenate Indian nations and cause **war**.

120 **Left** A Ghost Dance shirt.

121 **Below** This white buckskin dress of about 1890 was worn by a Kiowa woman who participated in the Kiowa version of the Ghost Dance. It bears simple colours and a moon and stars design. According to the visionary instructions given about how Ghost Dance garments should be made, there are no ornaments on the dress.

The whole world is coming.
A nation is coming, a nation is coming.
The eagle has brought the message to the tribe.
The father says so, the father says so.
Over the whole earth they are coming.
The buffalo are coming, the buffalo are coming.
The crow has brought the message to the tribe.
The father says so, the father says so.
Ghost Dance song believed to be sung by Kicking Bear, the Minneconjou Sioux leader

My children, my children
It is I who wear the morning star on my head
says the father, says the father.
Ghost Dance song

Gifts and giveaways

Gift giving and gift exchange among many Native peoples was a complex matter. It was influenced by the status of the giver and the receiver, the value of the goods given or exchanged, and whether a gift was expected in return. Among tribal peoples in North America, gift giving and exchange involved a huge set of mostly unspoken relationships.

Everyone had to share **food**, although the way it was shared was based on the status of the people. In the Plains tribes, women might give decorated clothes, robes, shirts and leggings – all made with great skill. Men might be obliged to give **horses** they had brought, traded or stolen. Everyone gave and still gives **blankets** and, in some areas, quilts. Whereas once parfleches filled with clothing and other goods were given away, today people fill plastic laundry hampers with lengths of cloth, dishcloths and towels to give away. In the pueblos, when children take part in their first ceremonial **dance**, their families throw sweets, fruit and bags of food to the people watching the dances.

Europeans and Indians had very different ideas about the giving and receiving of gifts and what that exchange meant. This caused misunderstandings about the implications and obligations of the exchange, which led to conflict between the two parties. Whites used the term 'Indian givers' as an insulting way of describing what the Indians expected in this two-way relationship of gift giving. The one area in which gift giving and receiving seemed to be fairly well understood was that of **diplomatic** gift exchange.

Gift giving brought honour and respect to

the giver, making the person who received the gift obliged to the giver. An anthropologist tells the story of a Hidatsa woman who gained retribution on a man who had annoyed her by giving him a beautiful **quilled** shirt and pair of leggings; in return he had to give her a **horse**.[23]

The quilt ceremony is about honouring people. 'When you are honoured, you know you are held in high esteem by the family', says *Spike Big Horn*.

122 Above Basketball Star Quilt, made in 1996 by Rae Jean Walking Eagle (Assiniboine/Sioux) for a high school basketball tournament giveaway. Star (or morning star) designs in particular are used in the Northern Plains on quilts made for honouring ceremonies.

When a veteran returned from **war**, he and his relatives gave gifts to honour those who had supported him. This was later transferred to other moments of achievement, such as graduation from school. A first ceremonial dance, a marriage or a basketball tournament might all require a giveaway, a kind of official public offering of gifts made by the people in the Northern and Southern Plains. In much of Indian Country, the honoured person or family and friends acting behalf of him or her, give gifts, rather than receiving them as in European societies.

Families pile up blankets, cloth, shawls and jewellery in order to show their support for a loved one in this way. In a baby naming **ceremony** or when someone is being given a traditional name, a Lakota family gives goods in honour of the person whose name is used.[24] For some people, giveaways are associated with the death of a family member. The relatives of a dead person might want to give away goods belonging to that person, either at a memorial feast a year after the death or after the services for the dead. See also **potlatch**.

At times, the Giving Away is hard, but also is an honour
for the treasured, or Giving Away when we are so Full,
the Harvest is the memory of the Living.
Elizabeth Woody, Wasco/Warm Springs/Navajo poet

Come   This is a give-away poem
I cannot go home
until you have taken everything & the basket which held it
When my hands are empty
I will be full
Chrystos, Menominee poet, 1988

Green Corn Ceremony

Several Southeastern Indian peoples (for example Choctaw, Yuchi and **Creek/Seminole**) hold an annual Green Corn Ceremony. Although there are frequent **stomp dances**, this is the main religious ceremony of the year for these peoples. It is an annual gathering of traditional peoples at which much of political, social and religious importance takes place. They hold ceremonies on traditional grounds kept for this purpose and the rituals are important for the ongoing life of the people. Although each of these tribes celebrate Green Corn in different ways, for all of them it is a time of healing, forgiveness and of reconciliation. Before the Green Corn Dance, no-one can eat **maize**. Afterwards, maize is eaten to show how it is a symbol of continued life and good for the people. Several Creek, Seminole and Choctaw Green Corn sacred ceremonial grounds throughout the South are now threatened by development. The tribes are struggling to hold onto them because of their significance in the life-renewal ceremonies of their people.

Haida

The Haida, **Tlingit** and Tsimshian are the three language groups that occupy the rugged islands off the **Northwest Coast**. Separated into two clans, the **eagle** and the **raven**, they trace descent through the female line. They travelled great distances in large carved dugout canoes, which were highly prized by other groups for **trade**. **Fishing** for **salmon**, halibut and sea mammals was the main **economy** of these people. Today fishing fleets can still be found in many coastal communities. Men fish and build **boats**, while women work in canneries. More recently, logging has become important and a number of bands have formed logging co-operatives. Although tourism has increased, unemployment has forced many to leave the **reservation** and go to the cities in search of work. Along with economic development issues, **land claims** and campaigns against logging and clear-cutting continue to be the central issue of the Haida and other communities on the Northwest Coast.

The Haida were master carvers and were highly acclaimed for their **art** that depicted animals or images from myths. They carved fine figures in wood, bone and horn; spoons, bowls and other domestic objects; wooden **sculptures**; and massive crest, 'totem' or house poles. Their important architectural achievements could be seen in their large cedar houses with carved support posts.

The Haida system of **potlatch** laid down a structure of social hierarchy based on both hereditary status and acquired wealth. It also reinforced a system of redistribution of wealth within the community.

Handsome Lake

The **Seneca** Handsome Lake was the brother of the traditional leader, Cornplanter and a hereditary chief of the **Iroquois** Confederacy. In 1799 he founded the modern Longhouse religion. His rise as a prophet began with a series of visions. Messengers from the Creator instructed him to tell the people to restore and keep their traditional **ceremonies**, to give up alcohol, sexual promiscuity, wife-beating, quarrelling and **gambling**. Instead the people were to start social reform among families and to oppose further European intrusions on their land and culture. His gospel, drawn from ancient Iroquois religious ideas and practices, was

123 Above Made in the 20th century, these corn husk **dolls** show construction and clothing typical of the 18th century. They are plainly clothed, like followers of Handsome Lake during the Longhouse festivals of the early 1800s. The male doll wears a white cotton shirt, black beaded leggings and brown cloth moccasins. The female doll wears a calico tunic, a black skirt with glass **bead**s on the hem and leggings of blue strouding (woven wool cloth) beaded at the bottom.

reinforced in part by similar **Christian** beliefs and customs and by the Iroquois' traditional faith in prophecy. Handsome Lake died in 1815 at Onondaga in New York. By the 1850s, his gospel had spread widely and the new rituals had become part of Iroquois religious custom. The moral code spread quickly and restored a ceremonial cycle whose survival today continues to make the Iroquois a distinct political and ethnic group.

The women faithkeepers asked Handsome Lake's grandson, James Johnson, to help set down his grandfather's teachings. James Johnson and Ely S. Parker (a Seneca scholar) finally recorded Handsome Lake's words in 1845. These teachings are often known as the 'Code of Handsome Lake', and are called the Good Message (*Gawi'yo*) by Longhouse people. The Seneca are the 'firekeepers' of the Longhouse religion. To this day they visit reservations to preach the Good Message of Handsome Lake.

This is from an English version of the Good Message of Handsome Lake:

It was the original intention of our Maker,
that all our feasts of thanksgiving should be
seasoned with the flesh of wild animals.
   But we are surrounded by pale-faces, and in a short time
the woods will all be removed.
Then there will be no more game for the Indian to use
in his feasts.
   The four Messengers [who appeared to Handsome Lake] said, in
consequence of this, that we might use the flesh of domestic animals. This will not be wrong.
   The pale-faces are pressing you on every side.
   You must therefore live as they do.
   How far you can do so without sin, I will now tell you.
   You may grow cattle, and build yourselves warm and comfortable
dwelling-houses.
   This is not sin; and it is all that you can safely adopt of the
customs of the pale-faces.
   You cannot live as they do.
   Thus they said.
   Continue to listen: It has pleased our Creator to set apart as
our Life, the Three Sisters [maize, beans and squash]. For this special favour, let us ever be thankful.
   When you have gathered in your harvest, let the people assemble,
and hold a general thanksgiving for so great a good. In this way you will show your obedience to the will and
pleasure of your Creator.
   Thus they said.
   Reg Henry, Cayuga faithkeeper

Headgear and headdresses

Native headgear shows much more diversity and variation from group to group than **footwear**. This might be because headgear is usually non-essential and can be adapted to style, fashion, climate, environment and culture. Headgear is associated with **ceremony**, and often shows status, achievement and relationship. In this way it says much more about the culture than footwear. Some men's headgear identified the

man's role or rank in society and told of his actions and achievements, for example in **feathers** fixed to the headpiece. Other headgear might have been practical, perhaps decorative, but designed for daily wear.
   Headgear used in ceremonies was thought of as special, almost sacred, and only to be handled or worn by people who had the right to do so. The Pueblo women wore painted *tablita* during certain **dances** and the Goose Society headdress was worn by Hidatsa women. In the Plateau region of North America hats made of hemp (or jute) and beargrass had designs woven into the cap and shell, with feather and **bead** attachments. Women wore these caps during the Longhouse religious rituals and ceremonies connected to root digging, weaving them like the root bags into which they gathered the roots. Nowadays, some women might wear them for **pow wow** dancing, although traditional religious people believe they should only wear them for traditional root feast activities. The wearing of one today designates someone honoured for her knowledge of the traditional skills and ceremonies. Many caps worn today are old ones, passed down by relatives; but in California the caps are being made anew by **basketmakers** among the **Yurok** and Karok women whose traditions demand them.

I have been learning to weave root bags… .
My teacher told me as we sat twining, 'We are making beautiful houses for our little sisters.' I… asked, 'Who are our little sisters? 'The roots –
pia-xi, khoush, sowit-k, wak amu', she answered.
Elizabeth Woody, Wasco, Warm Springs and Navajo poet

Women and men in the Northeast often copied European hats, 'Indianizing' them to suit their own purposes. In the 18th century, **Iroquois** women favoured plaid wool Glengarry caps, the common hat worn by Scots military men. Often mistakenly called 'Princesses' by Europeans, young Indian women wore a type of crown, often **beaded** or decorated with silver and ribbons, when they represented their tribe in public events of the late 19th and 20th centuries. In the 18th and 19th centuries, **Cherokee** men, such as **Sequoyah**, often wore a kind of wrapped trade cloth turban, sometimes decorated with the **feathers** of flamingos, spoonbills and red-tailed hawks.

124 Above A Tsististas/Cheyenne feather bonnet of the 19th century.

125 Above This commercially made baseball cap was **beaded** by Arvo Mikkanen, a lawyer and tribal judge of the Comanche Nation of Oklahoma. Modern Native peoples, like their predecessors, show their tribal affiliation or identity on all sorts of objects. These include car bumper stickers ('I'm Comanche Indian and proud of it'), T-shirts ('Don't Worry, Be Hopi'), hats and badges. Baseball caps have been popular with Indian men since the late 19th century.

126 Below A **Mi'kmaq** 19th-century women's headdress, made of velvet and **beads**. The shape may be derived from 18th-century French women's headdresses.

Beaded headbands, worn by **Algonquin** women and men, were mistakenly thought by whites to be headgear worn by all Indians. Indians in films, for example, commonly wear either beaded headbands or Plains 'war bonnets', no matter what tribe or kind of person they are supposed to represent.

Much headgear was also closely associated with hairstyles. Indian men from many tribes shaved their heads on the sides and wore their hair down the centre made to stand up straight. This famous 'Mohawk' hair style was popular among many Indians in the Northeast in the 18th century and again with young people in Europe and the United States from the 1970s (so-called 'punks'). Later, some tribal peoples stopped wearing their own hair shaved on the sides and 'roached' up the centre, instead wearing a

127 Left This Otoe roach spreader, c. 1820–25, is made of **elk** antler with a **buffalo** head design. It helped to hold apart the 'porky' or deer hair roach on the man's headpiece. **Feathers** – an **eagle** feather perhaps if the person had the right to wear one – were placed in the holder on the top of the roach spreader, between the fringes of animal hair.

headdress made of deer hair or the soft, long belly hair of the porcupine which gave the same look. It became an important hair style to wear with the **pow wow** fancy dance outfits in the 20th century.

Horses

Horses, first called 'sky (or holy) dogs', revolutionized the **economy** of the Plains. They came to be a measure of value, as deer and deerskins had been before them. Plains **economic** exchange was worked out according to how many horses some goods, prospective marriage partners and services were worth.

The decoration of horse equipment in Plains cultures, with ornamented saddles, and **beaded** and carved bridles, shields, swords and lance scabbards, shows how important the horse was in the Plains world. Plains Indians (such as the **Sioux**) painted and gave spiritual protection to horses before battle just as they did to human warriors. Crows (a so-called 'horse culture') are well known for the number and quality of their horses, and for the decoration of horse equipment for war, show and presentation.

128 Below A late 19th-century **beaded Blackfoot** man's 'pad' saddle. Women made the highly valued Blackfoot saddles, for their own families and for **trade**. As in other horse cultures, men's saddles were different to women's saddles and their horse equipment and horses had different decoration.

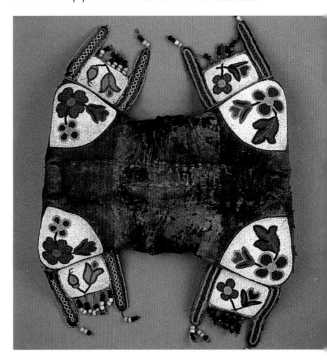

Crows still feature mounted horse parades at their annual celebration and gathering, the Crow Fair, but now also decorate and use cars in the way they did horses.[25]

Some peoples, such as the Nez Percé, developed specific pony breeds (Appaloosas or 'paint ponies') which, to the present day, are very valuable in the horse and cattle business. Crow, **Blackfeet**, the Nez Percé and Kiowas were called the 'Lords of the Plains', because of their command of the horse. These tribes, along with the **Navajos**, developed the tradition of the Indian **cowboys**, cattle raising and the rodeo after **reservationization** and their days of riding the Plains were restrained.[26]

130 Kwakwaka'wakw house, c. 1900.

129 **Below** Coastal **Salish** house posts.

House posts

House posts are often mistakenly referred to as 'totem poles' by non-Indians. They appear inside and outside the dwellings and gathering places of people on the **Northwest Coast**. The rights to have these sometimes elaborately carved posts were first acquired by supernatural heroes in legends. The rights were inherited – along with feast dishes – by **clan** chiefs and aristocratic families. The posts display the crests of chiefs and their families, and tell the stories of how they were acquired and the deeds of their supernatural ancestors.[27]

80

131 **Left** Bob Haozous, an **Apache** sculptor, mocks the relationship of '**cowboys and Indians**' in this 1988 steel **sculpture**, *Apache Pull-Toy*. Shot full of holes, the cowboy defends his toy from 'vicious Apaches' who fulfil their stereotype. Much of contemporary Indian humour involves the stereotyping of Indian behaviour.

Humour

Native humour appears in traditional stories and creation tales and in **ceremonies** and rituals. Storytellers detail the outrageous and socially unacceptable deeds of animal trickster figures such as **Coyote**, **Rabbit**, Crow and **Turtle**. Sacred **clown** figures, *katsinas*, and animal **dancers** act out humorous dramas before an audience that learns good behaviour by laughing at bad behaviour.

There has always been intertribal joking, usually about the strange habits and customs of the other tribes. Like all peoples, Indians joke about **food**, especially if their foods are strange or forbidden to other peoples. The largest group of jokes told by Indians across the country revolve around **Sioux** and **dog** eating. Although many tribal peoples all over the world eat dog, and, in fact, many (such as the Plains tribes) only eat it ceremonially, the dog's place as a domestic pet for Europeans has made people feel uneasy about eating it. For Indians, teasing Sioux about dog-eating amounts to a national sport. At a **pow wow**, some **Ojibwa** sing a mock 'honouring' song called 'How Much is that Doggy in the Window?' to their long-time traditional Sioux enemies. The Sioux retaliate by singing a song called 'Here Comes Peter Cottontail' to their Ojibwa enemy-neighbours, who are known as 'rabbit-chokers' because of their fondness for rabbit.

Finally, there is Indian humour that involves joking about white people. Artists and potters, at Cochiti Pueblo for example, make humorous **sculptures** of foolish figures from their own communities and of sheriffs, priests, **cowboys** and the white people who have come to their world. (See picture 71 on page 51.) Tales from the 18th century onwards record jokes that pass back and forth between these different peoples with different sets of rules about how to behave.

132 **Below** A Nuu-chah-nulth club of whalebone, c. 1778, from Vancouver Island. Before **bows**, arrows and guns, clubs were used for hunting, for war and for rituals in the **potlatch**.

Hunting

Hunting and **fishing** provided the **food**, clothes and shelter for Native peoples, and continue to provide it for some. Although the significance of hunting, as opposed to **agriculture**, has probably been overestimated for some Indians, some Native peoples in the **Arctic** and Northwest Territories and Plains rely almost solely on hunting for their provisions. Before the **fur trade** disrupted traditional hunting, it was an activity characterized by ritual practice and by a huge variety of tools and weapons.

People on the West Coast of Vancouver Island, Nuu-chah-nulth/Nootka, Makah and some **Inuit** hunted **whales**. Whale hunting needed hunting and leadership skills, the wealth to buy and keep a craft and crew, and the religious knowledge to follow the many ritual and religious practices necessary for whale hunting. The role was very well respected in the community. The hats they wore (decorated with scenes of whale hunting and ivory, bone, **shell** and **feather** ornaments) sheltered the heads of men, reduced glare on the open sea and were a sign of the prestige and position of those allowed to wear them.

133 **Left** This 19th-century **whaling** hat is sometimes called a Maquinna hat, named after an 18th-century chief. There is an inner hat, woven from cedar **bark**, and an outer 'basket' hat of twined spruce root, cedar bark and surf grass.

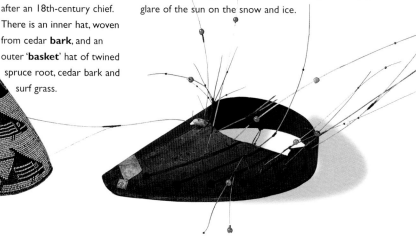

134 **Below** This Alutiiq/**Aleut** bentwood hunter's visor is decorated with bone and **feathered** objects that bring good fortune in hunting. It shields the hunter's eyes from the glare of the sun on the snow and ice.

Indian Territory

The notion of an 'Indian Country' to which tribes would be removed arose with the Louisiana Purchase of 1803. The idea was to have new lands to exchange for Indian Eastern lands, and the country immediately west of Missouri and Arkansas came to be that 'Indian Territory' in about 1830. Treaties with the tribes removed from the Southeast stipulated that their new lands would never be included in any state or territory, and 'the Indian Territory' would never endure white settlement.

The so-called 'Five Civilized Tribes' (**Cherokee**, Choctaw, Chickasaw, **Seminole** and **Creek**) were removed there, while other removed tribes were put in 'Kansas Territory' just north of Indian Territory. After the **Civil War**, the US government cancelled all of the **treaties** with tribes in the area, reduced their lands again and opened them up to other tribes. The Cheyenne, Arapaho, Caddo, Comanche, Wichita, Kickapoo, Otoe, Missouri, Shawnee, Eastern Shawnee, Modoc, Pawnee, Tonkawa, Kaw, Osage, Peoria, Potawatomi, Iowa, Sac and Fox, and Wyandot were moved from other territories and resettled there after 1866. Indian Territory then covered much of the present-day state of Oklahoma.

In 1889, the government opened up lands to non-Indian settlement, to allot Indian lands not from the Five Civilized Tribes under the Dawes General **Allotment** Act, and sell 'surplus' (unallotted) lands to whites. A plea from the Five Civilized Tribes to create the state of Sequoyah failed in Congress in 1905. The creation of the new state of Oklahoma in 1906 cancelled all agreements with tribes for the preservation of Indian Territory, Kansas Territory and Oklahoma Territory.

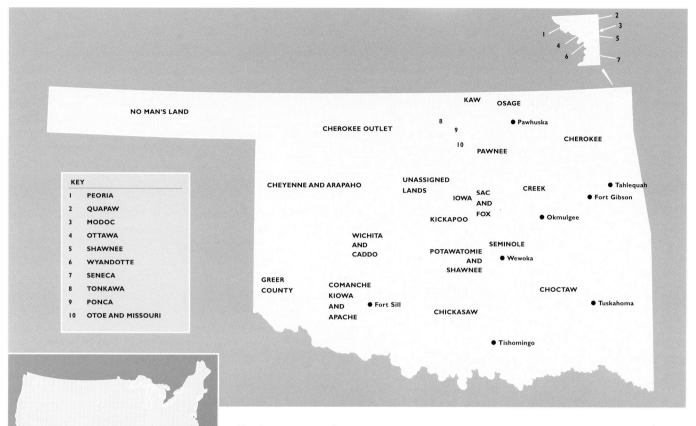

KEY
1	PEORIA
2	QUAPAW
3	MODOC
4	OTTAWA
5	SHAWNEE
6	WYANDOTTE
7	SENECA
8	TONKAWA
9	PONCA
10	OTOE AND MISSOURI

135 Above Indian Territory, 1886–1889.

Intermarriage

The Native peoples of North America intermarried with one another for centuries before Europeans, **Africans** and others arrived in North America. However, it was the invasion of North America and the intermarriage and sexual relations with non-Indians that created an enormous mixed-blood population – Indian, European and African – that began to change the political and cultural landscape of North America. Some thought that such interaction was predictable and desirable. Others thought it was disastrous, but inevitable. Europeans applied many different theories of race and culture to the different mixes of people developing in the 'New World', even though they themselves were composed of just such mixed populations.

T he day will soon come when you will unite yourselves with us, join in our great councils, and form a people with us, and we shall all be Americans; you will mix with us by marriage; your blood will run in our veins and will spread with us over this great continent.
Thomas Jefferson to the Indians in the West in 1808

European men mostly saw Indian women as sexual partners. Whether by force, with consent or to create political alliances, European men and Native women began to have sexual relations, creating the first of a new group of mixed-blood peoples. Such alliances, whether temporary or permanent, changed forever the terms under which Native peoples existed and survived.

According to the customs of many Native peoples, adult women were free to form sexual alliances with anyone they chose; marriage being a different category of behaviour. In matriarchal societies, children belonged entirely to women, as did the property and distribution of resources gained from **agricultural** or **hunting** land. Indian men would abide by the rules concerning women. So if the couple separated, the man would leave with only that which belonged to him when he arrived. If an Indian woman formed an alliance with a European man by choice, she would have had every reason to imagine that her rules would be followed. Europeans, however, often held different notions about inheritance, especially concerning children.

Just as European ideas about property, leadership and government differed greatly from the Native ideas, so did the alliances between men and women. European men often married or formed alliances with Indian women of status (the sister of a leader, for example) so that they could then – according

83

to their understanding of inheritance – secure a right to her property as well as access to the friendship of her male relatives. In a way, such actions acknowledged the importance of women. In the European mind, this alliance gave the male control of the property and of the children born from the relationship.

Conflict over the interpretation of different practices was inevitable. With European laws imposed on them, the Indians lost out and women's status was undermined. As late as the early 20th century, when oil was discovered in Oklahoma, it was common practice for white men to marry into high status female-centred Indian families. Under common property laws, they would then inherit the wealth which would have been reserved for the woman's family (under Osage practice, for example). In a number of famous instances in Oklahoma, men murdered Indian women so that husbands could inherit their wealth. So it was that women's high status was sometimes used as a way of removing Indian property and altering the position of women.

Moreover, people of mixed race (Indian, white and, in some instances, African) were thought of and treated differently than their supposedly 'full-blooded' relatives (Indian, African or white). In some instances, when their bloodlines included white genes, their status was raised. In others their mixed bloodlines caused them to lose status. Some used terms such as 'squawmen' for men who had sexual relationships with Indian women and 'half breed' became a negative term. Others thought that mixed bloods were the key to the 'civilization' of the Indian. In Canada, certain people of mixed Indian and European descent were called **Métis**. They have no formal **status** in Canada, but are recognized in the political process. In the United States, there is no formal recognition for a 'mixed-blood' tribe. Each tribal group treats mixed bloods differently, measuring the blood quantum of each part of an individual's genealogy and granting status/enrolment in the group based on that quantum (see page 40) and other forms of ancestral descent.

Inuit/Inupiaq

The Inuit are made up of several distinct groups: the Mackenzie Delta Inuit of the Western Canadian **Arctic** and the Yukon coast; the Central Inuit made up of the Copper,

Netsilik, Iglulik and Baffinland groups who occupy much of the Canadian Arctic from Victoria Island and Coppermine River in the west to Baffin Island in the East; the Caribou Inuit of the Hudson Bay interior; and the Inuit of Northern Québec and Labrador.

The Inuit **hunted** sea mammals with harpoons in kayaks or *umiaks*. On land, caribou was the most important prey. The Inuit lived almost completely on animal meat (which they ate raw), but also gathered berries and bird eggs. Sea mammal blubber provided an important source of nutrition as well as oil for lamps and heat.

Social groups varied with the seasons. Several families, generally related through the males, remained together throughout most of the year. Hunters shared the kills among the group of families. When **food** was abundant, larger social groups of 100 or more formed. Women were skilled in preparing winter clothing from caribou hides and spent much of their time repairing or preparing garments. Various pastimes were also part of community life. During the winter, groups held many festivals at which people played **drums** and **danced**. In some communities women performed throat singing. **Games** such as the cup and pin or string figures were also popular, as was storytelling.

Contact between the Inuit and Europeans goes back to the Norse settlements of Greenland and takes the form of both battles and **trade**. **Fishermen** and **whalers** of several European nations were working off the Labrador coast after 1500 and probably came into contact with Inuit. The earliest continuous contact began in Labrador where Moravian **missionaries** helped the British governor of Newfoundland to negotiate peace with the Inuit in 1765. They then began establishing missions, near which the Inuit began to settle. **Explorers** did not reach the Arctic and the Central Inuit until the 19th century. Early contact was brief and mostly for trade as the explorers were still looking for the Northwest Passage (a seaway from the Atlantic into the Pacific north of North America). Then commercial whaling started along Baffin Bay and Hudson Bay. This brought the Inuit and European whalers into close contact and a few worked on whaling **boats**. After using up the Alaskan reserves, American whalers moved into Canadian waters by 1890. There they wintered near the Mackenzie Delta Inuit, bringing **alcohol** and **disease**.

The whaling and **fur trade** era took its toll on the Inuit. Alcohol abuse, infant mortality, tuberculosis and other health problems brought some groups close to extinction. The Canadian government did little to help the Inuit and left them in the hands of the missionaries. By the 1950s, the Canadian government became more active in the Inuit communities, and took over services provided by missionaries, fur traders or police. The government built **schools**, encouraging settlement in permanent communities. Inuit abandoned their hunting camps and nomadic lifestyles for the lure of this subsidized housing and other services. Life has changed greatly for the Inuit, with modern technology replacing traditional Inuit ways. Snowmobiles replaced **dog** sleds, boats and motors replaced kayaks and air **transport** links Northern communities. Unemployment is high and jobs are seasonal. Some families still try to live off the land or return to the land for part of the year, hoping to retain or regain something of a traditional **subsistence**, land-based lifestyle.[28] Only in recent years have Inuit been able to demand control over their lives.

In 1991, approximately 30,000 people identified themselves as Inuit and 19,000 as partially Inuit. The Inuit remain a majority population throughout their traditional land. Taught in schools, Inuktitut is still the **language** of the Arctic. It has two written forms, one using syllabics and the other using the Roman alphabet. The Inuit Broadcasting Corporation produces newspapers, radio and television. **Land claims** settlements have given Inuit some measure of **self-government** and **economic** status. The Northwest Territories have now been split in two to create a self-governing Inuit homeland of **Nunavut** in the Eastern Arctic. This territory has status similar to that of a province in Canada.

This land of ours is a good land and it is big, but to us Inuit it is very small. There is not much room. It is our own land and the animals are our own, and we used to be free to kill them because they were our animals. We cannot live anywhere else, we cannot drink any other water. We cannot travel by dog-teams in any other place but our land.
Innakatsik, Baker Lake, 1989

Invention and innovation

Every culture has within it forces for change, innovation and invention, as well as the forces for resistance to change. Moreover, each has different levels of tolerance for such change. Both internal forces (such as the death of leaders and the appearance of prophets) and external events (such as war, famine and drought) push change, as do external forces such as **war**. Certain individuals and groups, moved by personal or practical needs, create the objects, the ideas or the events that start change. Some changes come from a need to solve problems, such as a **hunter**'s need to reduce glare in the **Arctic**. Other changes come from an individual's desire to do something new, or different, such as **Sequoyah**'s development of a written **language** for the **Cherokee** or the artist's need to change a traditional design. New technologies (for example guns or motorized vehicles) cause people to respond with further innovations. Natives have produced their share of inventions and changes.

136 Below Wood goggles, the first 'sunglasses', created by the **Inuit** to shade **hunter**'s eyes from the sun's glare on the ice.

137 Below The canoe and the kayak remain models of invention. Their basic structural forms were so perfect that they have never changed, even when the materials for building them (wood, hide and **bark**) were modernized (fibreglass). Kayaks, like this one from King Island, Alaska, remain enormously popular, although used more for **sport** by non-Indians than for **hunting** and **fishing**.

At first, I made Klikitat cedar root baskets using only the traditional mountain designs with horses or people in between… . Next I took an idea from the coastal baskets, putting an edging of animals around the top … with a black line above and below… . I moved from the old traditional designs to putting what I wanted on a basket… I began to use scissors instead of the knife my teacher used.
Nettie Jackson, 1992

138 Above In 1871, some of the hereditary chiefs of the *Haudenosaunee* (once 50 in number) gathered to recite the laws of the Confederacy, using the **wampum** belts that remind them of the history and the structure of the people. From right to left: Joseph Snow (**Onondaga**), George Martin Johnson (**Mohawk**), John Buck (Onondaga), John Smoke Johnson (wampum keeper and Mohawk), Isaac Hill (speaker and Onondaga) and Seneca Johnson (**Seneca**).

Iroquois Confederacy

The Iroquois Confederacy – sometimes referred to as the League of the Iroquois – was the political group formed by six nations, together called the Iroquois. The Iroquois call themselves *Haudenosaunee* ('people of the longhouse'). This is taken from the custom of building permanent towns with communal houses and ceremonial buildings called 'longhouses'. The members of the Confederacy saw themselves as a family with 'one body, one mind, one heart'. They shared religious and cultural beliefs and they acted as a single group in **trade**, **war**, peace and **treaties**.

The exact date that the Confederacy was founded is unknown, but by 1600, it comprised five separate nations: the **Seneca**, **Mohawk**, **Oneida**, **Onondaga** and **Cayuga**. Their original homeland is in New York State and Ohio, but all groups are now found in communities in Canada as well. By 1720, Tuscarora had joined the five nations, forced in defeat by Southern colonists and other Indians to migrate from North Carolina. *Deganawida* (the Peacemaker), a Huron prophet, came to end years of war and bloodshed among the individual nations. In 1799, a Seneca prophet called **Handsome Lake** travelled through the Iroquois territory in an attempt to restore traditional religious practice and to encourage the leaders of the various Iroquois nations to work together to replace violence with positive actions. He enlisted the assistance of the Onondaga Chief, Hiawatha, to spread his Great Law of Peace. The Nations came together into a Confederacy or League and structured themselves like the upper and lower house of some parliamentary systems. Governed by a Council of 50 chiefs (*sachems*), the League holds its main Council Fire (meeting place) at Onondaga. When a Chief dies, the senior woman in his **clan**, the clan mother, has the responsibility of choosing his successor, who governs (like his predecessor, whose name he inherits) until his death or removal by the clan mother.

The Confederacy supported trade, negotiated agreements and settled disputes among the six nations as well as with European colonists and other Indian nations. When the American colonies tried to unite during their war with Britain, some thought that the Confederacy might be a partial model for the new US government. During the American Revolution the Iroquois Grand Council declared neutrality. However, many Iroquois aligned themselves with the **British**. After the war, the state of New York took most of the Iroquois land. **Joseph Brant**, a British loyalist, negotiated lands in Canada as a result of the Iroquois participation in the war. In the 1840s, the Oneida were resettled to land in Wisconsin and in Ontario, Canada. The Grand Council again formed at Onondaga, New York, adding a new Council at Grand River, Ontario.

On many occasions the US and Canadian governments tried to break the power of the traditional Confederacy Council and install an elected system. In 1924 on the Grand River, Six Nation Reserve, the Canadian Royal Mounted Police arrested all the Confederacy chiefs and arranged elections. In 1959 the chiefs attempted to overthrow the elected government, but were arrested. Although an elected band council is still in place, the traditional Confederacy chiefs continue to hold Councils and discuss the business of the community. Today modern communities split their religious life between **Christianity** and the traditional Longhouse religion following the teachings of Handsome Lake.

Iroquois have always said that they are a sovereign nation and oppose many of the policies of the Canadian and US governments and the Indian Act. Traditionalists also believe that Iroquois should not participate in Canadian or US politics and oppose voting in elections and military service as a threat to their **sovereignty**. In the 1920s, the Six Nations Reserve issued its own passport and currently competes internationally in lacrosse.

Jay Treaty of 1794

The Jay Treaty granted Indians free passage between Canada and the United States. This was of particular importance to Iroquois because once the United States and Canada had been established, their peoples were split across the borders. Both nations had difficulty respecting the Treaty. For years, the **Iroquois Confederacy** held annual border crossing events in defiance of the violations of their **sovereignty**, finally forcing the US government to honour the Treaty in 1928.[29]

139 Right Rick Glazer Danay, a **Mohawk** artist, produced this work, *Mohawk Lunch Pail*, as a comment on Mohawk/**Iroquois** bicultural and binational identity. The Mohawk eats a good lunch (on the New York side), composed of a Canadian Moosehead beer. He is half Canadian and half American, he is half free and half captive, he is half high steel ironworker and half culturally 'Mohawk'. He is able to cross the US-Canadian border freely because of the Jay Treaty, whereas his ancestors were driven across that border because of their loyalty to the **British** during the Revolutionary War.

Treaty of Amity, Commerce and Navigation, 1794

His Britannic Majesty and the United States of America, being desirous, by a treaty of amity, commerce and navigation, to terminate their difference in such a manner, as, without reference to the merits of their respective complaints and pretensions, may be the best calculated to produce mutual satisfaction and good understanding; and also to regulate the commerce and navigation between their respective countries, territories and people, in such a manner as to render the same reciprocally beneficial and satisfactory; they have, respectively, named their Plenipotentiaries, and given them full powers to treat of, and conclude the said treaty, that is to say:

Who have agreed on and concluded the following articles:

Article I

There shall be a firm, inviolable and universal peace, and a true and sincere friendship between His Britannic Majesty, his heirs and successors, and the United States of America; and between their respective countries, territories, cities, towns and people of every degree, without exception of persons or places.

Article III

It is agreed that it shall at all times be free to His Majesty's subjects, and to the citizens of the United States, and also to the Indians dwelling on either side of the said boundary line, freely to pass and repass by land or inland navigation, into the respective territories and countries of the two parties, on the continent of America (the country within the limits of the Hudson's Bay Company only excepted) and to navigate all the lakes, rivers and waters thereof, and freely to carry on trade and commerce with each other.

No duty of entry shall ever be levied by either party on peltries [hides] brought by land or inland navigation into the said territories respectively, nor shall the Indians passing or repassing with their own proper goods and effects of whatever nature, pay for the same any impost or duty whatever. But goods in bales, or other large packages, unusual among Indians, shall not be considered as goods belonging *bona fide* to Indians.

In faith whereof we, the undersigned Ministers Plenipotentiary of His Majesty the King of Great Britain and the United States of America, have signed this present treaty, and have caused to be affixed thereto the seal of our arms.

Done at London this 19th day of November, one thousand seven hundred and ninety-four.

(Seal) Greenville

(Seal) John Jay

K

Katsinas

For six months of the year, from February (with the Bean **Dance**, called *Powamu*) to July (with the Home Dance called N*iman*), the *katsinas* come from their home in the San Francisco mountains and stay in Hopiland, dancing in the plazas and teaching the children the Hopi way. They come from Katsina Village in the sky with other *katsinas*, the Council of the Gods, to bring messages from and take them to the gods.

There are over three 300 *kacinam* in Hopiland. These masked spirits come in the winter to Hopiland to chastise and reward the people, to teach the Hopi ways, to make the crops grow by bringing **rain** and to accompany the Cloud People to the *mesas*. In their dances, a form of prayer, they bring the families, **clans** and villages together. Sometimes they bring presents, sometimes they behave in a frightening way. Often they behave like the **clowns**, misbehaving and acting in strange and wonderful ways – making fun of people, rolling in the dirt and worse.

Hopis don't worship *katsinas*. *Katsinas* are intermediaries between the Creator and humankind. They deliver the blessings of life – health and happiness and hope. *Katsinas* provide living examples of how life is conducted.
Ramson Lomatewama, Hopi educator and poet

L

Land

Despite their diversity, American Indians eventually shared a common experience. Their lives changed forever following the arrival of Europeans, as Indian land became American land.

Indians and non-Indians had different understandings of the land and their place on it. These include issues of 'ownership', the ways in which land is used, issues of control, the sacred nature of some land and the **Removal** from homelands.

The Great Being… gave us this land, but the white people seem to want to drive us from it.
Attakullakulla (Little Carpenter), Cherokee, 1769

Question: What did Indians call America before Columbus came?
Answer: Home!
Indian joke

The Rio Grande Valley is high and dry, laced with a few streams that carry precious water from the mountains that surround it. To the Pueblos who believe they have been here since they emerged from the *sipapu*, a hole in the ground, to the centre of the Earth – the centre which each of them inhabits now and forever, this land was sacred space, an indivisible entity of earth, plants, animals, humans and spirits. Spaniards saw a conquerable human and material resource which would enrich the Spanish Empire, individual men and the Holy Catholic Church through Christian conversion. Later immigrants saw a land of marketable, but unexploited commodities, human and material, as beautiful and unpopulated landscape.
Simon Ortiz, Acoma Pueblo poet

In our language, our name is *q'idicca?atx* (pronounced kwadich cha'ak) This means the 'People who Live Among the Rocks and the Seagulls'… . Our stories say that we have lived here since the beginning of time. We have always been whale hunters and fishermen… . Our people learned to make a living from the sea and to respect the power of the ocean and its inhabitants.
Greig Arnold, Makah carver, 1997

Native people throughout the Americas have always had an intimate relationship with their lands and with the places from which they come which give them nourishment, which give them life, which give them identity… . For Native American people, art and the ways in which they made a living from their lands, whether it was farming or hunting and gathering or fishing, and the expressions of various kinds of ritual and ceremonial ways of being, are all an integrated whole, which in a sense are reflection of a spiritual ecology… in which Native people throughout the Americas understood the relationship and expressed the relationship to their land and their place.

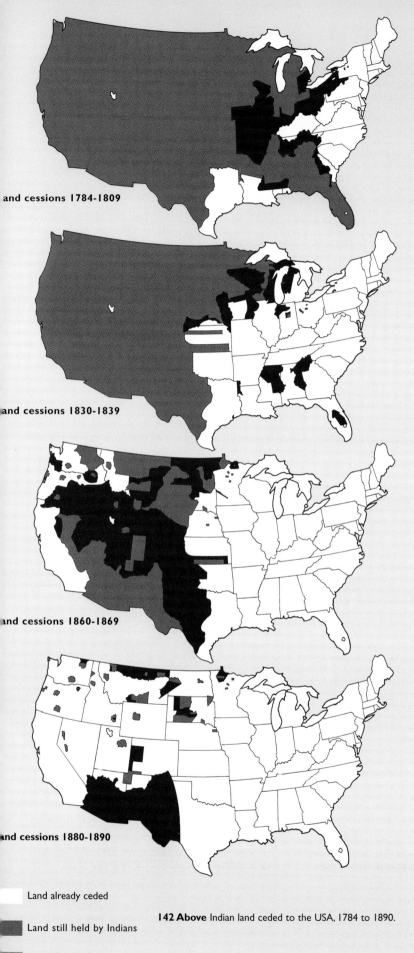

and cessions 1784-1809

and cessions 1830-1839

and cessions 1860-1869

and cessions 1880-1890

Land already ceded

Land still held by Indians

Land cessions

142 Above Indian land ceded to the USA, 1784 to 1890.

Through time, of course, and especially with the first contact with Europeans, this way of understanding, this way of relationship, changes sometimes dramatically.
Greg Cajete, Santa Clara Pueblo educator, 1995

It is important and a special thing to be an Indian. Being an Indian means being able to understand and live with this world in a very special way. It means living with the land, with the animals, with the birds and fish, as though they were your brothers and sisters. It means saying the land is an old friend and an old friend your father knew, your people always have known… we see our land as much, much more than the white man sees it. To the Indian people our land really is our life.
Richard Nerysoo, Fort McPherson

Land claims

In the United States, the Indian Claims Commission, established in 1946 to settle land claims that could previously only be settled by Congress, could award only a limited amount of money to tribes whose claims were successful. Until 1978, when the Commission's work ended, it came to be seen as a way of extinguishing aboriginal title. Many land claims that followed the break-up of Indian lands according to the General Allotment Act (see **allotment**) remain unsettled, as do the **reservation** rights to **hunt**, **fish** and use resources. The inability of most tribes to settle their land claims shows the difficulties of taking land claims to court when such claims are against non-Indians.

However, the courts have settled a few claims in favour of tribes. The US Supreme Court found that the State of Maine violated the Indian Trade and Non-Intercourse Act of 1790, which forbade the acquisition of Indian land by non-Indians without the approval of Congress. States, not Congress, took Mashpee, Penobscot and Passamaquoddy lands. As a result of the court's finding, the Penobscot and Passamaquoddy received a US$81.5 million settlement which enabled them to buy lands and develop **economic** structures for their futures.

The **Bureau of Indian Affairs** leased much of the remaining land held by Indians for 99 years at favourable lease rates to non-Indian businesses, ranchers, hoteliers and domestic residents. As these leases came up for

89

renewal from the 1960s to the 1980s, newly reinvigorated tribes have refused to renew them or have renegotiated them for better financial and legal terms. Thus, Native nations in Palm Springs (California) and Salamanca (New York) have held up property sales and exchanges for years until they have received more favourable leases on lands that belong to them.

Although the government, states and business have tried to resolve land claims cases by making compensation payments to tribes, some tribes have refused to take money in return for land. The **Sioux** case for the Black Hills, their sacred Paha Sapa, is one example. When gold was discovered in the Black Hills of South Dakota in 1871, the federal government tried to buy the land from the Great Sioux Nation, but the nation refused money for the land it believed to be sacred. The government broke the Treaty of Fort Laramie, removing the Black Hills from the nation's land settlement, but continuing to offer money as payment. The Sioux have refused it to date.

In Canada, there are two types of land claims. The first are 'comprehensive claims' based on aboriginal title, where the title to the land has never been removed. The second are 'specific claims', where the title is in dispute. The cornerstone of the legal argument for comprehensive claims is the **Royal Proclamation** of 1763. Where no formal **treaties** exist between Native bands and **British** and Canadian governments in most of Northern Québec, the Northwest Territories and most of British Columbia, groups claim that they never surrendered their lands. They claim land rights because they occupied Canada before the Europeans. The Indian Act made it illegal to raise money to pursue land claims until 1951, when the Act was amended. In 1973, the Supreme Court of Canada agreed that aboriginal rights did exist, and the long, slow process of negotiating settlements began. There were millions of dollars at stake as Native groups sought rights to resources as well as land.

The first claim settled was with the **Cree** in northern Québec. It was very controversial because it involved the development of a huge hydro-electric project. Later, groups in British Columbia, the Northwest Territories and the Yukon filed claims. The British Columbia claim by the Gitxsan-Wet'suwet'en

people (settled recently), is seen as a landmark decision. This is not only because it recognizes aboriginal title, but also because it affirms that the title must be upheld and protected under the Constitution. It states that the First Nations' spoken history is acceptable evidence and is as important as written legal records of the past.

Before the 20th century, about half of Canada's Native bands had signed treaties that surrendered certain rights in exchange for promised lands, money and other guarantees. Since the 1970s, Native groups have launched hundreds of specific claims over treaties. A number of groups have become frustrated that the government has been slow to settle these claims and have become militant, protesting with marches, and road and rail blockades. The most dramatic confrontation over a land claim was near the town of **Oka** in Québec in 1990. Heavily armed **Mohawks** blockaded the town in protest over a proposed golf course that would disrupt some of their **sacred lands**.

Languages

Before **contact**, Indian languages were as diverse and numerous as the tribes themselves. Many Native people spoke several languages, including sign and **trade** languages, which they used when communicating with other tribes.

Missionaries and the government led a cultural assault on Native languages, forbidding the speaking of those languages in **schools** and even on the **reservations**. For a few peoples, such as the **Cherokee**, development of a written language (**Sequoyan**), was combined with the rare support of the Church in using the tribal language in a religious context, in order to keep the language alive. Language was usually the main target for those who wished Indians to 'assimilate' and be 'civilized'.

Many languages, such as those spoken by Timuacan peoples in the Floridas, died with their people in the latter part of the 17th century. Most coastal **Algonquian**, California Indian languages and those from Oregon (Wappo, Yuki, Chimariko, Shasta, Takelma, Kalapuya, Coos, Chumash, Costanoan, Esselen, Siuslaw and Yana) cannot be restored, because there are no Native speakers remaining. In many places, only a few Native speakers of a language are alive.

At the beginning of the 20th century, most Indians spoke a tribal language and English was their second language. At the turn of the century, over 300 languages were spoken by Indians. In the last years of the 20th century, the only languages used by over 50,000 speakers are **Navajo** and **Ojibwa**.[30]

The introduction of a new people, a new culture, changed their whole outlook on life…. Handsome Lake predicted… that this new culture would introduce their language which in time will completely erase our own Native language from our minds.
This will be the last of Natives as a people.
Reg Henry, Cayuga faithkeeper, 1990

Linguists predict that Yup'ik Eskimo, Cherokee, Choctaw, Mikasuki, Cocopah, Keresan (Santo Domingo, Jemez), Havasupai-Walapai-Yavapai, Hopi, Tohono O'odham, Yaqui, Navajo, Mescalero, **Apache**, Tiwa, Western Apache, Yaqui and **Zuni** in the United States, and **Cree** and Ojibwa in Canada can survive into the 21st century.[31]

Most tribal peoples are making major efforts to revive and support their languages, because they know that tribal language – in the words of the Cherokee Language and Culture Preservation Bill – is the 'single most important attribute of cultural persistence'. Many tribes have language committees, cultural preservation offices, dictionary and language projects, and projects for the introduction and use of languages in schools. Now there are a number of professionally trained Native linguists and many others committed to the preservation and survival of Native language.

A few tribes besides the Cherokee have written languages. Almost everyone is aware that both new and traditional forms of language are passed on through the processes of song, story and **dance**.

The Mesquakie language, our ways, our religion are woven into one…. With another language, we cannot perform our religion.
Don Wanatee, Mesquakie, 1969

My parents are traditional, and I grew up with ceremonies and chants. I'd speak Navajo in front of a lot of friends at school, and they referred to us as 'sheep-camp girls'. What stays with me is a saying, 'Don't ever be afraid of having an accent. It just means you are worth two people.'
Susan Baldwin, Dilkon, Arizona, c. 1992

Literature

Although some Native peoples recorded their stories in pictures of various kinds before Europeans came to the Americas, most storytelling was by word of mouth (the oral tradition). Dramatic performance in **ceremonies** and in storytelling was the main body of literature for every tribe, although the styles, content and contexts for those performances varied from group to group. Indians have been writing in English, Spanish and French, but primarily in English, since the early days of the **missionary** invasion in the 18th century. From that time, Indians began writing down the stories that had remained only in memory and verbal form. They also began writing in a European way. From **Elias Boudinot** onward, many Native journalists documented the lives, histories and stories of Indians in the United States and Canada. Samson Occom (1723–92), a Mohegan Methodist missionary, first published sermons on the conditions of Indian life in 1772. From the mid 19th century, Native writers such as Charles Eastman, **Sioux**; Humishuma (Chrystal Quintasket), Okanogan (1888–1934); John Joseph Mathews, Osage (1894–1979); and John Rollin Ridge, **Cherokee** (1827–69), have brought a rich body of written literature to the American public in the form of autobiography, novels, poetry and humour. They have also turned material from the oral tradition into an accessible written form for an Indian and non-Indian audience. Native writers of the 20th century, such as Will Rogers, Cherokee (1879–1935); N. Scott Momaday, Kiowa; Leslie Silko, Laguna Pueblo (born 1948); James Welch, **Blackfoot**/Gros Ventre (born 1940); and Louise Erdrich, **Ojibwa** (born 1954), have gained worldwide audiences and literary awards for their work.[32]

Emily Pauline Johnson was born on the Six Nations Reserve near Brantford, Ontario. She was the daughter of a hereditary **Mohawk** Chief *Teyonnhehkewea* and an English woman. Johnson assumed her great-grandfather's Confederacy title and signed all of her poems

largely on Indian themes. She retired from performing and settled in Vancouver in 1909, collaborating there with Joe Capilano, a Squamish Chief she had met in London. Her work with him led to the much acclaimed *Legends of Vancouver* (1911). In 1912, she published *Flint and Feather*. She died of cancer in 1913. Johnson was the first Indian woman to publish books of poetry and collections of short fiction, and one of the first writers to explore the theme of mixed-blood Indians and their search for identity and place.

Joy Harjo, a member of the Muskogee tribe, was born in Oklahoma in 1951 and raised in New Mexico. She has written several books of poetry, including her award-winning *In Mad Love and War*, *The Woman Who Fell from the Sky* and *She Had Some Horses*. Most recently, she edited a new anthology of work by Native women, *Reinventing the Enemy's Language*. She has taught creative writing at several universities. Whilst a student at the Institute of American Indian Arts in Santa Fe, she discovered the value of poetry at a time when Indian politics were changing. At the heart of Harjo's poetry is compassion, grace and, in her own words, the need to express 'how justice can appear in the world despite forces of confusion and destruction'. These same ideas are important to her band 'Poetic Justice'. She is very inspired by the musical work of Jim Pepper, a Kaw jazzman, and she puts her words to a mix of jazz, blues and traditional music.

The music that speaks for us is a blend of influences that speak of community, love for people, for all creatures, for this crazy beautiful history and the need to sing with and of the sacred. These musics are our respective tribal musics... born of the indomitable spirit of a tribal people in a colonized land, a music born of the need to sing by African peoples in this country, a revolutionary movement of predominately African sources influenced by Europe and the Southern tribes; and rock and blues, musics cradled in the South that speak of our need to move with heart and soul through this land, this spiral of life. We are forged by this dance for justice and the absolute need to sing.
Joy Harjo, Muskogee poet and musician

141 Above Joy Harjo, Muskogee poet and musician.

'E. Pauline Johnson' and '*Tekahionwake*'. Often billed as the 'Indian Princess', Johnson performed part of her programme in fringed buckskin. In 1894, she travelled to London to give recitals and published her first book of poetry, *The White Wampum* (1895), based

battle marked the end of freedom for the Northern Plains Indians and became a symbol for both Indians and whites of how far apart they were. New myths about the cavalry, Sitting Bull, Crazy Horse, Custer and Buffalo Bill all came from this incident.

The victors could hardly have predicted what followed: Crazy Horse's assassination, the Wild West Show stardom (and later murder) of Sitting Bull, the **allotment** of the Indian lands under the Dawes Act and the final killing of the Minneconjou Sioux over the **Ghost Dance** resistance of 1890.

For both whites and Indians, Little Big Horn remains a significant battleground. The site lies on a Crow reservation and is part of the US National Park system. It was called the Custer National Monument until 1990. Indians everywhere petitioned for a name change to the 'Little Bighorn National Monument'. Everyone wants the story told the way they remember it. The Little Bighorn River still flows with blood.

Tomson Highway, a **Cree** from Northern Manitoba, is the eleventh of 12 children. He earned two undergraduate degrees in music and one in English and is a gifted pianist. A Native theatre group in Toronto performed his 1986 play, *The Rez Sisters*. His sequel, entitled *Dry Lips Oughta Move to Kapuskasing*, was an immediate hit and won the Canadian Dora Mavor Moore award for Best New Play. His work captures the humour and reality of Native life on the reserve.

Little Bighorn

Known to whites as 'Custer's Last Stand', the battle of the Little Bighorn in 1876 was the dramatic beginning of the end for the Indian Wars of the Plains and the final closing of the reservations. The trail that led to the Little Bighorn included the Fort Laramie Treaty in 1851, which established tribal boundaries in the Northern Plains, the 1864 massacre of Cheyenne at Sand Creek by the US Army, the 1868 Treaty establishing the Great **Sioux** Reservation, and the discovery of gold in the South Dakota Black Hills in 1875. **Sitting Bull** and Crazy Horse, leaders of different Sioux peoples, were doomed to battle General George Armstrong Custer in the last fight against **reservationization**. The Sioux and Cheyenne outmanned and outgunned Custer's cavalry and his Crow allies, but this

My friend, I do not blame you for this. had I listened to you this trouble would not have happened to me. Sometimes my young men would attack the Indians who were their enemies and took their ponies. They did it in return.

We had buffalo for food, and their hides for clothing and our tipis. We preferred hunting to a life of idleness on the reservations, where we were driven against our will. At times we did not have enough to eat, and we were not allowed to leave the reservation to hunt.

We preferred our own way of living. We were no expense to the government then. All we wanted was peace and to be left alone. Soldiers were sent out in the winter, who destroyed our villages. Then Long Hair [Custer] came in the same way. They say we massacred him, but he would have done the same to us had we not defended ourselves and fought to the last. Our impulse was to escape with our squaws and papooses, but we were so hemmed in we had to fight.

After that I went up on the Tongue River and lived in peace. But the government would not let me alone… I came here with the agent to talk with the Big White Chief, but was not given a chance. They tried to confine me. I tried to escape and a soldier (a Sioux) ran his bayonet into me.

Crazy Horse, on his deathbed, to Agent Jesse Lee, 1877

93

Long Walk of the Navajo, The/Bosque Redondo

In 1864, more than 8,000 **Navajos** and 400 Mescalero **Apaches** (long enemies of the Navajo even though they shared a common Athapaskan language) were held at Bosque Redondo, a reservation in Eastern New Mexico. They had been marched there by Kit Carson and Union military forces in the Southwest. Bosque Redondo proved to be the Navajo equivalent of the Trail of Tears. The Long Walk, a forced migration, was the tragic end of a long and bloody conflict between Navajos and others for control of the lands and minerals in Navajo country. Bosque Redondo proved a disaster. As many as 2,000 died, suffering **disease** and winters with little housing, clothing or **food**. A few thousand Navajos escaped the round-up. Eventually, these remaining people and the Navajos at Bosque Redondo pleaded for their return rather than exile to **reservations** far from their homeland. Mescaleros fled Bosque Redondo in 1865. In 1868, the remaining Navajos were allowed to begin the slow march home to rebuild their lives.

T he mourning of our women makes the tears roll down into my moustache.... I want to go and see my own country.
Barboncito, Navajo war leader, 1868

Lumbee

Lumbees, who now number more than 40,000 people, are the largest non-**federally recognized** group of Indian people in the United States. With much controversy over their origins as a people and their identity as Indians, their history remains muddied. For at least two centuries, the ancestors of Lumbee people – named after the Lumber River that flows through the area in which they live – have resided in North Carolina. According to their spoken stories, they have several possibilities of origin: as **Algonquian** peoples who lived in coastal North Carolina and merged with the descendants of the so-called Lost Colony of Roanoke; as Siouan or Cheraw or other tribal remnant peoples who fled the **disease** and encroachments that accompanied white settlement; or as mixtures of the two groups named above. What is certain is that, whoever they were as Indians, they mixed and **intermarried** in their

North Carolina setting, with whites and with **Africans** after the 1700s. Whatever Native languages they spoke and whatever Native lifestyles they led, they had merged with those of the people with whom they intermarried. Still, they remained separate from white communities, and were always treated and recognized as non-whites. Known for their resistance to racism, they organized a massive protest against the Ku Klux Klan in 1858, driving the Klan out of Robeson County.

In the 20th century, they were known as Croatan, **Cherokee** and the 'Indians of Robeson County'. In 1953 they took the name Lumbee, and have since worked hard for the education of their people as well as for federal recognition that so far has been denied them. In many ways, the Lumbees are typical of a number of communities, largely on the East Coast of North America (such as the Wampanoags in Massachusetts and the **Abenakis** in Vermont) who have persistently claimed Indian histories and connections, but who, for the most part, have been denied federal recognition and federal services.

Maize

Maize (called 'corn' in the United States) is cultivated from the area south of Chile in South America, north to Montreal in Canada.

It is grown in both high and in low altitudes, in wet and dry climates, on high plateaus and in tropical forests. Its grains vary in size. The stalks can be 1–3.5 m high and the ears 12–15 cm long. Wild maize has been dated to 80,000 BC, long before human inhabitation. Domesticated in Mexico, maize (*zea maize*) was introduced to the American Southwest at least 6,000 years ago. Along with **beans** and **squash**, it is the most important **food** plant of Native peoples in the Americas and one of the three most important grains in the world.

In the 17th and 18th centuries, 'Indian maize' was one of the major export crops of North America, and remains a major grain in world **trade**. Even now, ecologists and agricultural specialists insist that we have much to learn from both the cultivation and preservation methods of so many varieties of maize by Native peoples.

Most Native peoples intercrop, that is plant other species along with maize. When maize is interplanted with beans or other legumes, its stalks provide support to the climbing bean vines. The legumes also add nitrogen to the soil. Almost all Indian farmers plant in hills. Low-growing crops, such as squashes and pumpkins, can be interplanted between the hills, thus choking out the weeds. It also, as is often the case in Mexico and Central and South America, allows edible green crops, called *quelites*, to thrive.

Each Native group adapted maize to suit its agricultural needs. A Hopi blue maize is adapted to deep seeded planting in hilled sand conditions. In Hopi country, the sand stays moist at a depth of 20–30 cm. The Hopi maize has a root and shoot elongation much tougher and faster growing than other varieties. Locally cultivated plants are distinctive plant populations adapted over centuries to specific climates and soils and selected to fit certain conditions.

143 A ladle (c. 1850) used by Seminole for stirring and eating *sofky*, a hominy soup made by Muskogean people.

The culinary preferences of particular cultures have favoured the forms, tastes and colours of some plants over others. Hopi maize is red, white, blue and yellow as a result of selective growing. Blue, red, white, yellow and black varieties mirror the sacred colours of the universe.

There are six colours of corn: yellow, white, blue, black, red and speckled. And each colour stands for a direction: north, south, east, and west, up and down… . White is for the east, where the sun rises, and the blue is for the west. In a **ceremony**, when they're about to blow tobacco smoke and incense to the six directions, they sing the song of corn and growth, and here is one:

Ha-o, my mother, ha-o, my mother,
Due west, blue corn ear, my mother,
Due eastward, blooming blue-bird flower,
Decorate our faces, bless us with flowers.
Thus being face-decorated,
Being blessed with flowers,
We shall be delighted, we shall be delighted.
Ha-o, my mother, ha-o, my mother.
Due east, white corn ear, my mother,
Due south, red corn ear,
Due northward, blooming maiden blossom,
Due above, black corn ear, my mother.
Due downward, blooming sunflower,
Due below, sweet corn ear, my mother,
Due upward, blooming, all kinds of flowers.
Agnes Dill, Isleta Pueblo

By 1500, the Iroquois had flints, dents, popcorns and sweetcorns, and grew several varieties of each. In the Northeast, archaeological evidence shows that enough maize could be stored to feed thousands of people for over a year. The tribes went to war when the **British** and Spanish destroyed or confiscated corn stores. The British succeeded in weakening the **Iroquois** who fought for the American side in the Revolutionary War by burning their maize stores. Maize remains central in Iroquois life today as it was in the 18th century. Whereas women had the primary responsibility for all cultivation until the mid 18th century, now both men and women tend the fields. Iroquois people still cultivate many old varieties of maize and store it in a traditional manner (in braids) after harvest. Foods made from maize remain important in the ceremonial and daily diet, and Iroquois still make objects from the husks such as **dolls** and **masks**.

In the Southwest, Southeast and Northeast, maize is the main religious and ceremonial symbol. Cornmeal accompanies prayers made to the spirits. **Dances** and prayers for healing take place around it and it appears in **art** and stories.

One **Navajo** story says that the wind created people from two perfect white and yellow ears of maize. Among the Pueblos of the Southwest, a baby's naming ceremony is accompanied by maize pollen scattered over the ground, thrown to the air and rubbed into

the hair. Some of the *katsinas* bring and give corn. A young **Apache** girl, in her puberty ceremony, is covered in cornmeal. The Iroquois have an important ceremony for Green Corn, which, as in the Southeast, reconciles all bad feelings between people.

Corn is the basic ingredient that all of us, as Indian people, believe in. We use it in our ceremonies; we use it for subsistence; we use it to feed our animals. So the corn plays a very significant role in our daily lives. We start with it, we end up with it.... We give thanks to the Creator for providing this to us. Corn... we use in our songs, we use in our dances, we use in the daily life of all of us.
Walter Dasheno, Governor, Santa Clara Pueblo, 1995

But for me, I cannot forget our old ways. Often in summer I rise at daybreak and steal out to the cornfields, and as I hoe the corn I sing to it, as we did when I was young. No-one cares for our corn songs now.
Maxiwidiac or Buffalo Bird Woman, Hidatsa, 1921

I start planting, helping my father, when I was about 12 years old... my father... always tell me, 'You better do it right now, because Mother Nature is right there looking at you, so you'd better talk to Mother Nature so she can give you some food, some good vegetable.... He said someday when you become a farmer, be sure and get up early in the morning, about 4:30. If you plant corn in the field, come down and talk to them. Talk to all little spirit around there, so they can hear you talk your Indian language. Talk to them in Indian and pray and say your Indian prayer early in the morning.' So that's why we always have a good crop.
Ramos Oyenque, San Juan Pueblo, 1995

Before I go out into my field, I sing a song .... My cornfield has a prayer.... I offer corn pollen to Mother Earth.... I use Corn Pollen to communicate with the Holy People. She gives me dried cornhusk so people can smoke tobacco at ceremonies.... I also grow corn so my family eats roasted corn, kneel-down bread or mutton stew with corn.
Jesse Biakeddy, Navajo, Big Mountain, Arizona

144 **Below** Maize from Ramos Oyenque's fields at San Juan Pueblo.

145 **Left** A Navajo maize farmer in Canyon de Chelley, Arizona.

146 Above This modern version of the Corn Mother was made by Pablita Abeyta (*Tah-nez-bah*), a Navajo ceramic sculptor. Many native people, including Hopi, Cherokee and Arikara, believe in a Corn Mother who gave birth to them and made the land that provides for them. The extensive and continued use of Corn Mother's image on ceremonial clothing, in ceremonies themselves, in prayers, songs and dances reminds us that the crop remains important to Native people.

147 Above Onondaga women in the 18th and 19th centuries used a double-headed stick to pound and grind shelled, dried maize in a wooden mortar, such as this. Cherokee, Creek, Choctaw and Seminole women used similar pounders, usually made from the hard and durable hickory tree.

Masks

All over the world, people hold **ceremonies** and ritual **dances** for healing, for **war** or peace, for hunting and **fishing**, and for weddings, births and funerals. Masked characters join in these dances. Humans take on the roles of the animals or spirits that must be called upon or driven out in order to put things right. Although not all Indians use masked ritual dramas, many do. For those people, the masks themselves become part of their spiritual and cultural heritage, living things that must be handled with respect and care.

Seneca societies used **medicine** masks, carved from a living tree, along with **drums**, snapping **turtle rattles**, canes, songs, dances and plant medicines in healing ceremonies. To many **Iroquois**, masks are among the most sacred of objects, inappropriate for display in a **museum** or in a book. Some Iroquois continue to use masks in the practice of the Longhouse religion. The **Cherokees** made carved wooden masks, called 'booger masks' by the first anthropologists who studied them, to embody the spirits who came to frighten, heal and instruct during Cherokee ceremonies. However, Cherokees today do not use these masks, although they still refer in story, song and ritual to some of the creatures (such as **buffalo**) and spirits that the masks represent.

Inuit and tribal peoples from the **Northwest Coast**, **Navajos** and **Apaches** use masks in their religious and social rituals. On the Northwest Coast, the Canadian government recently returned to the Kwakwaka'wakw many masks it had taken away when it banned the **potlatch**.[33]

148 Left This Nunivak mask from the **Inuit** of the Bering Sea was probably worn at feasts. In the mask, the human spirit and animal spirit (*inua*) merge and reverse themselves, surrounded by the **fish**, **whales** and tools that characterize the **hunter's** world.

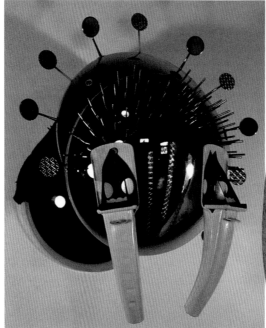

149 Right This Punk Walrus Mask/Spirit (*Pooka Timerik Inua*), *c.* 1987, was made by Larry Beck, a Yup'ik artist. Beck's masks, made of 'found' materials, bring to life animals from his **Arctic** world, with their *inua* (spirit) intact.

I'm an Eskimo, but I'm also a 20th-century American... my found materials come from junk yards, trash cans [bins] and industrial waste facilities, since the ancient beaches where my ancestors found driftwood and washed up debris from shipwrecks are no longer available to me... even though I use Baby Moon hubcaps, pop rivets, snow tires, Teflon spatulas, dental pick mirrors and stuff to make my spirits... because, below these relics of your world, reside the old forces familiar to the *inua*.
Larry Beck, Yup'ik artist

151 Above Bella Coola sun mask.

The *matachinas* (masked) dance, brought to the Americas by the Spanish, may have been taught to Indians as a way of making them accept the power and rule of Spain and of **Christianity**. Indians in Mexico and in New Mexico have turned the dance into a drama about the encounter between them. Usually danced on Christmas Day, it features the masked *Monarcha* (King), two *abuelos* (grandfathers), a bull and an unmasked young girl, who represents *Malinche* (the Spanish name for the conqueror Cortez's Indian mistress and translator). The young

150 Right Lillian Pitt, from the Warm Springs/Wasco people of Oregon, makes modern masks. This one is constructed with the Japanese *raku* method of ceramic firing. Pitt creates spirit masks from the stories and legends of her tribal past and from the physical characteristics associated with **Inuit** and Yup'ik masks.

girl represents innocence and goodness. The *abuelos* function as **clowns**, dancing among the other characters, keeping order and teasing the **tourists** in the audience. They also symbolically kill and castrate the bull, which represents Spain and evil. Some say they learned the dance from Moctezuma, the last Aztec emperor. In some pueblos, it is very 'Indianized', with the dancers wearing Pueblo ceremonial costumes and dancing to drums. In others, it is very Hispanic and Catholic, with *Malinche* wearing a white communion dress and dancing to fiddle music.

152 Below In this picture from the *matachinas* **dance** at San Juan Pueblo on Christmas Day 1992, the masked *Monarcha* dances behind *Malinche*, who wears a Pendleton blanket shawl, a white communion dress and Pueblo-style deerskin leggings.

Matrilineality and matrilocality

Unlike the patrilineal Anglo-American society, in which women and children took the name of their husbands and fathers, some Native people, such as the **Cherokee**, were matrilineal. Cherokees received their **clan** affiliation (**Wolf**, Paint, Blue, Wild Potato, etc.) from their mothers, and considered a person's only blood relatives to be those on the mother's side. This matrilineal kinship played a part in the status of women in Cherokee society. Men in matrilocal societies went to live in the homes of their wives, and a mother and her family had sole authority in raising children. Many Native peoples (such as **Iroquois** and **Navajo**) had matrilineal societies until the **Christian** and European laws of property and male descent were forced on them.

B y the time Napi came over to this side of the ocean, the Creator had already made more people. But the women couldn't get along with the men, so Napi sent them away in different groups. Not long after, he got together with the chief of the women so that they could decide about some important things. The chief of the women told Napi that he could make the first decision, as long as she could have the final word; the old people say that ever since then it has been this way between men and women. Napi decides many things for the men and women, and the chief of the women countermands him, making women have better skills than the men. Then she decides that men and women will live together after Napi put them apart. Now at that time men were living real pitiful lives. The clothes they were wearing were made from stiff furs and hides. They couldn't make moccasins or lodges and they couldn't even keep themselves clean. They were nearly starved. They were very anxious to join the women.
Beverley Hungry Wolf, a Blackfeet writer, in her version of a creation story, 1980

Although matrilineality was predominant in Indian societies, some tribal peoples were male-centred. These tribes had male gods, spirits and origin stories (see **creation stories**), and had government, inheritance and residence patterns determined by the male line of descent.

Medicine

Medicine is the English word by which Indian traditional healing – mental, spiritual (religious) and physical – became known. Native medical practice and scientific knowledge, based on plants, is connected to and even inseparable from spiritual healing. American Indians were skilled at using plants for medicinal purposes. Their knowledge of plants' different properties gave them a pharmacy of cough, cold and fever remedies, laxatives, emetics, antiseptics and pain killers. Research on a number of these plants now verifies their traditional Indian uses. American Indians were not only aware of the medicinal properties of a plant's roots, leaves, **bark**, berries and flowers, but also of how the properties of one plant enhanced the properties of another. Thus, they frequently made medicines of combined ingredients. Indians knew which plants could be eaten raw and which had first to be prepared in such a way as to reduce the plant's natural poisons. They knew how mature or how young a plant should be to be effective. They understood the dosages needed and they always ensured that a plant was not harvested in a way that would interfere with its own future propagation.

One plant used by many Native peoples for different purposes was mayapple (*Podophyllum peltatum*). Many tribes used the plant as a laxative, an emetic and remedy against intestinal worms. The Penobscots of New England prepared a mayapple ointment to use as a treatment for warts and skin cancer. In 1820, it was added to the United States *Pharmacopoeia*, an official registry of medicinal substances. Mayapple is also still used in several commercially prepared laxatives and for skin problems. Researchers believe it be to effective against some tumours and cancers.

Medicine bag, medicine bundle

Medicine bags and bundles have always fascinated non-Indians (although only a few Native cultures possess and use them) and so **museums** have often collected them. Medicine bags and bundles carry the tools and objects needed to protect an individual or a group. The bag or bundle and what it contains might come from a **dream** or vision, from a protective spirit or from someone or something with power. It could be filled with items of importance to the individual who carries it, for example special stones, parts of animals, **feathers** and painted objects. Like crosses to **Christians**, these objects (often called fetishes, charms or amulets) have special meaning and special protective powers to those who believe in them.

Anyone might carry a bag, but bundles are usually carried by someone who has been specially chosen to do so, either by a medicine man or by the previous bundle carrier. As bundles are sacred, they are brought out only occasionally and in a ceremonial context. They cannot be opened by anyone not responsible for them. They can only be seen by those participating in a traditional religious **ceremony**. Many peoples, such as the **Navajo**, have begun to recover bundles and objects (*jish*) used for healing which were taken from them. On their return, they have either been dismantled and destroyed, because they have been away from the medicine people for such a long time that they are contaminated, or they are 'reconsecrated' and used once again by those who understand their uses and powers.

Medicine men and women

The term 'medicine man' covers a wide variety of people who, in different tribes take care of the physical and spiritual welfare of their people.

The much used, often misused, terms of 'shamans' and 'medicine men' have different names in different cultures, but the term 'Indian doctor' in English covers most of them and their practices.

Medicine men and women carry the sacred knowledge and history of their people. They know the stories, songs, **dances**, **ceremonies** and rituals connected with the origin of humans, plants and animals, and their relationships. They understand the forces in the universe that can cause illness and disharmony and those that can heal and restore peace. Many believe that **Coyote**, the trickster, was the first doctor and that he created them.

Not all medicine people look after and heal the body, not all look after and heal the mind and spirit, but all know that body, mind and spirit are connected. Each of their particular practices are built on that understanding. Some specialize in particular conditions and problems, others specialize in diagnosis. Some **Navajo** *hataali* (singers) know only specific rituals for certain kinds of healing. After the problem has been diagnosed, by a hand trembler or a crystal singer for example, a person would go to a certain *hataali* who would conduct the 'sing' appropriate to that problem. In the Lakota way, some healers would conduct certain ceremonies because spiritual illness had manifested itself in a physical way. Others would be more like a minister, rabbi or priest, constantly overseeing the spiritual health of his or her people.

Among the Natives of California and the Navajo of the Southwest, some of the most respected medicine people were women. Changing Woman, the 'mother' of the Navajo People in their origin stories, gave them many ceremonies and stories for healing. She was herself a medicine woman. A girl usually begins to learn medicine from her grandmother at an early age. The Navajo women, who were weavers, had extensive knowledge of plants and the properties of many plants that are dyes. They also know the specific songs and ceremonies that will heal. Women may hold **medicine bundles** and special objects (*jish*) for healing. They may be herbalists themselves or be helpers or apprentices to others. They may be diagnosticians, working out what is wrong with a patient and what ceremony and procedure will provide the cure.

Of course, as with all cultures who practice or believe in traditional spiritual and physical medicine, there can be a 'dark side' to the practice of that medicine. The knowledge of the forces that affect the body and mind can be used for evil purposes, and Indian cultures do have sorcerers (so-called 'witch doctors' or 'magicians') who do not use their knowledge for good. Most groups forbid gaining and using such knowledge for evil and have stories that tell of the punishments for such practice.

Metal/metalwork, minerals and metallurgy

Before the arrival of the Europeans and their industries, Native peoples extracted minerals and worked metals of all sorts. Copper was abundant all over North America, and may have been used as early as 3,000 BC. In the Southeast, Adena and Hopewell peoples (sometimes called Moundbuilders) made copper into jewellery, including spiral-shaped earspools, gorgets (breastplates or neckpieces) and bracelets, **beads** and tools (**fish** hooks and axe heads). Copper appeared on **pottery**, together with **shells** and mica. Ancient people mined copper from surface mines or gathered it from rivers and hammered it, probably using heat in the process. In the North, near Lake Superior, copper and lead mining was common. In British Columbia, Alaska (on the Copper River) and the Yukon gold, silver, copper and lead did not require smelting. Cold-worked copper existed widely in Tsimshian Territory, with beads and bracelets found there as early as 500 BC. Copper proved to be an important material in the Northwest tribes, in the manufacture of coppers for the **potlatch** and for the display of wealth.[34]

In the Southeast, the Pueblos mined lead and, like their neighbours to the South in Mexico, used lead as pigment for fired pottery. However, this was not a healthy practice as the pottery leaked lead into the diet. The Spanish commandeered their lead mines to make bullets, and the Pueblos abandoned lead paints and took to vegetable-based pigments for their pottery. In this way, they produced the extraordinary pigments and painting styles distinctive to Pueblo clayware. Indians traded with Europeans for valuable iron goods, and scavenged metals from trade **boats** and expeditions. They remade metal goods such as gunstock, pots and tacks into items for their own use (see **recycled materials**).

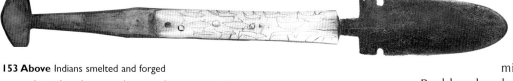

153 Above Indians smelted and forged copper, but others hammered, engraved and cut copper. Most often it was used for tools and weapons, but sometimes also for decorative work. Copper knives, like these, were made before worked iron and were an important **trade** item.

154 Below An early 20th-century **Navajo** ring and necklace. Navajos took the tools and techniques of Spanish silverwork and turned them into a uniquely Navajo **trade**. This was made possible by the silver and turquoise mines in the Southwest. The designs and symbols used were important to Navajos, such as the **squash** blossom and the *naja* or inverted rainbow seen in this necklace.

Native silver (mined or melted down from coins) was an important commodity. It was valued in the same way that gold was by the Europeans. Indians in the Southwest learned the metal stamping and casting techniques of the Mexicans and developed silverwork into a major **art**form and **trade** that continues today. In the Northeast, too, silverwork was used in trade and presentation. Indians combined traditional designs with European techniques and styles to create brooches, gorgets and other items. The Indians in the Southern Plains and Southeast became expert at a form of metalwork with German silver, or nickel silver, an alloy of zinc, copper and nickel, using it to make objects associated with the **Native American Church**.

Métis

The Métis were a distinct society that emerged in the 19th century in Western and Northern Canada. They are of mixed Native and European heritage. The word Métis comes from the French use of the Latin *miscere*, meaning 'to mix'. Much of this population is French-speaking. The rise and spread of the **fur trade** in the Hudson Bay and the St Lawrence trading systems in the Canadian Northwest began this population, usually born to Native mothers and Scots, French or English fathers.

Métis cultural roots rest near the Red and Assiniboine Rivers (Winnipeg today). **Buffalo hunting** and trapping were central to their identity. A distinctive clothing style evolved, mixing European and Native heritages.

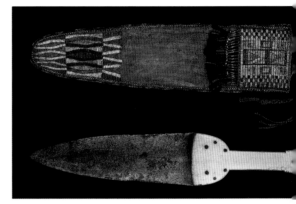

155 Above Métis loomweavers made detailed and complex objects, using the tiny **quills** that other Indians found hard to use with Native tools. This knife sheath, with loomed quills laid onto a buckskin frame, was probably made in about 1860 for a Sheffield knife traded to Métis for furs.

Men wore a long hooded coat (*capote*) with a brightly coloured sash or belt, trousers and moccasins. Women wore European dresses, with shawls or **blankets** covering their head and shoulders, with moccasins. The red sash (*ceinture de fleché* or L'A*ssomption* sash), which was adopted from the French and worn by many Indians from the fur trade era onwards, is an important symbol to Métis. Women were skilled **beadworkers** and they decorated moccasins, pouches and other items with floral designs. Fiddle **music** and step **dancing** became popular, a legacy of French and Scots heritage that remains important today in Métis communities.

In 1812 and again in the 1860s, the Métis found their way of life threatened. This was due to an influx of settlers onto lands given

156 Right An photograph of Louis Riel, the Métis leader, taken in 1868.

157 Below Maxim Marion, a Métis guide, is typical of mixed-blood children who became both a source of dispute and a bridge between their relatives. These children were 'between two worlds'. They understood the cultures of both their mother and their father and so became translators, guides and negotiators. This picture dates from 1872.

in 1812 and 1869 by the Hudson's Bay Company to Scots settlers, 'the new Canadian government'. Métis communities turned to **farming** as the buffalo and other wildlife were hunted. They demanded **land rights** along the Red River in the Northwest, a movement of 1869 known as the Red River Rebellion.

It was during this period that Louis Riel emerged as a community leader in the Red River Settlement. He was educated in Montreal, was fluent in French, English and **Cree**, and his education and background made him an obvious leader in the land struggles. The

uprising in 1869–70 forced Riel into exile. Manitoba joined the Canadian Confederation in July 1870. Even though he was exiled and so could not take up his seat, Riel was twice elected to Parliament in Ottawa. He returned to Canada, to the Métis settlement in Batoche, Saskatchewan, in 1884. In 1885 he and his armed supporters proclaimed a provisional government there, demanding the right of the Métis to govern themselves as well as to be represented in the Canadian Parliament. After several weeks, the Métis lost the rebellion at the Battle of Batoche. Louis Riel surrendered and the federal government hanged him for treason. Canada has since recognized the importance of Louis Riel in the struggle for nationhood. His statue was recently erected on the grounds of the Manitoba Legislature in Winnipeg, and the Canadian government apologized in 1998 for hanging him.

In 1991 approximately 75,000 people identified themselves as Métis, but it still remains unclear who should be considered Métis. Many people who are simply a mix of European and Native have begun to call themselves Métis, but they may not necessarily share the cultural heritage of the historical group. This definition can create tensions. A number of Métis organizations came together to define Métis as 'an aboriginal person who self-identifies as Métis and is a descendant of those Métis who were entitled to land grants or scrip under the provision of the Manitoba Act of 1870, the Dominion Land Act'. In 1984, the Métis were officially included as a community in the Canadian Constitution.

Although there may be many people in the United States who are relatives of the Canadian Métis – usually referring to so-called 'landless Chippewa' in Montana and to the **reservation**-based Turtle Mountain Chippewa in North Dakota – the term still has little 'official', even unofficial, meaning in the United States.[35]

103

Mi'kmaq/MicMac

The Mi'kmaq homelands lie on the East Coast of North America. The Mi'kmaq are closely related to neighbouring Malecite/Maliseet, but are a more coastal people. In a Mi'kmaq **creation story**, Glooscap, the Mi'kmaq trickster/creator, transformed animals into their present shapes and taught humans how to make tools.

In the winter small groups of related families would gather. In the summer larger groups met, living in portable **bark**-covered wigwams. The sea was important for food and **transport**. Mi'kmaq made birchbark canoes, snowshoes and sleds like the other Algonquian peoples in the Northeast. They wore highly decorated hide clothing with dyed **quillwork**. After **contact** with Europeans, they used cloth decorated in a distinctive Mi'kmaq style with **beads**, ribbons and embroidery. The women's traditional high peaked caps of beaded and embroidered dark cloth (adapted from French women's clothing of the 17th century) and the adoption of Gaelic-influenced fiddle **music** and **dancing** show the considerable French influences on Mi'kmaq culture.

Each chief (*sagamore*) in the Mi'kmaq tribes held power over the group. In the 17th century a *sagamore* called Membertou recorded the first contact with the **explorer** Jacques Cartier in 1534. Intensive French colonization began in the early 17th century and the Mi'kmaq became French allies and partners in the **fur trade**. Their associations with the French drew them into conflict with the British and their **Iroquois** allies. Disputes between the British and French came to a temporary halt with the Treaty of Utrecht in 1713, and the French gained temporary control over Atlantic Canada. Tensions brought about the formation of the Wabenaki Confederacy, an alliance of Northeastern Algonquins, Mi'kmaq, Maliseet, Passamaquoddy, Penobscot and **Abenaki**. The **British** signed **treaties** with the Mi'kmaq in 1752; these formed the basis for the **Royal Proclamation** of 1763. Settlers poured into Mi'kmaq country and the Mi'kmaq lost much of their land, their role in the fur trade and their population due to **disease**.

Today 27 bands of Mi'kmaq live in three Maritime Provinces, in Québec and in Newfoundland. Their treaties have stood the test of time and Mi'kmaq traditional **hunting** and **fishing** rights have been protected by the Supreme Court of Canada. Many communities today are involved in the lumber industry, fishing, lobster trapping and the crafts industry. However, unemployment is still high on reserves and many people have moved to cities for work.

Politically very active, the Mi'kmaq created the Union of New Brunswick Indians and the Union of Nova Scotia Indians to help settle **land claims**. Today the Council acts as the political and religious leadership for the community.

Missions/missionaries

Missions and missionaries, Catholic and Protestant, became one of the main and effective tools of the conquest of the Indians. From 1524, when the Spanish **explorer** Cortéz first introduced missionization as a way to conquer Mexico, to the present day, when vast efforts continue in the Southwest to missionize the **Navajo** and Hopi, missionary activity has always accompanied the dismantling of traditional Indian society. The missionization of Indians, in South and North America, was thought of as pacification – peaceful conversion – as it was not supposed to need **war** in order for it to succeed. Often, however, Spanish efforts at conversion led to military action.

158 Left An 18th-century **trade** silver cross, probably brought by French Catholic brothers from France and given to **Mohawks** in Canada.

Many missionaries in Indian Country had military back-up, although missionaries and military men often felt that they were at odds with each others' methods and goals. In many instances, however, missionary zeal to convert and civilize Indians interfered with military and civilian force. This was the case of the Moravian, Baptist and Methodist

159 Right James Luna, a Luiseño (named after San Luis/Saint Louis) or 'Mission' Indian and artist from California, often explores aspects of Indian history. In *California Mission Daze*, he creates a graveyard. This is much as he imagines those graveyards next to the missions created by the friars for those Indians who died during their service to the missions.

160 Below California 'Mission' Indians, who were superb **basketmakers**, made this woven hat, with crosses woven into the basketry in the style of the hats of Spanish friars.

missionary stand against the Jackson administration and the state of Georgia in the issue of **Cherokee Removal**. Reverend Samuel Worcester was imprisoned by the state of Georgia for his acts in defence of the Cherokees. He insisted that **Christian** pacification was already working and he took cases to the Supreme Court to prove that point.

The people who came here with us have done grave injury to the Natives of this land. This brought great discredit to our teaching, for [the Indians] said that if we who are Christians caused so much harm, why should they become Christians?
Fray (Friar) Francisco de Zamora, 1601

An Indian listened to a long missionary sermon about Heaven and Hell and finally said to him, 'Pastor, when you die, will you go to Heaven?' And the minister said, 'Absolutely, I will go to Heaven.' And the Indian said, 'Well, if you are going to Heaven, then I believe I will go to Hell.'
An old story that Indians like to tell

Even before the Spanish established a permanent settlement in the Rio Grande Valley, between 1598 and 1680, Franciscan friars were sent to convert Indians. Their missions forced a different social order on the people and made them abandon their old way of life. They destroyed religious objects and shrines sacred to the Indians. Although there were laws to protect the Indians, missionaries and the colonists who followed them demanded labour and tributes from them in the form of **food** and **blankets**. The Pueblos resisted these efforts to change their lives, even taking to war in 1680 (the Pueblo Revolt) and driving the friars and the Spanish armies out of the Pueblo world, only to have them reintroduced 13 years later.

The Franciscan, Junipero Serra, went into California in 1769 with troops from the Vice-Regency of Spain. He built a mission system that depended on Indian labour and Indian lands. In the South and in the rich coastal areas of California, Indians were forced to support the military encampments, missions and towns developed by the Spanish. The Spanish and, later, the Mexicans moved Indians to villages near the towns and missions to continue their labour for the 'cross and the crown' and to work for the new generations of ranchers and businesspeople.

Mohawk

The Mohawk occupied Eastern New York and were the most easterly nation of the **Iroquois Confederacy**. Their original name means 'people of the flint'. The Dutch and British called them 'Mohawk', meaning 'man eaters'. In the Confederacy Council, Mohawks are one of the three elder brothers along with **Seneca** and **Onondaga**. They have nine chiefs. They led the move to create the Confederacy and they remain dominant in Iroquois **diplomacy**.

As with all Iroquois nations, the Mohawk are **matrilineal**, with a life based on **agriculture**. They were among the first Iroquois nations to come into **contact** with Europeans. By allying themselves with Europeans, especially the Dutch, they could control access to **trade** routes. Mohawk communities adopted many of the the Huron and Neutral nations, which were dying out from **war** and **disease**. In the 18th century many Mohawks were converted to Catholicism by French Jesuit missionaries called 'black-robes'.

The British tried to win Mohawk support. During the American Revolution the Confederacy Council voted to remain neutral, however many tribes took sides in the conflict that tore the Confederacy apart. When the **British** lost the war, the Mohawks were forced out of the Mohawk Valley and followed **Joseph Brant** to negotiated lands in Ontario. Other Mohawks fled to Montreal, later settling at Tyendinaga, Oka and at Akwesasne. In 1993, a small group relocated back to the Mohawk Valley in New York State.

A century ago, Mohawk men found a niche as high steel construction workers and can be found working on large projects in the United States and Canada.

Museums

The history of Indians and the history of museums are almost inseparable. The first museums in North America (Peale's Cabinet of Curiosities in Baltimore and the Smithsonian Institution) and in Britain (the Ashmolean) were built around their display of ancient artefacts gathered by naturalists and **explorers** on their travels. The earliest museums considered Indians to be part of the natural universe. They displayed geological specimens, animals, plants, Indian artefacts and skeletal remains. The presence and evidence of ancient people in North America intrigued and baffled early scientists or 'naturalists', and they collected specimens of all known species to study.

Explorers, artists and military men also collected objects **traded**, given by Indians or taken by force. In addition, **missionaries**, who urged Indians to give up the objects associated with a pagan culture, piled up collections of Indian artefacts.

Displayed first in private exhibitions, whether in the Great Houses of Britain or in Thomas Jefferson's Monticello, these objects then found their way into newly developed museums. Only in the late 19th century did the collection of American Indian objects become deliberate, and then associated with the archaeologists, anthropologists and private collectors such as General Pitt-Rivers, George Gustav Heye and Prince Maximillian von Wied. The Peabody in Boston, the American Museum of Natural History in New York, the Pitt-Rivers in Oxford, the Volkerkunde in Vienna, the museum at Cambridge University and the Carnegie in Pittsburgh, the Royal Ontario Museum and the Canadian Museum of Civilization all joined the Smithsonian and the British Museum as places where one would find Indians and all with which they were associated. These places became, alongside universities, centres for research on indigenous peoples of the world. Many places built their reputations on their displays of and research on Indians. The museum associated with the University of California at Berkeley even put an actual Indian on display when it 'collected' Ishi, the 'last' Yahi Indian in California.

In the 20th century Native peoples began to question the ethics of collecting and displaying human ancestral remains, asking for their return to Indians. People all over the world then began to call for the return of objects obtained by **war** or force as well as the objects that represented important cultural and religious property. Thus, Indians

161 Above Cree from Hudson Bay made this set of nesting **birchbark baskets** decorated with porcupine **quills**. In the early 19th century an **exploring** sailor, Captain Middleton, acquired them. He inscribed them to 'Miss Nellie Middleton', but gave them instead to Sir Hans Sloane, the man whose collection established the foundation for the British Museum in London.

162 Right An early bone spoon (1702) from New England, from the collection of Sir Hans Sloane.

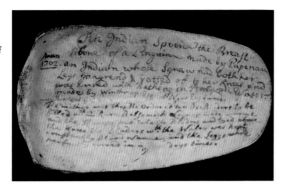

and museum curators, acknowledging that museums can return something – both materially and intellectually – to Indian Country. Some people have undertaken professional training in the last 15 years so that they can interpret and preserve Native history and cultural materials from a Native point of view.

Many museums in Britain, Canada and the United States now work closely with Native scholars, both academic and community-

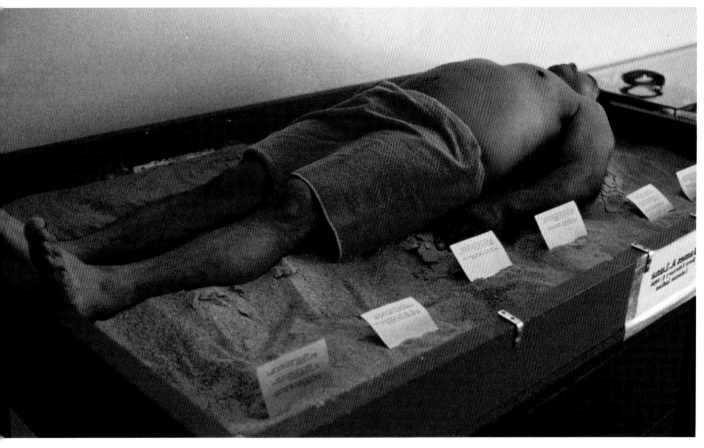

163 Above James Luna, in his 1987 performance theatre work, *The Artefact Piece*, makes himself into an object in a museum case. Around him are personal artefacts, such as his diploma, tapes from his music collection and family photographs. Commenting on non-Indians' obsession with dead Indians, Luna's work is about the relationships between Indians, Indian 'art' and museums.

in the United States encouraged the Native American Graves and Repatriation Act 1990 to be passed by Congress, so that they might recover both their sacred and culturally important objects from museums.

Indians in many areas have now established museum-like institutions (cultural resource centres) which better fit their notions of what a cultural store should be. These are places where Native people interpret their lives and histories for an Indian and non-Indian audience. Many Native peoples now work closely with anthropologists, archaeologists, historians

based, to share materials and to produce exhibitions and programmes that reflect a new understanding of Indian life and history.

The British Museum's Ethnography Department collaborated with **Inuit** in the development of an exhibition 'The Living **Arctic**' in 1987. The Smithsonian's new museum, the National Museum of the American Indian, is curated largely by Natives. It promises to offer a partnership between Indians and museums that will reflect new ways of working and thinking about Native peoples.[36]

Music

The way the Indian people, long ago, made their songs was by looking at what the Great Spirit gave them to understand in their minds… to make songs out of what they saw. Like the leaves when the wind blows, they're shaking; they make a little noise. That's how they got the idea to put bells on their legs. And sometimes you see a fowl, like an eagle, an owl, a chickenhawk. The Indian people looked at them, the way they'd sway their wings, how they'd go down and up. That's how they'd make the pitch of their songs… and everything they'd see; when they looked at the sky, the clouds, they'd make songs out of those… . And they'd think that there's kind of a holy spirit going round, and that's how they'd make their songs.
Fred Benjamin, a Mille Lacs Ojibwe elder, 1984

Indian music, like Indian **dance**, is connected to specific tribal traditions, usually religious. Music accompanied **ceremonies, games,** stories and dance. Tribal groups developed musical forms very specific to them, modified and adopted from other groups (Indian and non-Indian) with whom they had **contact, trade, intermarriage** and even **war.** The distinctive regional and tribal styles exist and thrive, along with more '**pan-Indian**' and intertribal music, such as **pow wow** war dance songs.

Whenever corn [maize] is being ground, there are certain things that go with it, and so the woman never tires out in grinding corn. She can grind it for three or four hours straight, because while she grinds, the men come and sing. And in the grinding songs they tell you almost what to do. And you have to grind to the beat, to the rhythm of the songs… . And in the singing, it tells you to keep grinding, and you grind in rhythm. It's a beautiful song. I think it's all in Laguna.
Agnes Dill, Isleta Pueblo

Most Native peoples sing Protestant and Catholic hymns and gospel music in the various Indian **languages**. There are special tribal versions of mainstream songs, such as 'Amazing Grace'. **Mi'kmaq, Métis, Creeks, Cherokees** and **Ojibwa** adopted fiddle music from French, Scottish and Irish traditions. They even took the Gaelic styles of step dancing from those traditions. In the

Southwest and California, Mexican Indian and Spanish music from 19th-century Mexico influenced and merged with some California Indian music.

Indian professional musicians have mixed European and Indian styles of music and instruments, incorporating rock and roll, rhythm and blues, jazz, reggae, folk and even classical music. Guitars, synthesizers and keyboards, in addition to the horns and strings adopted in the 19th century, supplement **drums, rattles** and **flutes**.

'Traditional' Native music has experienced a revival. Modern Native music, meant to appeal to a non-Indian audience too, has also grown. There are Native recording companies and Native radio stations. Indian musical events, such as pow wows, are likely to feature everything from flute players to blues singers along with different styles of traditional tribal dance music.

We make all our own songs. The songs just come to you. You have to wait for them. We practice and teach each other. Our songs are in Cree and the other ladies are real good. They learn to sing the songs in Cree and we sing some songs in Nakota.
Celina Jones, Cree, leader of the Crying Woman drum group, Fort Belknap, Montana

When the dance is over, Sweetheart, I will take you home, in my one-eyed [one headlight] Ford.
…
I'm from Oklahoma, Got no-one to call my own, So, I come here looking for you, *heya.*
…
I don't care if you're married, I'll get you anyway.
…
BIA, I ain't your Indian anymore, So farewell, goodbye to you, *heya.*
Oklahoma-style intertribal social dance songs, sung in English, called 'Forty-Nine's'

108

Names

Names given to the indigenous peoples of the Americas, at various places and times, by specific groups of people:
aboriginal/aborigine, Amerindian, *barbaros* (Spanish for 'barbarous'), First Americans, First Nations, Indian, indigenous, *indios* (Spanish for 'in or with God'), Native American, Original, redskins, savage/*sauvage*.

I'm just glad Columbus wasn't looking for Turkey!
Indian car sticker, c. 1975

Names given to some specific Indian peoples or types of people, often generally applied to any male, female or child:
brave, buck, Chief, King, maiden, papoose, Princess, squaw, Queen.

Names translated from French or Spanish, or in English about misunderstood or caricatured physical characteristics or relationships:
Blackfeet/Blackfoot, Flatheads, Gros Ventres (French for 'big bellies'), Nez Percé (French for 'pierced noses'), peaux rouge (French for 'red skin'), redskin.

Names given to **sports** teams and mascots in the United States:
Braves/Chief Noc-A-Homa, Chief Wahoo, Indians, Little Red, Redskins, Savages, Seminoles/Sammy Seminole.

Names given to specific groups of indigenous people, alongside the names those people called and call themselves:
Aleut – Alutiiq, Unangan, Suqpiaq, Sasignan
Cherokee – Tsa-la-gi – Aniyunwiya
Cheyenne – Tsististas
Chippewa – **Ojibwa**/Ojibwe – Anishinabe, Shinnob (Ojibwe slang)
Crow – Absaroke
Huron – Wyandotte – Wendat
Iroquois – Haudenosaunee
Navajo – Diné
Nootka – Nuu-chah-nulth
Petun – Tiontati
Pojoaque Pueblo – Po'sua'geh (Spanish for 'town dwellers'), San Juan Pueblo – Oke Okweenge, Santa Clara – Kha'po
Winnebago – Ho-Chunk.

In Canada, the current term for specific tribal peoples recognized by the Canadian government is 'First Nations'. This term is seen by Native people as an acknowledgement of the **sovereign status** of the Native people and the nation-to-nation relationship of the Native peoples, their governments and the national governments of the countries. Much like any **diplomatic** acknowledgement of one country to another, France to England for example, 'First Nations' suggests that these people were 'first' on the land that was once all theirs. This means that these nations enjoy equal status. In everyday speech about Native peoples, Canadians tend to use the words 'Native', 'aboriginal' and 'First Nations'.

In the United States, the current 'official' term for North American indigenous people is 'Native American'. First developed out of a concern that 'Indian' was inappropriate, the term 'Native American' allowed people to avoid specifying 'North American Indians, Aleuts and Eskimos' (the three distinct groups that were formerly classed together under the word 'Indian'). However, in official regulations and law the term 'Native American' now applies to all government-recognized 'Indians' as well as to Native Hawaiians. Most American Indians prefer to refer to their tribal names, using the general term 'Indian' and, more rarely, 'Native American' in everyday speech.

Names in North America that come from Indian sources:
Alabama – Alibamu
Alaska – Alutiiq or **Inuit**
Illinois – Illini
kayak – Inuit
Massachusetts, Michigan, moccasin, raccoon, **squash**, pecan, toboggan, caucus, chipmunk, moose – Algonquin
Nebraska – Sioux or Otoe
Ohio – Iroquois
Oklahoma – Choctaw for 'red people'
Tallahassee – Muskogee for 'old town'
Tennessee – Cherokee/*tanasi*.

Words from other Native languages became part of the standard US vocabulary as early as the 18th century. Most of these words remained as neutral descriptive words. For example the Algonquian 'moccasin' came to mean any style of Indian hide shoe and 'papoose' became a way of describing a baby or any Indian baby no matter what the tribe. However, the word 'squaw', which was an Algonquian word that meant 'a married or distinguished woman', came to have a negative meaning as an insult to Indian women. In the 19th century, there were two very separate images of Indian women common among non-Indians. The first was that Indian women were violent, degraded and filthy creatures, who were brutal to captives. The second was that Indian women were beautiful and pure princesses, like **Pocahontas**, who were kind to whites. These romantic ideals often had the fair-skinned Princess suffer a tragic death, separated from her usually white lover by a cruel world. Sadly, the once honourable Algonquian word 'squaw', widely adopted to apply to non-Algonquian Native women, remains a term of derision for Native women.

Native American Church and the 'peyote' religion

Native religious practices, whether ancient or new, always aroused suspicion and fear in non-Indians. **Missionaries** and military leaders saw it as a form of resistance as well as 'savagery'. From the **Handsome Lake**/Longhouse religion of the **Iroquois** to that preached by the Shawnee Prophet, from the **Dream Dance** of the **Algonquian** peoples to the **Ghost Dance** of the Plains, religious belief inspired Indians to fight and resist white encroachment on their **land** and on their lives. No religious movement inspired more negative reaction from whites than the Peyote Way.

Peyotism is a religious practice in which the hallucinogenic cactus is used to bring on dreams and visions. It started in Mexico and spread to the Mescalero **Apaches**, Comanches, Caddoes and Kiowas in the mid 19th century. By the late 19th century, thousands of Winnebagos, Menominees, Pawnees, Cheyennes, Arapahos and Shoshones had converted to peyotism. In the mid 20th century, more than 80 tribes were involved in some sort of peyotism. In 1944, to survive opposition to it, followers of the Peyote Way developed the practice into a formal religion called the Native American Church. They stated their need to protect their sacrament, peyote, in the same way that the use of sacramental wine was protected under the First Amendment to the US

Constitution. The multi-tribal officials of the Native American Church tried to put themselves and their religion under the protection of the US government by incorporating the Native American Church in the state of Oklahoma.

Several tribal governments passed regulations prohibiting the use of peyote, as did states and territories. Peyotists and tribal nationalists joined together to protect their Constitutional rights to the freedom of religion. The fight of the Native American Church for survival led to increased lobbying for political rights of all sorts. In 1964, the California Supreme Court upheld peyotism, a decision that was seen as a victory for religious freedom. Despite their religious practices being legal, members of the Native American Church remain stigmatized in US society, and are often denied jobs by public institutions, such as state governments and schools.

164 Right Members of the Native American Church put images of 'peyote' or 'water birds', and other ritual images of the Native American Church, on jewellery such as these German silver earrings and on **drums**. Connected with the cleansing power of water in prayer, the birds act as spirits to convey prayers and visions.

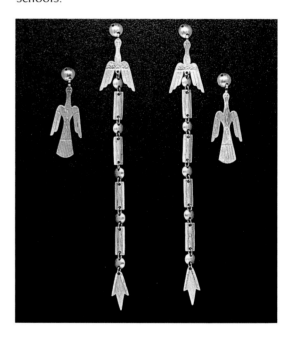

Navajo

Navajo, Diné or 'The People', believe the Holy People created them and placed them on Earth. They emerged through a reed, having journeyed through the underworlds (the Black World, the Blue World and the Yellow World). Finally they came to the present world (Dinétah) in Northwest New Mexico. The 'Holy People' served as disciples to Mother Earth by taking the form of wind, **rain**, thunder, lightning and snow. They defined the Navajo homeland by designating the Four Sacred Mountains – Sierra Blanca Peak to the east (Colorado), Mount Taylor to the south (New Mexico), San Francisco Peaks to the west (Arizona) and the La Platas to the north (Colorado). *Shii'kayah* ('my home') is what the Navajos call this landscape of valleys, plains, *mesas* (hills) and mountains.

Now the largest American Indian tribe in the United States, the modern Navajo Nation has shaped itself through three centuries of changing relationships with their Pueblo neighbours. War with the Spanish, and, later, the United States, forced education, religious change and **relocation**. Most Navajos now live as part of large extended families. Although jobs for wages are the main source of income, most families still **farm**, keep livestock, weave and make jewellery. The Navajo Nation has its own **sovereign tribal government** recognized by the Treaty of Bosque Redondo (see the **Long Walk**), made with the United States in 1868. It operates its own **schools**, police and courts, a tribal college system, industries and businesses, spread over Arizona and New Mexico.

As humans, we are part of Mother Earth. Animals and insects emerged through the four worlds from the pit of the earth. The Holy People created First Man and First Woman, who gave flesh to the Navajo people. We are told our legs are made from earth, our midsection is from water, our lungs from air, and our head is made out of heat and it is placed close to the Father Sun. We are known as the On-Earth Holy People. For that reason, our skin is brown like the earth. A child has certain similarities to the Mother.
Bennie Silversmith, medicine man and herbalist, Pine Springs, Arizona

Navajos have been subjected to strict government policies on land and land use. They still object to the policy of forced stock reduction due to overgrazing in the 1930s and 1950s. They believe that a reduction in the number of sheep causes the rains and vegetation to diminish. In addition, many Navajo were relocated in the 1950s to traditional Hopi lands by the government. This was encouraged by the large mining companies that wanted access to the emptied lands. They joined the Navajos who had been living on lands partitioned to the Hopi Reservation when it was formed in 1882.

Each tribe believes the land has always been theirs. From 1930, the Hopi government tried to recover those lands where Navajos were living – even though they had been designated a 'joint use' area. The government split the jointly used lands into equal parts and forced 8,000 Navajos to relocate.

To the federal government, there is the written law…. For centuries, to us, the law is what is out here… the law of Mother Earth. The Holy People placed us here as a people and we abide by their instructions. When you live in harmony with the land, no-one fights, no-one argues and everyone is happy. That is *hozhone*. But when people begin to argue and fight, the Wind People report to the Holy People of our discontent, That's when rain is withheld…. I think Mother Earth hears about this dispute and doesn't appreciate it. We don't get as much rain as we once did.
Jesse Biakeddy, Big Mountain

Northwest Coast

The area generally called the Northwest Coast is made up of rainforests that follow the Pacific shore from Southeast Alaska to Northwest California. Native cultures in these areas have access to rich resources from the sea and forests. Coastal groups also extend inland up the major rivers. A variety of **languages** and customs exist among communities, but they share a similar cultural pattern. In this region, 17 languages were once spoken. In the North are the **Haida** and Tsimshian (divided into three languages) and the Tlingit of Alaska. In the central region are the Kwakwaka'wakw (three languages), Nuu-chah-nulth (two languages) and Bella Coola (a Northern group of **Salish** speakers). In the Southern area are the speakers of six related languages called 'Coast Salish'.

The sea provides **salmon**, clams, sea lions and seals. Large cedar trees are used to build houses and for carving. There are complex political structures, with chiefdoms and inherited classes of nobility and commoners. Their lavish **ceremonial** life included huge feasts to show status, distribution of goods and **dancing**. Since the end of suppression in the Northwest – during which the government removed ceremonial regalia and banned the **potlatch** and traditional **subsistence** methods – a cultural resurgence is taking place, with **art** traditions noted worldwide.

Fishing and some logging continue to be the main **economies** of the area and **land claims** remain one of the key issues affecting Northwest Coastal groups. The entry of British Columbia into the Canadian Confederation in 1871 shifted responsibility for Natives to the Canadian government. The Nishga and Gitsan-Wet'suwet'en took their land claims cases to the Supreme Court of Canada. In 1997, the Court decided that they had aboriginal title to the land and that history passed by word of mouth could be used as evidence. In addition, the **Haida** and Nuu-chah-nulth have led highly publicized demonstrations protesting against logging in their traditional territory. Northwest Coast groups are also active in national debates on constitutional issues and **self-determination** issues in Canada. The Sechelt, a Coastal Salish group, negotiated their own self-government agreement with the Canadian government. They are now free to develop their lands as they wish because they are exempted from the Indian Act. The government has also transferred ownership of the reserve lands to the band.

165 Below Nunavut, the Inuit homeland, created in 1999.

Nunavut

In 1999, the **Inuit** homeland of Nunavut ('Our Land' in the Inuktitut language) came into existence. The Inuit of the Western **Arctic** signed an agreement in 1984, surrendering their aboriginal title (ancient right to the land) in exchange for US$445 million in compensation and title to 770,000 square miles. The agreement gives the Inuit rights to the resources below the surface of the Arctic as well as **hunting** and **fishing** rights. The lands formerly known as the Northwest Territories are now split in two, separating the Inuit from the Dené, **Métis** and settlers. This division creates an Inuit majority homeland with political and economic **sovereignty** similar to a Canadian province. The split is costly as no political, social or economic structure existed in the territory and has to be created from scratch. Although at the beginning, the territory is 95 percent dependent on the rest of Canada for maintenance, there are plans to develop the **economy**. The new capital is in Iqaluit, a community of 3,552 people.

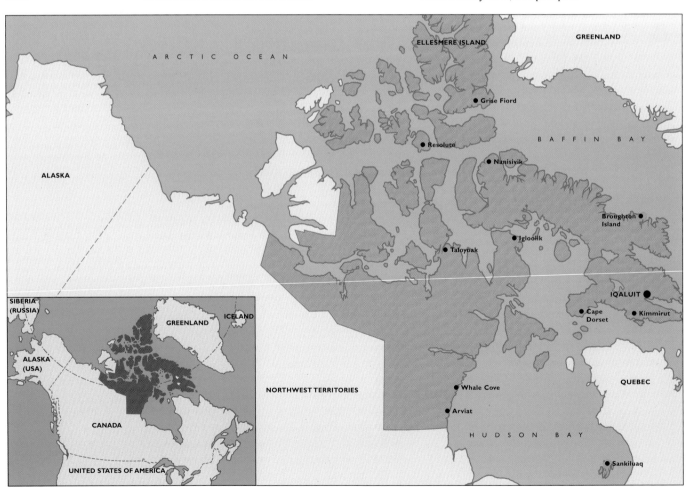

Ojibwa/Anishinabe/ Chippewa/Saulteaux/ Nipissing/Mississauga

The early homeland of the Ojibwa was along the Northern shores of Lake Huron and Lake Superior. The major **fishing** and cultural centre was located at Sault St Marie. Their territory then extended dramatically and some moved southeast into the **Iroquois** lands of Southern Ontario. Others pushed west to Wisconsin and Minnesota, displacing the Dakota people.

The **fur trade** lured many groups far north and west in search of new trap lines (the areas and technologies for trapping fur-bearing animals) and some even spread onto the Plains. The Ojibwa groups then adapted to their new environments and cultural differences emerged between groups. The Ottawa (Odawa), whose lifestyle and language were virtually the same as the neighbouring Ojibwa and Potawatomi people of Lake Michigan, occupied much of the Northern shore of Georgian Bay as well as the Bruce Peninsula bordering on the Huron and Petun people. The three groups remained allied in a loose Confederacy known as the Council of Three Fires.

When Europeans arrived, many separate groups gradually became known collectively as the Ojibwa. Although the groups did not have a common national identity, a cultural and national identity is forming today in Canada under the term 'Anishinabe (Original) Nation' for all groups speaking the Ojibwa **language**. Linguists class the Ojibwa, Ottawa and Algonquian into a single language group with numerous dialects. In Canada, the **Cree** are also almost indistinguishable from the northern Ojibwa and many communities today are considered Oji-Cree, having members from both groups.

Intermarriage and common cultural traditions link these communities. Each community had its own chief and hunting territory. Bands stayed in family hunting units for much of the year, assembling in great numbers only during late spring and summer. The patrilineal society, divided into **clans**, had an informal leadership, with chiefs holding power by virtue of skill in **hunting**, **warfare** and medicine. By the mid 17th century, the fur trade took over the **subsistence** lifestyle, based on hunting, **fishing**, the tapping of maple sap for sugar and the harvesting of berries and **wild rice**.

Traditionally, Ojibwa made birch**bark** canoes to travel rivers and lakes. In the winter, people travelled by snowshoe and sled. Ojibwa wigwams, both temporary and portable, reflected their mobility. They used dome-shaped structures with layers of birchbark and moss as insulation. By the 19th century, tipis covered in birchbark became popular. Women made winter clothing from tanned hides of moose and deer and hats and mittens lined with **beaver** or **rabbit** fur. Clothes were decorated with dyed porcupine **quills** and, when traders arrived with **beads**, with elaborate beaded patterns.

Large summer camps allowed for feasting, **dancing**, lacrosse playing, **gambling** and for young people to meet and arrange marriages. Storytelling was also an important pastime with tales of supernatural beings such as Nanabush (the terrifying Windigo, a giant with a hunger for human flesh), the thunderbirds (that controlled the weather) and the Mishipisu (a large water serpent). They believed that every object or animal possessed a spirit (*manitou*) and offerings such as tobacco had to be given to calm them. The ultimate and most sacred force was the *Kitchi Manitou* (the Great Spirit), often identified as the sun. Widely respected for their spiritual power, many asked the Ojibwa to cure illness and provide charms for hunting. They developed a formal organization of shamans (Indian doctors or healers) called 'Midéwiwin' or the Grand Medicine Society. Its primary purpose was to heal, but it became the main expression of the Ojibwa religion.

Today, Ojibwa people struggle to protect hunting and fishing rights and to settle **land claims** issues. Casinos are also rapidly changing the life on many **reservations**.

Oka

After the Europeans' arrival, the strategic position of the town of Oka (close to where the Ottawa and St Lawrence Rivers meet) helped the **Iroquois** to control the **fur trade**. However, in 1717, the King of France granted the lands to a **missionary** group, the Seminary of St Sulpice. Although many **Mohawk** peoples were converted to Catholicism and taken to the mission, other Mohawk people already lived in the area and challenged the mission's ownership of the

166 Above In 1990, Alice Olsen Williams (Anishinabe) of Curved Lake, Ontario, made this quilt called *The Tree of Peace Saves the Earth.* The quilt uses pictures from a traditional **Iroquois** story with a new image of the Oka dispute. The Tree of Peace, emerging from the mud on the back of Grandmother Turtle (Earth) and spreading its White Roots of Peace among the nations, shoots up through the Canadian Parliament building. Beneath the tree, **war** clubs are buried. On top, the **eagle's** heart is a circle with the Four Directions and colours, a symbol often used by US and Canadian Indian political activists.

Oka lands. In 1841, the Canadian government confirmed that the land belonged to the religious order, but the right of Native people to live on the land was never disputed. This conflict arose again in 1881. Some Mohawk families moved to Gibson, Ontario; others decided to stay. In 1912, the Judicial Council decided that the land belonged entirely to the Seminary.

The Mohawks of Kanesatake (Oka) and two other Mohawk communities repeatedly made **land claims**, stating that they had first rights to significant areas of land. The most fierce conflict over this land erupted on 11 March 1990, over the plans to expand Oka's golf course onto land considered a sacred religious burial site. Mohawks and other Natives erected a road blockade. The Québec Provincial Police were summoned to tear it down, and a police officer was shot and killed. Although the siege ended after 78 days, the land issue at Oka still remains unresolved to the satisfaction of both communities.

Oneida

Living between the **Mohawk** and **Onondaga** Nations are the Oneida. Their original name means 'people of the standing stone'. They have nine chiefs represented in the Confederacy Council and are the 'Younger Brothers' along with the **Cayugas**. Together with the Tuscaroras, they sided with the colonists in the American Revolution, playing key roles in guaranteeing victory on behalf of the Americans and enduring terrible loss of life in the process. The 1784 Treaty of Fort Stanwix was to have guaranteed them lands in exchange for their loyalty. However, New York State ignored this treaty and the Oneida steadily lost land. Most were removed to either Wisconsin or Ontario, although some remain in New York.

Throughout constant change and **Removal**, the Oneida have struggled to preserve their **language** and their cycle of Longhouse **ceremonies**. Today casinos provide important sources of income and employment for the Wisconsin Oneida.

Onondaga

The Onondaga Nation ('People of the Hills') occupies the geographic centre of the **Iroquois Confederacy**. Within their communities, all nine **clans** are found. The Onondaga were among the strongest voices supporting a position of neutrality during the American Revolution. They were attacked by the revolutionary forces whose leaders assumed they were supporting the **British**. After the war, they entered into **treaties** with New York State that gave them lands near Syracuse, New York, while some members relocated to the Grand River in Canada. The Onondaga continue to host meetings of the Confederacy and act as 'fire keepers' who keep the symbolic Council fire burning.

The Onondaga have long rejected attempts to install an elected government and instead have kept their traditional systems. Since the 1960s they have also been a major force in the fight for **sovereignty** and have challenged military service and other government and state controls over them, their land and their religious life. Since 1994, they have refused any state or government grants of money which they believe would compromise their independence and sovereignty. They have launched **land claims** to regain their original territory.

P

Pan-Indianism

Indians had been meeting and mixing with one another for centuries before **contact** with Europeans. Many developed mutually understood **languages**, such as **trade** languages and sign language, to communicate with each other. They shared and traded songs, **dances** and stories. Different groups formed alliances and friendships. Some eventually lived and merged with each other, having been driven from their homes by famine, **disease**, drought and **war**. When **schooling** was made compulsory in the late 18th century and when various groups were forced together through imprisonment, **Removal** and **reservationization**, a type of forced intertribalism became common.

New types of 'Indian' behaviour emerged. Indian peoples who were once very different began to adopt each other's vocabularies (like the so-called meaningless sounds and words of **pow wow** songs), clothing styles (such as ribbon shirts), **foods** (such as frybread) and even jokes. This common behaviour is often called 'pan-Indianism'. It has often been used in an insulting way to describe actions, social styles and language that is not particular to one tribe, but which is mixed. It has been applied to people who do not speak their tribal languages and who were raised not with a specific culture (such as Otoe, **Navajo** or Karok), but as 'Indians' – vaguely Siouan or Plains in cultural style (those being the dominant styles in pan-Indianism). However, instead of weakening specific tribal cultures, these new intertribal behaviours have often brought Indians together, and given them a strong unified voice on political issues.

Parka

'Parka' is the general **Inuit**/Inupiaq name for an overcoat. It is used in English to describe a hooded coat now made in cotton and synthetic materials as well as the traditional hide, and worn by Inuit of the **Arctic** and non-Indians. Although styles of parkas differ in the various areas of Canada, Greenland and the United States, they are important among all the Inuit. Parkas are necessary for survival in the Arctic and making them, even the new 'show' parkas, exemplifies a woman's role and her skills as a seamstress. The demand for 'fancy' parkas from the oil and communications line workers from the United States and Europe, who went to the Arctic in the 1950s, helped to rejuvenate nearly abandoned skills. Some styles of parkas embody a woman's role as giver of life, with the apron flap (*kiniq*) as a symbol of childbirth. The long back tail represents animals, the Inuit source of fur, oil, hide, bones and meat. The carrying pouch (*amauti*) works like a **baby carrier**, but is built into the garment.

167 Left A Copper **Inuit** woman's parka and pants. Copper Inuit live in the far west of the Canadian **Arctic**, in the Northwest Territories, now the territory of Nunavut. In world of tundra, forest tundra, fresh water lakes and rivers and ocean, people use the rich animal life of musk ox, caribou, seal, mink, squirrel, wolverine, **wolf** and freshwater **fish** to support their needs for **food**, clothing and shelter. For clothing nowadays, Copper Eskimos also use **dog** skins, commercially tanned hides and imitation fur.

Ｈow sweet he is when he smiles
With two teeth like a little walrus.
Ah, I like my little one to be heavy
And my hood to be full.
A *Thule Inuit lullaby*

168 Right Nora Ann
Rexford-Leavitt, Inupiaq,
from Barrow, Alaska, made
this new woman's fancy
parka in 1997. Made from
wolf, wolverine, muskrat and
calfskin, the **wolf** ruff helps
protect the face from the
cold **Arctic** wind. Wolf and
wolverine furs do not ice up
with condensation from
breath.[37]

169 Below This waterproof
Aleut gut parka was made
by cleaning yards of intestine
(perhaps walrus), drying and
bleaching it, cutting it into
strips and sewing it together
with sinew. Aleut **medicine**
men and dancers in
ceremonies may have
worn them. They are
sometimes worn on St
Laurence Island to honour
the walrus god, the master
of the sea. They are often
decorated with **feathers**
and animal/bird parts.[38]

Photography

American Indians are among the most
photographed peoples of the world. From
the time photography was invented in the
mid 19th century, people built their artistic
reputations on their pictures of Indians. Men
such as Edward Curtis began, like the
painters before and after them, to document
and stage a beautiful world that they
believed was on the verge of extinction. Their
photographs continue to offer a portrait of
Indians that most people (including many
Native people) use to define the 19th-
century and present-day Indian world.

Native peoples' attitudes to the camera
were complex. Many believed it to be a
powerful magical 'soul-stealer' from which
they must hide. Others saw it as an intruder
in their ceremonial, family and community
life. Others would come to be grateful for its
record of their ancestors and hang those
pictures on their walls. Later in the 20th
century, many banned the camera and
outside photographers from their villages,
their **ceremonies** and their private lives.

Since the early part of the 20th century,
the number of Native photographers has
grown. Some, out of a passionate interest in
their own communities, document the daily
lives of their people. One such photographer
was Horace Poolaw (1906–84), a Kiowa, who
was an aerial photographer in the **Second
World War**. When he returned home, he
wanted to show life as the Kiowas,
Comanches, **Apaches** and Delawares in
Southwestern Oklahoma were living it in
those times – as a remarkable mixture of old
and new, traditional and progressive,
Christian and pagan, and **farmers** and
horsemen. From the memorial feast at the
Rainy Mountain Baptist Church to Lizzie
Little Joe with her high heels and **baby
carrier**; from Poolaw and his friends in the
nose cone of a B-52 bomber to his Mexican
captive grandmother, the best **beadworker** in
the town; from the beef jerky drying at one
families' butchering site to the parade
featuring three Kiowa Princesses, Poolaw
made an enormous record of the changes
and character of the world he understood.

Some took pictures of the world as
outsiders. Others made their pictures a
commentary (often humorous) on the history
and politics of Indian life and on the history
of photographing Indians.[39]

170 Right *Watcheye II: Mary Matinaas* (1996) is a silver print by Greg Staats, a **Mohawk** and professional photographer, who was born in 1963 on the Six Nations Reserve in Southwestern Ontario. Staats' work includes portraits, especially of elders, who he sees as a 'living history; a link with the past and into the future'.

171 Below *The Iroquois is a Matriarchal Society* by Shelley Niro, a **Mohawk**. Her work explores issues of identity, stereotypes, history and the environment through the use of humour. She shows the contrast between the idea of the **Iroquois** as a matriarchal (see **matrilineality**) society and this Iroquois woman under her hair dryer.

172 Above Kiowa Group in American Indian Exposition Parade, Anadarko, taken in 1941 by Horace Poolaw.

Pipes

Most Native peoples engaged in some form of smoking for ritual, **diplomatic** and social purposes. Consequently, pipe-making and the accessories associated with pipes developed into an important artform.

On the Northern Plains, many peoples used pipes, usually made of wood with a stone bowl. Smoking the pipe, whether alone or with several people, was a means of seeking assistance from spirits and the **tobacco** used was a form of prayer or way of communicating with those spirits. Many peoples used the **medicine** pipe in healing. Europeans mistakenly called all pipes 'peace pipes' because Indians would use the smoking of the pipe, passed among groups of men in discussion, as a symbol of good feeling between the parties.[40]

I watched the old Sioux men carve and learned from them. The quarry is sacred ground. I make my offerings before I go. Back at my home, I say a prayer with the stone. The Sioux have always carved. In earlier times, a holy woman gave us the pipe, with instructions as to how we should live; the pipe has meaning to our people today. The pipe provides guidance, shows us a way of life. When we travel, we place the pipe on the dashboard of our car, and they watch over us.
Amos Owen, Dakota elder

The Lakota considered smoking with others a way of affirming the truth and believed that the 'Way of the Pipe' was given to them by White Buffalo Calf Woman.

Then she gave something to the chief, and it was a pipe with a bison [buffalo] calf carved on one side to mean the earth that bears and feeds us, and with twelve eagle feathers hanging from the stem to mean the sky and the twelve moons, and these were tied with a grass that never breaks. 'Behold!', she said. 'With this you shall multiply and be a good nation. Nothing but good shall come from it.' Then she sang again and went out of the teepee, and as people watched her going, suddenly it was a white bison galloping away and snorting, and soon it was gone.
Black Elk (c. 1863–1950), Lakota medicine man

173 Below An **Ojibwa** pipe and bowl.

174 Below An early **Mi'kmaq** stone pipe bowl.

175 Above A Plains pipe bag, shown from the back, where it can be tied to a belt.

The Lakota had men called pipe carriers, who carried the pipes used only in **ceremonies** in highly decorated **beaded, quilled** and painted pipe bags. These bags also held tobacco and various small tools associated with smoking and cleaning the pipe. The stem and the fragile bowl are kept separately and joined only when they are used in ceremonies.

176 Right The classic and best-known image of Pocahontas in the court dress, fashionable hat and ruff of Elizabethan England. Like two other images of Pocahontas, a popular engraving of *Pocahontas Saving Captain John Smith* and the painting *The Baptism of Pocahontas*, this one has no basis in reality as no-one made portraits of her from life.

ɔove A Plains pipe ʒorated with **beads**, ʌnd **metal** tinkling Ꭲhis is shown from k, where it can be a belt.

Ætatis suæ 21. Aº. 1616.

Matoaks als Rebecka daughter to the mighty Prince Powhatan Emperour of Attanoughkomiouck als Virginia converted and baptized in the Christian faith, and Wife to the worꝰ Mʳ Tho: Rolff.

Pocahontas

Pocahontas, or *Matoaka*, was born in about 1595, the young daughter of the leader of several **Algonquian** tribes in Southeast Virginia. When the **British** came to her country in 1619, she became a figure in 'American' legend, known less for her real role in history than for her symbolic role representing the relationships between the new colonists and Indians. Few facts are known about her. Captured by the British visitors in order to force land agreements with her father and his tribesmen, she was eventually married to a colonist, John Rolfe, in order to forge an alliance between the British and the Indians. She travelled to England with Rolfe. She was baptized as a **Christian**, presented in the Court of Elizabeth I, had a son, caught smallpox and died in England in about 1617.

Captain John Smith's version of Pocahontas' story in his *Generall Historie of Virginie* of 1624 tells of a girl smitten with Englishmen, who intervenes in Smith's

177 Right In 1997 Murv Jacob, a **Cherokee** artist and illustrator, took the standard painting of Pocahontas in her Elizabethan clothing, and restored her in his fantasy painting to a true daughter of the Southeast. Still in her English and **Christian** clothes, she now appears on the arm of **Rabbit** (the trickster hero of Southeastern Indians), instead of with John Rolfe or John Smith. Jacob has darkened her skin and made her features more Indian. Rabbit wears his traditional 16th-century style Cherokee clothes, including his **dance** apron and engraved gorget made from freshwater pink mussel **shell**.

execution by throwing herself between him and her father's tomahawk. Her father, the Powhatan, is forced to make peace with the Englishmen. Pocahontas marries John Rolfe, goes to England and becomes a Christian.

An Indian, specifically an Algonquian, version of the story presents a very different picture. In that version, Powhatan chooses John Smith to be adopted in a ritual way into his family. As a woman of some status, the daughter of the tribe's leader would have acted as his 'mother' so that he could be reborn, after his ritual death, as one of the tribe. At that time, Algonquian, **Iroquoian** and **Cherokee** people honoured the wishes of women with respect to the fate of captives. Women could determine whether captives would live or die. Captives chosen to live could be adopted as a son or daughter by a childless woman or one who had lost a child

to **disease** or **war**. Whatever the case, the adoption **ceremony** often involved symbolic death and rebirth. That is what happened to John Smith. Rather than Pocahontas betraying her own people, as Smith portrayed it, she was attempting to make him become one of them. This would have forced the British and the Indians to cease competition and behave like relatives toward one another, with mutual responsibilities and obligations.

The story of Pocahontas as told by John Smith, in school books, in hundreds of paintings and pictures, and recently by the Disney Corporation in a 1997 film, is very nearly an American **creation** or **origin story**. The story of Pocahontas made legitimate the European presence and the mixing of European and Indian heritage. Pocahontas makes the colonists (and so the takeover of Indian lands) welcome.[41]

Political activism, 1880–1980

Indians engaged in political action from their first **contact** with Europeans. Indians have always tried to intervene in the political decisions that affected them, by actual physical resistance in the first few hundred years, by **diplomacy** in the 19th century and by intellectual resistance and reform in the early 20th century. Writers, doctors, lawyers, social workers and politicians have followed and replaced the **war** chiefs as the defenders of Native rights.

Members of the Omaha LaFlesche family – Susan (a doctor), Suzette (a journalist) and Francis (a scholar) – put their talents to use in influencing the outcome of the 1879 court decision over *Standing Bear v. General George Crook*. When the Ponca people were removed from their Nebraska homelands, reformers were sure that the Omahas would be the next to follow them. When Standing Bear and other Poncas tried to return home, they were arrested. The LaFlesche family and other activists backed the Ponca cause. The *Standing Bear* case went to court and proved to be one of the most significant legal decisions in civil rights law for Indians, as it established that an Indian is a person before the law and has the right to seek legal redress before the court.

At the start of the 20th century, a group of Indian activists, including Carlos Montezuma and Charles Eastman, organized the Society of American Indians (SAI). These educated people gathered to lobby for Indian **self-determination**. Gertrude Simmons Bonnin (*Zitkala-sa*) (1876–1938), a Yankton **Sioux** woman, joined them in their cause. She helped organize the modern Indian reform and **pan-Indian** movement and began taking an active role in the SAI's business. Eventually, she moved to Washington, D.C., where she wrote works supporting Indian **citizenship**, and **land** and **water rights**. In 1926, she formed the National Congress of American Indians, which is still a major Indian lobbying group, and became its President with her husband as Secretary.

In the mid 20th century – after the devastating period of **reservationization** – activism once again took shape. In November 1969, a small group of Indian activists and students, later joined by another 100, went to the abandoned, former prison island of

178 Above The famed photographer Gertrude Kasebier took this photograph of young Gertrude Simmons Bonnin (*Zitkala-sa*), a classically trained violist, in 1898. Bonnin often wore traditional Native dress when she lectured.

Alcatraz, demanding that it be given over to Indians by the government. Alcatraz was occupied by Indian groups for over two years, and it became a national focal point for the issues of Indian political and cultural nationalism. Ultimately, the courts refused to uphold their claims, and the last remaining occupiers were removed by force.

During the same period, the American Indian Movement (AIM) grew from the civil rights movements of the 1960s (including the blacks, Hispanics, women and anti-war protesters). Members of the AIM took up Native issues such as education, self-government (see **self-determination**), oppression, poverty, religious freedom and the control of natural resources. The emergence of pan-Indian activism and even the militancy of groups such as the National Indian Youth Council, Indians of All Tribes and the AIM drew urban Indians and reservation-based Indians together in a new kind of nationalism. They were determined to protect their land and identity.

Some political protests were dangerous. In Wisconsin, Oregon, Washington, South Dakota, the District of Columbia and Québec, Canada, Native men and women faced government agents, the National Guard, the Royal Canadian Mounted Police, SWAT teams of police and armed non-Indian civilians in numerous disputes. The most prominent of the AIM protests were the 1972 March on Washington (known as the Trail of Broken Treaties Caravan or The Longest Walk), the occupation of the BIA Offices in 1972 and the 1973 occupation of **Wounded Knee** on the Pine Ridge **Sioux** Reservation.[42]

The last 30 years have seen debates over Indian rights to use methods of **hunting** and **fishing** (for example spear fishing and gillnetting) which are now forbidden for non-Indians, religious rights and the government's intervention in or neglect of Indian affairs. Essentially, the women and men who fought these battles have been fighting for the preservation of their heritage and traditions.

Just as the **Second World War** produced a new and invigorated leadership, such movements and actions rallied national support around Indian issues and created yet new leaders and generations of Indian activists to campaign for Indian causes. Activist movements also helped increase the numbers of Indian lawyers and other professionals. Thus, the battles were moved from the barricades and marches to the courts and educational institutions.

Population

Estimates of Indians in America (north of Mexico) before European **contact** range from 1 million to 18 million. It is probably somewhere in between, perhaps under 8 million.

During the first contact in 1500 and 1900, the Indian population declined heavily. Devastation, such as **disease** and **war**, took the Indian population from 500 distinct groups of people to 300 **federally recognized** tribes (some incredibly small in number), many unrecognized peoples and as many **urban Indians** in just over two centuries.

Many questions remain unanswered. How many Indians were there in North America or

South America at the point of first contact with Europeans? How did Indians come to be in North and South America? How many Indians died from disease, war, famine and **Removal**? How many Indians were **reservationized** and how many existed in North America at the turn of the 20th century? How many Indians exist now?

There is much research on the population before Columbus. The people who study populations, the history of diseases, economics, archaeology, social history and political history all have different ways and reasons for counting Indians. To determine how many Indians were at any given place at any given time, who lived, who died and how, scholars have analysed information from Indian winter counts and government censuses during Removal. They have studied grave sites following smallpox epidemics, court records, voting behaviour, land records and employment statistics.

In 1900, there were about 400,000 Indians counted in both the United States and Canada. Most scholars and government officials predicted the extinction of Indians. However, from that time, Native populations started a slight recovery, and the estimates of the numbers of North American Indians, **Inuit**, **Aleut** and **Métis** (in Canada) range widely over the next three-quarters of a century. The 1990 US census counted 1.95 million Indians; a little over half of those who called themselves Indians were enrolled members of federally recognized tribes. Even the federally recognized population has grown as the Indian birth rate rises regularly. The next census in the year 2000 anticipates 2 million Indians. However, the Native population in the United States and Canada is tiny compared with other ethnic groups. Many problems (mostly because of old ideas about race and ethnicity, and the Native resistance to counting by governments) make it difficult to know just how many Native people there are in North America.

Potlatch

Gift giving has always been an important aspect of Indian culture. In the Pacific Northwest of the United States and Canada, it is known as potlatch. **Haida**, Makah, Kwakwaka'wakw, Nuu-chah-nulth, **Tlingit** and Tsimshian communities participated in potlatches. The gifts included **blankets**, furs

Pottery

Pottery, like **basketry**, is one of the oldest and most widespread of Native crafts, which is connected to the very source of life. The Pueblo pottery is a good example of the world of Indian pottery. The Tewa word for clay, *nung*, is the same as the word for people. For the Pueblos, people are clay (see **adobe**), and thus making pottery from Mother Clay is a sacred act. Gathering clay and making a dish is intimately connected with and must be accompanied by prayers and good thoughts for the well-being of the world, just like **dances** and songs. Over the centuries, before **contact** with Europeans, Pueblos and others made pottery for everyday use, for storing water and cooking food. They, like other peoples who made pottery, traded their pottery with other tribes for goods – hides, **feathers**, **shells**, minerals such as turquoise, dyes and food.

When the Spaniards came, they demanded from the people pottery to match their needs – flat dishes, smaller water jars, cups, soup plates and dough bowls for the raised wheat breads introduced into the Pueblo world. So the Pueblos began to make a great range of pottery goods to meet those needs. In the late 19th and 20th centuries, new demands from new markets and a shift from a trade to a cash **economy** changed the objects produced. **Tourists** wanted less expensive objects, so potters made small animal figures, matched sets of dishes modelled after china, representations of trains and candlesticks.

179 Left This Kwakwaka'wakw anvil with the Thunderbird design was designed for breaking coppers. These were made from traded sheet copper and perhaps from Native copper.

and skins, jewellery, money and, in the 20th century, appliances. Native people on the **Northwest Coast** made 'coppers' for use in the potlatch. The coppers, which had names, were large **metal** shield-like pieces passed down to male relatives, distributed, traded for blankets or broken down during potlatches. Coppers were often carved, painted or hammered into traditional designs that reflected the **clan**, family crests and historic stories of the persons giving or breaking the copper. In a way, they reflected the giver's honour and wealth. Today artists made small coppers as jewellery, decorations and as reproductions for **tourists**.

The potlatch kept the community hierarchy and allowed individuals to gather wealth and move up in status. It was an important system of redistribution. Hosts would give away most, if not all, of their material goods to show good will to the rest of the community and to keep or gain status.

Laws in Canada (in 1884) and the United States (in the early 20th century) banned the potlatch to control Indians and reduce traditional systems of tribal government. After decades of repression, the potlatch was allowed in the United States in 1934 with the Indian Reorganization Act and in Canada in 1951 with the revised Indian Act. The potlatch remains central to community life.

180 Above A bowl from the excavated Hopi village of Sityatki, c. 1600.

As the Spanish had commandeered Pueblo lead mines, they went from using mineral-based paints to the vegetable paints for which they are now well known. They used the manures of the newly introduced sheep, cattle and **horses** to create new, black polished ware.

181 Above A bowl made by Nampeyo (1860–1947) of Hano, a Hopi-Tewa woman who created what **art** historians would later call the Sityatki Revival of Hopi pottery. Inspired by seeing the excavated potteries found accidentally by Hopis and then later by archaeologists in the 1890s, Nampeyo, with her husband, began to reconstruct old traditional forms not produced for centuries among the Hopi. Her old and new designs revised and preserved the symbols of her people's culture. The work of Nampeyo and another Pueblo woman from San Ildefonso called Maria Martinez aroused much interest in Pueblo pottery. They inspired many others to revive traditional forms while contributing enormously to the **economic** survival of their people.

Although pottery was made mostly for the tourism and **art** market, it was still used within communities and for **ceremonies**. Many potters and ceramic sculptors have returned to a more traditional way of making pottery, reviving the prayers and the rituals needed to accompany the process.

> *Nan chu Kweejo,*
> *na ho uvi whageh oe powa,*
> *du huu joni heda di aweh joni*
> *hey bo hanbo di koe gi un muu.*
> *Wayhaa ha yun maa bo,*
> *we un tsi maai pi.*
> Clay Mother,
> I have come to the centre of
> your abode, feed me and clothe me
> and in the end you will absorb me
> into your centre.
> However far you travel,
> do not go crying.
> *Nora Naranjo-Morse's version, learned from her mother,*
> *of a prayer Pueblos offer to Clay Mother*

Whenever you... get the pottery clay, you take your cornmeal (for prayers). You can't go to Mother Clay without the cornmeal and ask her permission to touch her. Talk to [her]. She... will hear your word and she will answer your prayer.
Margaret Tafoya, Santa Clara Pueblo

182 Above The Hopi potter, Nampeyo of Hano.

183 Above Russell Sanchez, a potter from San Ildefonso Pueblo takes issue with the motto of the state of New Mexico ('Land of Enchantment') in his jar, 'Land of Entrapment'. The water jar (*olla*) was imported by the Spanish. This one portrays three figures on crosses in a glazed area. The lip or centre of the jar goes back to the centre or navel of Mother Earth (the *sipapu*), 'where we all belong in the end', according to Russell. Russell comes from near the Los Alamos Nuclear Laboratory that developed the atomic bomb, and his art often records how Mother Earth has suffered.

Pow wow

The term 'pow wow', **Algonquian** in origin, meant a person of power, perhaps a '**medicine** man' or a gathering for healing **ceremonies**. It has now come to mean an organized gathering of tribal people where friendships are renewed and **dancing**, feasting, competitions, shows, **trade** and cultural exchange take place. Usually held in the summer months, pow wows are common in communities all over North America and have become part of an intertribal or multi-tribal expression of Indian identity.

I was told this at one of the White Shield pow wows… this old man came up and he said, 'Do you know how this giveaway came about? Over there in New Town |Fort Berthold Reservation in North Dakota, Mandan and Hidatsa|, corn |maize| is sacred to them. One summer when the corn was ripe our |Dakota| scouts were out toward their area and they came to this corn field, so they gathered up all the corn and bundled it and packed it on the horses and they headed back over here. When there got back over here, our leaders said, 'No, those are their sacred things, we never should have taken them. You know we respected each other's religion, that something we never fight over.' And so our people got together and they sent a messenger down there telling them we were coming. So, they were glad, so when we got there we gave gifts to the people showing them that the boys did not know what they were doing. We brought gifts to them and they brought food, and they were thankful.

They got their corn back, so they put on a big pow wow for everybody. The Sioux camped on one side of the river, and during the day they had horse races and games all day and then they had a big feed at supper in the evening. Then after supper everybody danced and had a good time. For three or four days they did that. Then at the end of the pow wow, the get-together – that's what a pow wow is, a gathering – they gave us gifts and showed appreciation that we weren't going to fight or anything, that we respected them.

So then our people said, 'You come down to our place next year, and we'll have a pow wow' and that's how the pow wows and giveaways started here.
Elmer White, Dakota

Dances at pow wows are performed in full costume. These include men's and women's, girl's and boy's traditional dances, fancy dances, round dances, straight dances, grass dances and jingle-dress dances. The dances performed vary from region to region, but have their roots in traditional dances. The Grass Dance is developed from a very old Plains tradition. The jingle-dress dance is said by some to have been a gift to the people of Whitefish Bay in Northern Ontario. The Fancy Shawl dance is said to have come from the Plains where the young women would gather to show off their newly painted **buffalo** hides and robes.

Communities now have different reasons for pow wows. Some are **tourist** attractions or for fund raising, others are a gathering of friends and families. Some are used for cultural renewal and have elders' workshops and other teaching sessions. Others are competition pow wows, where dancers come together to compete for prize money. An important part of the pow wow are the singers and the **drums**. Groups of singers, called 'a drum', are invited to participate and provide songs for the dancers. Food and craft booths are also essential parts of pow wows. Dancers and spectators can be found munching on buffalo burgers, Indian tacos, frybread and bacon, maize soup, pies and scones (in Canada), lemonade and ice cream. Crafts and food vendors, dancers and drummers often travel a circuit, the 'pow wow trail', during the summer months, going from one pow wow to another.

184 Above Traditional straight dancers at the 1992 Delaware pow wow at Copan, Oklahoma. Unlike 'fancy dancers', traditional **dancers** carry clubs and sticks, wear natural, undyed bird wings and **feathers**. Sometimes they wear large natural feather bustles, animal skins, **headdresses** and face paint.

Pueblo Revolt

When the Spaniards came to colonize New Mexico in 1598, they [the Pueblo Indians] tried to get along with them. But like most European powers, the Spaniards tried to dominate the Pueblo people. The Spaniards forced the Pueblos to give them food and to work as free labour. The Spanish tried to make the Pueblos get rid of their religion and accept the Spanish religion. The Pueblos suffered silently until a time in 1675 when the Spanish governor and the Catholic padres realized that the Pueblos were not really accepting the Spanish religion. So the Spaniards arrested 47 Pueblo leaders. Four were condemned to be hung and the others were whipped publicly on the plaza in Santa Fe.

Among those whipped was a person from San Juan by the name of Po'ping. The Spanish called him Popay and that is the way he is recorded in history because the Spanish wrote the history. Anyway, after Popay came home he began to think about the indignity that he had suffered. He decided he should organize other tribal leaders to do something about the Spaniards. Eventually, the Pueblo leaders decided they would go to the Spaniards and the priests to tell them to leave Pueblo land. This would not be a bloody revolt only if the Spaniards did not want to leave would they be killed. Runners took a deerskin strip with knots in it to each Pueblo. They told the Pueblos that each morning as the sun came up, they were to untie a knot. And on the morning that the last knot was untied, the revolt would begin.

On 10 August 1680, the Pueblos began to go to their padres and other Spanish families to ask them to leave or suffer the consequences. As a result, 21 priests were killed and something like 200 Spanish people. Many settlers left their homes and came to Santa Fe for protection inside the Governor's Palace. The Pueblos converged on the Palace and fought against the Spaniards for several days. Finally the Pueblo warriors decided to dam the water that was flowing through Santa Fe. After a few days the Spaniards were suffering from thirst. On 21 August, they began to evacuate Santa Fe. The Pueblo warriors watched them leave and did not attack. The Pueblo Revolt was the only successful revolt by a Native people against the European powers. The Spaniards left New Mexico and the Pueblos had their land again. And it was like this for 12 years.

Joe Sando, tribal historian, Jemez Pueblo, 1992

185 Above Tommie Montoya, a young Pueblo artist, did a series of pencil drawings in 1980, the 300th anniversary of the Pueblo Revolt. This drawing, called *Catua and Omtua, Pueblo Runners from Tesuque*, shows the runners from Tesuque Pueblo carrying the message (see **calendars**) to all the villages about the planned actions against the Spanish.

Quillwork

Like most Native craftwork, quillwork – common from the far Northeast to the far West – is not just decorative. The application of porcupine and (less frequently) bird quills onto items of clothing, tipi liners, and **buffalo** or **elk** robes was often a sacred responsibility for the women and their way of praying for someone's good health and welfare. Women on the Plains developed quilling societies and, later, beading societies, whose responsibility it was to protect the process of quilling.

Grass Woman, the daughter of Black Coal, was one of the last of the seven medicine women who carried the Quill Society's medicine bundles. The seven medicine women supervised the making of quill ornaments used to decorate tipis, moccasins, buffalo robes and cradles with designs representing prayers for health and long life. The women made gifts of quillwork so that blessings would follow the people as they travelled the four hills of life. The ceremonies of the society have disappeared with other aspects of Arapaho life, and our grandparents say they long for the old ways.
Debra Calling Thunder, Arapaho, 1993

In the late 19th century, **beads** were cheaper and easier to acquire than quills, so the quilling societies became dormant for a while. Some quillwork has continued, for example Plains women today are trying to revive the **art** and the spiritual connections it held in Plains life.

For the people who hold to this art form very strongly, quillwork still has strong spiritual and religious overtones that are integral to the art. I have a lot of respect for the people from the Sioux tribes and the respect they hold for that art form. That respect is what I try to introduce to my students… there's a lot more of the artist at work than just making a craft, just making a living. If you can go into it first with an understanding of the spiritual part of it – understanding the animal, understanding the people who put these things together and what the objects were intended for – you will hold the art of quillwork in your heart. I will tell my students – about my experiences hearing porcupines sing, and talking to porcupines and understanding what they have to offer. Porcupines are not just an animal.
Joanne Bigcrane, Pend d'Oreille, 1994

Rabbit

Rabbit, like **Coyote**, Spider, **Raven** and other characters in the origin stories (see **creation stories**) of Indian people, is a so-called trickster hero to Southeastern Indian peoples and to some Southwestern and Northeastern peoples. He is very similar to the character in the **African** tales of Bre'r (Brother) Rabbit, in that he jokes, lies, charms and befriends his way into and out of trouble. For **Cherokee**s, in particular, the Rabbit is a great singer and **dancer**, having taught the people many of their songs and dances. He is also a great storyteller, having invented many of the great lies that humans now believe.

186 Left In 1992 Murv Jacob, a **Cherokee** artist, illustrated an old Cherokee story about one of Rabbit's adventures. The **wolves** capture Rabbit who is coming from a **dance**. They tell him that they are going to eat him. However, Rabbit tells the wolves that, before he dies, he wants to teach them a new dance. Mesmerized by his songs, they dance happily. He slips through their legs and escapes, laughing at their gullibility.

Rain

For **agricultural** peoples and all those who are dependent on a supply of fresh water, rain is very important. Throughout the centuries, humans have prayed, danced and sung for rain. For most Native people – from the Hidatsa to the **Cherokee** to the Navajo – the **ceremonies** to bring rain are a sacred responsibility. In the dry lands of the Southwest, almost every aspect of life – clothing, **pottery**, **dances**, songs, prayers, and stories of the origins and nature of the world and its plants, animals and humans – reflects a concern about rain. For example, **Zunis** and Pueblos offer cornmeal, which is sacred to them, to the ancestors and spirits who provide all that sustains life. Quite common near the hearths and doorways of Pueblo homes are pottery bowls that hold sacred cornmeal, for the daily prayer offerings. Terraced Pueblo cornmeal bowls represent the world, with steps up to the clouds and ancestors who bring rain (see **clowns**).

An anthropologist asks a Pueblo man why all Pueblo songs, dances, prayers, and pots are about rain. He replied that people pray, sing, dance about what they don't have enough of, saying to the anthropologist, 'Why, all your songs are about love.'
A story some Zunis like to tell

187 Above A cornmeal bowl made in 1991 by Josephine Nahohai of Zuni Pueblo. The tadpoles and creatures on it are associated with water. As in all things connected with water and with corn, this bowl is also associated with fertility, so it could be given to a newly married couple as a wedding present.

Rattle

Most Native instruments are percussion instruments. **Drums** and rattles are the most common. Rattles are made from the most local and often the most sacred of materials. They are then filled with stones, seeds or shot, held in the hand and shaken. Many on the Plains were made from rawhide, wood or a gourd (see **squash**). At the turn of the 19th century, deprived of traditional materials with which to make rattles, many people made them out of tin cans and **metal** salt shakers (as in Oklahoma-style Gourd Dance rattles). During the **Second World War** in the Pacific, Southeastern tribal peoples made dance rattles out of hollow coconuts, instead of turtle **shells**, and often continued to make them out of coconuts after they had returned home.

Many Indians wear deer dewclaw rattles tied to leather bands around their legs. Others make them from **recycled** metal pieces (such as tin-lids), shells, bones and hooves, fixed to cloth or hide and worn on the body and used as percussive instruments when the body moves (as in a dance).

For many, the rattle makes a powerful and magical sound. Some Anishinabe even describe the sound of the gourd rattle or shaker as 'the Sound of Creation'.[43] The sound of a rattle can imitate or signal the presence of a supernatural power or spirit. It can also be the sound of **rain**, thunder, lightning, bird call, wind, breath or running water.

Rattles, like drums and bone whistles, are used in curing spiritual and physical illness. They are carved or painted carefully in a ritual way because they are used in a **ceremonial** context. Designs often come from supernatural powers in **dreams**.[44]

The *tsi'ka* is a kind of prayer that things will go well and nothing will go wrong. It is always done with a rattle, never a drum.
Helma Ward, Makah, 1991

188 Above Dancers from Santa Clara Pueblo in a Corn Dance (*kho'he'je*) held on Santa Clara's Feast Day, 12 August 1991. The men are wearing **bandoliers** of **shells** across their chest and carrying gourd rattles covered with clay from the river. The same clay wash covers parts of their bodies. Their sashes (**rain** belts) and their kilts are covered with symbols of rain and water. The rattles, shells from the ocean and gourds from a relative of the **squash**, imitate and call the thunder and lightning.

Raven

Raven, like **Coyote**, **Rabbit** and Spider, is a creator and a trickster. According to some **Inuit** and Northwest Coastal peoples, he brought light into the world. On the **Northwest Coast** his image can be found on **rattles** used for healing. The colour black symbolizes the power that Raven brings.

189 Below A bird-handled rattle, carved with a frog, a human and other animals, from the **Northwest Coast**.

When Raven reached the pea-vine he found three other men that had just fallen from the pea-pod that gave the first one (first man)... . Raven remained with them a long time, teaching them how to live. He taught them how to make a fire-drill and bow... . He made for each of the men a wife, and also made many plants and birds such as frequent the sea coast... . He taught the men to make bows, arrows, spears, nets and all the implements of the chase and how to use them; also how to capture the seal which had now become plentiful in the sea. After he taught them how to make kayaks, he showed them how to make houses of drift logs and bushes covered with earth.

An Inuit story

190 Below Some Native people, such as the **Yurok**, Tolowa and Karuk from Northern California, use rattles – **shells**, in this instance – over their whole bodies as the percussion for **dance**. Yuroks connect shells with water, the ocean and the creation of all things.

191 Below Indians did not need brass tacks to secure leather to wood, so they used them for decorative grips for war clubs and knives. This **Blackfeet** knife has brass tack decoration on the handle.

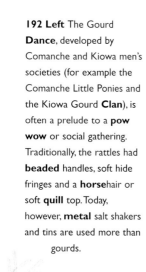

192 Left The Gourd **Dance**, developed by Comanche and Kiowa men's societies (for example the Comanche Little Ponies and the Kiowa Gourd **Clan**), is often a prelude to a **pow wow** or social gathering. Traditionally, the rattles had **beaded** handles, soft hide fringes and a **horse**hair or soft **quill** top. Today, however, **metal** salt shakers and tins are used more than gourds.

193 Below A wooden **war** club associated with Red Jacket.

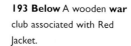

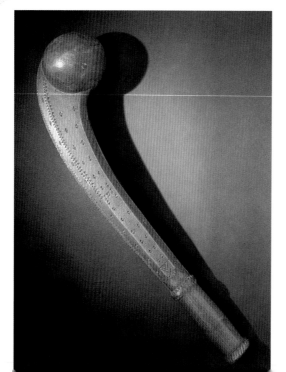

194 Above In this 1828 painting of Red Jacket by Robert Weir he carries a **diplomatic** gift, a pipe tomahawk, and wears the Peace Medal given him by George Washington, who betrayed him and his people, not fulfilling the pledges he made to protect his Seneca allies.

Recycled materials

Indians used and reused materials of all kinds. Native peoples took what was rubbish to Europeans and turned it into things that were of use and importance to them. Natives converted scrap copper and iron of all sorts (from kettles and tools, for example) into **metal** decorations for clothing and weapons.

Captured rifle stocks were transformed into **war** clubs. Gun barrels and metal scythes were made into **awl**s and scrapers for taking the flesh and hair off animal hides. People scavenged shipwrecks and abandoned camps for cast-off, worn out bits and pieces.

Items of considerable value to Europeans, such as gold coins, meant little to Indians not yet in a cash **economy**. They too were turned into distinctive ornaments and tools.

Red Jacket

Red Jacket (*Sagoyewatha*) (1756–1830), a **Seneca**, was a man of such intellectual and political skills that he was 'raised up' as a non-hereditary chief.

Although he was forced to join the majority of his people in a **British** alliance against the American rebels, he warned the **Iroquois** people against all European alliances.

After the war, he became grudgingly reconciled to the new government and many Seneca felt he had betrayed

195 Right The **Creek/** Muscogee chief Josiah Francis went to England in 1814, at the end of the Red Stick Wars, to regain **British** support for his people. Unable to return home because of his support of the rebels, he made this Southeastern-style finger-woven **bandolier** pouch of blue worsted wool. Eventually, Andrew Jackson's Navy captured and hung Francis.

them by bowing to Washington's power. However, he always strongly rejected white efforts to wipe out Seneca culture and power.

Our seats were once large and yours were small. You have now become a great people, and we have scarcely a place left to spread our blankets. You have got our country, but are not satisfied; you want to force your religion upon us. We do not wish to destroy your religion or take it from you. We only want to enjoy our own.
Red Jacket, to a representative of the US *government*, 1841

Red Stick Wars

In the history of warfare between the United States and Indian tribes, few battles cost more Indian lives than the one that ended the Red Stick Wars (1813–14). After Britain defaulted on its Native allies in the South during the War of 1812, the struggles between Indians and the new 'Americans' escalated in the Upland South. There was much discontent among the tribes and a series of battles between Anglo-American invaders, Muskogee (**Creek**) Indians and Muskogee rebel warriors (known by whites as 'redsticks' for the red clubs that they carried).

The war began on 22 July 1813, when the Muskogee rebels, guided by religious leaders, attacked in a determined and unified effort to remove US agents and the Muskogee chiefs from tribal lands. By the time the battles ended in Tohopeka on 27 March 1814, 80 percent of Red Stick warriors were dead. As a result of this defeat, Creeks gave up 14 million acres of land. This was the largest amount of land ever surrendered by a Native group to the government. The peace **treaty** signed at Fort Jackson ended the wars by re-drawing the boundaries between the United States and the Muskogee Nation.

131

196 Above A Navajo
political activist and
relocation resister, Katharine
Smith, Big Mountain, Arizona,
in 1991.

Relocation

The policy called 'relocation' involved Indian peoples moving from rural **reservations** to the cities. It came with another new policy called '**termination**', which was designed to remove as many reservations as possible from the list of tribes for whom the government was responsible according to its **treaties**. These policies, together with the collapse of **farming** and **subsistence**, and the **Second World War**, caused the massive resettlement of Native peoples to cities. This pattern of urbanization now has over 50 percent of Indians living off reservations in cities throughout the country. These people are called '**urban Indians**'.

The relocation of the 1950s changed the lives of Natives as much as the **Removal** of the 18th and 19th centuries. The **Navajos** and the other tribes that experienced the most relocation, lost their matrilocal style of residence and their control over their **economies** and distribution of goods. Urban life also put great pressure on all Indians to deny their Indian identity. They often felt rejected by reservation Indians and separated from traditional religious and cultural life. Although relocation traditionally included job placement, training and subsidies, Indians may have traded rural

poverty for urban poverty. They had fewer resources than other groups, and Indian families, larger than most, still lived below the poverty line at twice the national rate.

Native peoples all over the United States and Canada have continued to suffer other forms of relocation. **Seneca**, Makah, Colville, **Salish**, Kootenai, **Cherokee** and Mandan-Hidatsa (and in Canada, **Cree** and **Inuit**) were relocated because of hydro-electric power utilities and **dams** sited on their traditional lands. At Colville, for example, even traditional burial grounds were relocated to other sites. In the 1950s, the Canadian government 'relocated' Inuits from Northern Québec to the high **Arctic**. Inuits who lived traditionally in extended family units were often separated in the relocation, and game once hunted in Québec did not exist in the new colonies. In the late 1980s, faced with the massive failure of the programme, the government agreed to send home any Inuit who wished to return. The US government also abandoned the policy of relocation, although over half the reservation population chose to relocate voluntarily in the 1980s as people lost land, searched for work to fit their newly gained skills or moved for military service.

Removal

W̲e are almost surrounded by the whites and it seems to be their intention to destroy us as a people... . We had hoped that the white man would not be willing to travel beyond the mountains. Now that hope is gone. They have travelled beyond the mountains and settled on Cherokee land. They wish to have that usurpation sanctioned by treaty. When that is gained, the same encroaching spirit will lead them upon other lands of the Cherokees. New cessions will be asked. Finally the whole country, which the Cherokees and their fathers have so long occupied, will be demanded and the remnant of the Ani-Yuni-wiya, 'The Real People', once so great and formidable, will be compelled to seek refuge in some distant wilderness. There they will be permitted to stay only a short while, until they again behold the advancing banners of the same greedy host.
Dragging Canoe, Cherokee, 1776

After the Revolutionary War, increasing numbers of settlers moved out of the original colonies toward the West. Although most of the 116 treaties signed before 1820 involved the handover of a great deal of **land**, settlers wanted even more. Treaty promises to protect the tribes from further loss of land faded. Leaders such as the Shawnee *Tecumseh* (1768–1813) and his brother, *Tenskatawa* (the Prophet) (1775–1836), tried to unite tribes in military and religious rebellion against these new invasions, but they failed. The so-called 'opening of the frontier', triggered by the Louisiana Purchase, made westward expansion onto more Indian lands inevitable. Voluntary Removal was encouraged as a way of preventing further violence, but compulsory Removal (enacted by the Indian Removal Act of 1830) was enforced despite much debate and resistance in Congress. Most tribes resisted Removal, and there were enormous, often bloody, inter-tribal disputes

197 Below Removal routes of the Cherokee, Choctaw, Chickasaw, Creek and Seminole peoples.

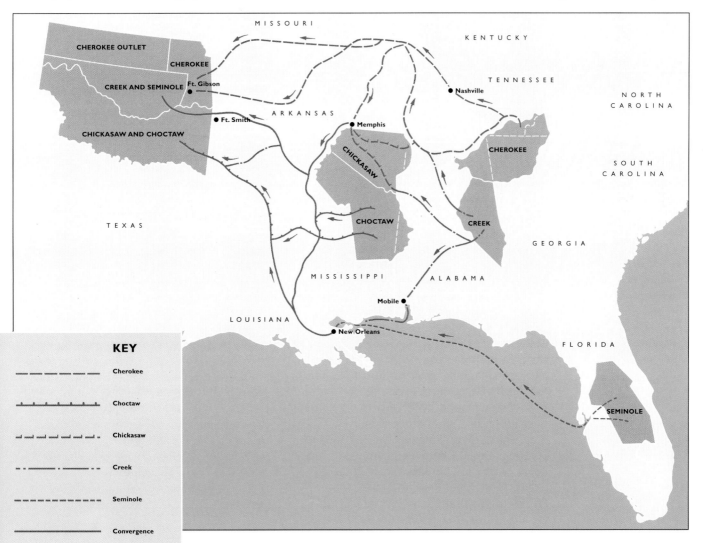

KEY

– – – –	Cherokee
–·–·–·–	Choctaw
–··–··–	Chickasaw
–·· ·––··	Creek
– – – – –	Seminole
————	Convergence

between those who would give in to Removal and those who would not.

In the 1820s, the state of Georgia enacted laws to drive the Cherokees from their homelands, land made even more desirable to whites by the recent discovery of gold and by its suitability for farming cotton. The Cherokees took their case to the US Supreme Court, which found the Georgia laws unconstitutional (in *Worcester v. Georgia* and *Cherokee Nation v. Georgia*). The Supreme Court ruled that the Cherokee Nation was a **sovereign** 'domestic dependent nation' and, therefore, exempt from Georgia law. President Andrew Jackson, the 'Father of Democracy' to non-Indians, refused to enforce the Court's ruling. When it became clear that the government would never uphold the decision of the Supreme Court, a few Cherokees (including Major Ridge and **Elias Boudinot**) began to consider negotiating Removal. They felt that they would save Cherokee lives if they went where they were promised no more white men would follow. Although their Treaty Party had little support among Cherokees, US commissioners met with them in 1835 and negotiated the Treaty of New Echota. It provided for the exchange of all Cherokee territory in the Southeast for a piece of land in **Indian Territory** (today Northeast Oklahoma). Most Cherokees in the East (including Principal Chief John Ross) signed a petition protesting that the treaty had been made by an unauthorized minority, but the US Senate approved the document.

In the summer of 1838, government troops began rounding up Cherokees and imprisoning them. Families were separated. Soldiers burned Cherokee cabins and crops. Some groups of Cherokees were forcibly moved west. Chief Ross appealed to President Van Buren to allow the Cherokees to carry out their own Removal. In the winter of 1838–39 the Cherokee Nation moved west, where they joined a smaller number of so-called Old Settler Cherokees already there. Even the wealthy Cherokees who had embraced the way of life promoted by the government, were forced from their homes by the Georgia Guards. The Cherokee Removal became known as the Trail of Tears (in Cherokee, 'The Place Where We Cried') because of the dreadful suffering they endured. Between 25 and 50 percent of those who began the journey died from **disease**, malnutrition, starvation or execution.

The Cherokees are nearly all prisoners. They have been dragged from their houses and camped at the forts and military posts all over the Nation. Multitudes were not allowed time to take anything with them but the clothes they had on. Well-furnished houses were left a prey to plunderers who, like hungry wolves, follow the progress of the captors and in many cases accompany them. It is a painful sight. The property of many has been taken and sold before their eyes for almost nothing, the sellers and buyers being in many cases combined to cheat the poor Indian. Private purchases, or at least the sham of purchases, have in many instances been made at the instant of arrest and consternation: the soldiers standing with guns and bayonets, impatient to go on with their work, could give but little time to transact business. The poor captive in a state of distressing agitation, his weeping wife almost frantic with terror, surrounded by a group of crying, terrified children, without a friend to speak one consoling word, is in a very unfavourable condition to make advantageous disposition of his property even were suitable and honest purchasers on the spot. Many who a few days ago were in comfortable circumstances are now the victims of abject poverty. Many who have been allowed to return to their homes under passport to inquire after their property have found their houses, cattle, hogs, ploughs, hoes, harness, tables, chairs, earthenware, all gone. It is altogether a faint and feeble representation of the work of barbarity which has been perpetrated on the unoffending, unarmed and unresisting Cherokees. I say nothing yet of several cold-blooded murders and other personal cruelties.
Evan B. Jones, Baptist missionary and Cherokee supporter

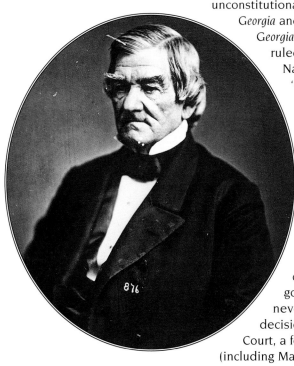

198 Above John Ross, the **Cherokee** Nation's first Principal Chief, was born in 1790 at Turkeytown, Alabama, to a Scottish father and a Cherokee mother. Ross held the Office of Principal Chief of the Cherokee Nation for 38 years through the stormy periods of Removal and the **Civil War**. In his personal appearance and upper-class lifestyle, John Ross seemed far from traditional, but he remains today a great hero to Cherokees everywhere because of his support for Cherokee **sovereignty**.

There was much sickness among the emigrants and a great many little children died of whooping cough.
Rebecca Neugin, a Cherokee girl removed during the Trail of Tears

If I could… I would remove every Indian tomorrow beyond the reach of the white men, who like vultures, are watching, ready to pounce upon their prey and strip them of everything they have or expect from the government of the United States.
General John Ellis Wool, Director of Removal, 1836

Repatriation

From the 17th century, the US government urged Indians to put aside their old religion and even to destroy the artefacts associated with that religion. In the meantime, traditional practice was eroded by active policies such as '**civilization**', 'assimilation' (see **acculturation**) and '**allotment**'. Native people found it increasingly difficult to keep up their traditional religions, believing that their Gods had abandoned them. Ceremonial objects were sold, taken or given away. Although many later generations would want these objects returned from **museums** and collectors, only a few, such as the Hidatsa in the 1930s, would be successful until the government would take legal action. When the great drought in the late 1930s threatened the survival of the Hidatsa, they succeeded in recovering their sacred Waterbuster Bundle from the Museum of the American Indian in New York. This **medicine bundle** had always brought the Hidatsa **rain**. It had been transferred to the museum

by its keeper, Wolf Chief, who believed that when he died no-one would care for it. It was the first object repatriated to Indians by an American museum.

Today, following the Native American Graves and Repatriation Act of 1990, many tribes hope to regain objects once separated from them and to recover and bury once again ancestral remains. They want to practise their religious rituals and to put right hostile relationships. The Act makes it necessary for government-funded museums and institutions to list and return if requested to do so skeletal remains, ceremonial/sacred objects and cultural objects that can be identified with specific **federally recognized** tribes. These repatriations only apply to the United States (not to Canada or to other countries).

The objects most vigorously pursued for repatriation from museums have been Zuni *ahay:uda* (war gods) and **Iroquois wampum** belts. Long before the enactment of the Native American Graves and Repatriation Act, the Grand Council of the *Haudenosaunee* tried to retrieve wampum belts held in museums. Two institutions in the state of New York – the New York Historical Society and the Museum of the American Indian (now the National Museum of the American Indian of the Smithsonian Institution) – held a number of significant belts in their collections. As of 1998, these have been returned, along with other belts from other museums, to Iroquois in Canada and the United States.

199 Above A Spanish soldier made this *bulto* or **sculpture** of the Archangel St Michael in 1779 for the altar screen of the newly built church at Zuni Pueblo. In 1879, the Smithsonian Institution anthropologists removed the statue from the church and sent it back to the **museum** in Washington. In 1992, when Smithsonian scholars discovered that it has been inappropriately and illegally removed, the National Museum of American History returned the *bulto* to Zuni.

The Act and attempts at repatriation have been widely criticized by archaeologists, anthropologists and museum officials who question how such repatriations will affect research, learning and legal notions of property. Indians do not all agree on repatriation, particularly concerning skeletal remains, the handling of ceremonial and sacred objects that have long been out of traditional caretaking, and the spiritual and cultural consequences of repatriating remains and objects. However, most agree on the moral need to repatriate religious objects.

200 Above In this 1989 photograph, Jake Thomas (a traditional chief of the **Cayuga** and of the Grand Council of the **Iroquois**) and Roland Force (then the Director of the Museum of the American Indian) examine a number of **wampum** belts to be returned.

Reservations

Since the creation of the United States in 1776, the government has forced tribes to give up millions of acres of land. In the 19th century tribes were forced to accept reservations as the price for guarantees of **sovereignty**, personal safety, land, water and other resources as set out in treaties. Rounding up the resistant Plains tribes and putting them on reservations was, for many, the last act of the 'civilization' campaign begun by the government in the 18th century.

Reservations, however, were not the only models for Indian residence. In the New Mexico Territories, many of the most recent reservations were based on old land grants from Spanish royalty, themselves often based on aboriginal territories occupied for thousands of years. After California was made a separate state, Indians who had no **treaties** with the government were moved to or allowed to stay on **federally recognized** old **mission** farm and ranch lands (*Rancherias*). These were **terminated** in the 1950s and half restored in the 1980s.

201 Above This ledger drawing (c. 1875), *A Cheyenne Warrior Killing a Soldier*, shows a Native version of resistance to land cessions, reservationization and defeat by the government.[45]

E	O	T	H	U	K		B	M	N	N	T	T	Y
O	H	I	C	A	N		E	O	A	E	I	O	A
A	T	C	H	E	Z		O	H	T	U	M	B	M
E	U	T	R	A	L		T	I	C	T	U	A	A
I	M	U	C	U	A		H	C	H	R	C	C	S
O	B	A	C	C	O		U	A	E	A	U	C	E
A	M	A	S	E	E		K	N	Z	L	A	O	E

Royal Proclamation

The defeat of the French in Canada by the **British** General Wolfe in 1759 ended French domination over the interior and maritime areas of North America. The 1763 Royal Proclamation established Canada as a British colony and was meant to make peace after years of conflict between the French and British. The Proclamation specifically recognized Native control over all unsettled **lands** and developed ways of negotiating these lands. It was decided that all lands would have to be purchased from Native groups once terms had been agreed. Once America gained independence from Britain, the Royal Proclamation no longer applied to the lands of the United States, but the Proclamation continues to form the basis for **land claims** cases in Canada. First Nations in Canada argue that the rights granted in this document are still in force despite all the federal or provincial government policies that followed, including the Indian Act.

202 Above This was painted in 1992 by Robert Houle, a Canadian Native artist. It uses a famous painting by the American artist Benjamin West, *The Death of Wolfe*, centred between the tribal names of extinct or nearly extinct groups of Indians. West painted large historic scenes, the most well-known being one of the death of the **British** hero General James Wolfe in the decisive battle for Canada between the French and the British in 1759. Wolfe is shown as a Christ-figure, the Indian represents America, and the painting probably represents the conquest of America.[46] Houle's reinterpretation of West's painting gives a tragic version of how the British Empire advanced.

Sacred sites, sacred objects

Sacred sites are the places where people's origin and **creation stories** tell them they began or where significant events and moments in the creation of the world took place. Thus, the city of Jerusalem is sacred to Jews, **Christians** and Muslims, because events central to their religion took place there. Often, a sacred site is linked with a natural phenomenon, such as a volcano (Mount St Helen's to the Pomo), a mountain (Mount Taylor to the **Navajos**) or an entire area (the Black Hills to the Lakota **Sioux**), or with a an astronomical or geological phenomenon (such as rock formations). In some cases, the sacred site is made by humans to commemorate or re-enact a sacred event. For example, a *kiva* to the Pueblos represents the Earth's Navel (*sipapu*) through which they emerged into this world.

People continue to travel to these sacred sites to hold **ceremonies** and protect them from acts that would contaminate or interfere with their special powers. Thus, there are conflicts between Indians and governments, businesses and private individuals who threaten to demolish, build on or alter those sacred sites. Vision quest sites, sites with rock paintings or picture writing, sweat bath sites, ceremonial grounds (such as Sun **Dance** lodges and stomp grounds), areas where sacred plants and other materials are gathered and mythic origin sites remain of great concern to Native peoples.

Sacred objects have a power that comes from their origin as a gift from a supernatural spirit. Most **medicine bundles**, for example, contain that sacred power, which is why so many tribal peoples (including Navajos, Hidatsas, Pawnees and Cheyennes) have tried to get medicine bundles returned to them from **museums**.

Salish

The Southern coast of British Columbia and south into Washington was the homeland of the Coastal Salish. Six distinct Salish **languages** were spoken, excluding the Northern group at Bella Coola.

Most Coastal Salish groups had typical **Northwest Coastal economies** based mainly on the sea and rivers, which provided **fish** and mammals. The communities had leaders rather than chiefs. The system was flexible

and allowed talented people to move up and gain status. A leader spoke only for his extended family or household. Households were the largest political groups and villages consisted of a group of households.

Unlike other groups near them, the Salish did not have large, dramatic **ceremonial art**. Common were carved **house posts**, grave figures and smaller works of art such as **rattles** and the combs and whorls associated with weaving. The Salish were skilled weavers, making beautiful practical **baskets** of split cedar root decorated with geometric designs in cherry **bark**. They also made loom-woven cedar bark capes and **blankets** for everyday use and 'nobility blankets' from goat or **dog** hair.

Salmon was important to the Plateau groups. Their economy was based on the seasonal patterns of the salmon's movement, with people living in small mobile bands from spring to autumn. In the winter, several bands would join together to form a larger village with permanent houses. They lived on mainly stored **food**. Fishing was mostly a men's activity and they **hunted** small game throughout the year. Women spent a great deal of time preparing and preserving the catch along with berries and roots for the winter months.

The US/Canadian border slices through the centre of the lands occupied by the Interior Salish. Four Salishan languages are spoken on the area called the Canadian Plateau, and others exist in the south. The Salish (misnamed Flathead) peoples of the Plateau in the United States live, following the Hellgate Treaty of 1855, in Western Montana. The government forced them there to join with the Kootenai people to whom they are related culturally. They inhabit agricultural land, rich in timber, water and fish. Through education they have tried to re-establish their **self-determination**, including running a very successful and expanding tribal college. They have also tried to maintain their tribal culture by keeping alive their language, art and ceremony.

Salmon

In the same way as **maize** was important to Northeast, Southwest and Southeast peoples and **wild rice** was to the **Ojibwa**, so salmon was central to Native peoples in the Northwest and Alaska.

Then there's our ceremony for the salmon. We respect the salmon, we call them 'Salmon People'… . The people gather with their ritualist in the Longhouse on the Tulalip Reservation. It's a big wooden structure, oblong, about 100 feet long… . Open fires provide heat and light. The people sing the old songs. Each one carries a hand drum, and they drum to the beat of the song they are singing. Then a young man comes in to announce that… our guest is coming ashore. So the young people bring the King Salmon, the first salmon of the season, to shore on a canoe… . They circle the longhouse four times – that is a magic number in our culture – chanting:

This is King Salmon,
Upland it goes,
Upland it goes.
King Salmon this is,
King Salmon this is.

Then we… have a feast honouring the spirit of the salmon. After the feast, the skeleton of the salmon is… returned to the waters, to his people… the spirit informs the Salmon People that it has been treated respectfully in Tulalip so the salmon will return another year to be food for the people.

Vi Hilbert (taq^{w}šoblu), Lushootseed, 1990

Schools

In the 15th century there was much debate in Spain over whether Indians had souls and so could be educated and **Christianized**. This resulted in early attempts by **missionaries** in South America and in 'New Spain' to teach Indians to read. In the 17th century, Louis XIV ordered missionaries to educate Indian children in the St Lawrence, Mississippi and Great Lakes regions 'in the French Manner'. They were taught the French language and customs, handicrafts, singing, **agriculture** and traditional academic subjects. The **British** (both Protestant and, in Maryland, Catholic) established schools to educate the 'savages'. Their attempt to educate Native people was really a way to get land grants and funds from colonial rulers. A number of prestigious US institutions – William and Mary, and the Universities of Harvard, Pennsylvania, Dartmouth and Yale – were established on that basis. The numbers of 'savages' educated in these systems was tiny (fewer than 50 via Dartmouth even until 1970).

In some ways, Indians tried to counter the Europeans' schooling. In a story often printed in the late 18th century, some Indians decline a Quaker offer to send children for education:

We know that you highly esteem the kind of learning taught in those colleges, and that the maintenance of our young men while with you would be very expensive to you. We are convinced that you mean to do us good by your proposal and we thank you heartily. But you who are wise must know that different Nations have different conceptions of things, and you will, therefore, not take it amiss if our ideas of this kind of education happen not to be the same with yours.

We have had some experience of it. Several of our young people were formerly brought up at the College of the Northern Provinces. They were instructed in all your sciences. But when they came back to us, they were bad runners, ignorant of every means of living in the woods, unable to bear either Cold or Hunger, knew neither how to build a cabin, take a Deer, kill an Enemy, spoke our language imperfectly. Neither for Hunters, nor Councillors, they were totally good for nothing. We are, however, not the less obliged by your kind offer, tho' we decline accepting it and to show our grateful sense of it, the Gentlemen of Virginia will send us a dozen of their Sons, and we will take great Care of their Education, instruct them in all we know, and make Men of them.

In 1840, the **Cherokees** decided to set up their own free state school system. By 1846, 21 state schools were running alongside 10 missionary schools. In 1847, after **Removal,** the Council wanted to train more Cherokee teachers for the state school system, so it started two secondary schools called seminaries, one for girls and one for boys. These seminaries were approved by both English-speaking and traditionalist Cherokees. The traditionalists hoped this new effort would lead to more instruction in the Cherokee language.

Cherokees had long been believers in universal education for men and women (unlike many white societies). In an age when women generally received only a basic education, students at the Cherokee Female Seminary near Tahlequah had to pass an entrance exam and study geometry, algebra, physiology, geography, Latin, English grammar and history. Students also learned

203 Above The **Cherokee** Female Seminary was established in 1850 near Tahlequah, Oklahoma (the Cherokee capital in **Indian Territory**) by Chief John Ross, the Cherokee Council and **missionaries**.

the domestic arts and social skills to prepare them to become 'ladies'. These new schools were deeply **Christian** and European in their approach to education and toward 'Indians'.

School was another way of making Indians change. Indians were sent to school in order for them to become like whites (ironic when **Africans** were forbidden an education by supporters of slavery). They were to change from 'pagan wanderers' to responsible citizens, whether as **farmers**, ministers, seamstresses or millers and sawyers (as set out in the 1794 **treaty** with the **Oneida**, Tuscarora and the Stockbridge). Indians came to expect schooling and later they demanded it as part of the social and political contracts with the invaders. Treaties often guaranteed some form of education. This, along with the

civilization policy of the United States, made schools the 'Americanizers' of Indian young people.[47]

Indians became captives of boarding schools. Parents had to send their children to school. The government would even use military force to place children in school, and written and spoken stories tell of children 'kidnapped' from their homes to be put in boarding schools far away. Many ran away repeatedly, never losing their Indian ways of thinking and being. Others, forbidden to speak their **languages**, wear Native dress and practise Indian singing and **dancing**, became assimilated (see **acculturation**). Children were even placed with white families after completing school, so that their education in white culture would be complete. In another

204 Left Woxie Haury, Carlisle Indian School, in 1897. Photographs from many schools show before and after shots of Indians. The 'before' portrait has the Indians wrapped in **blankets**, with **feathers** in their hair. They look dirty, hungry, perhaps dangerous. The 'after' portrait shows stiff young people, brown faces and new haircuts above the starched collars and shirtwaist dresses.

way, school also fostered a **pan-Indian** identity, as children from many different tribes attended the large boarding schools and the schools encouraged mutual interests and **intermarriage**.

We were now loaded into wagons hired from and driven by our enemies… . We were taken to the schoolhouse… into the big dormitory, lighted with electricity… had never seen so much light at night… . Evenings we would gather… and cry softly so the matron would not hear and scold or spank us… . I can still hear the plaintive little voices saying, 'I want to go home. I want my mother.' We didn't understand a word of English and didn't know what to say or do.
Helen Sekaquaptewa, Hopi, 1906

First, I will tell you about the Cherokees… . I think they improve. They have a printing press and print a paper which is called the *Cherokee Phoenix*. They come to meetings on Sabbath Days… . I hope this nation will soon become civilized and enlightened.
Sally Reece, a 12-year-old Cherokee student, in 1828

By 1928, however, the government had concluded that the boarding school system had failed to educate Indian students, and to improve their health or their ability to work. Military service during the **Second World War** had a profound effect on Indian education. Veterans returned to communities, often taking advantage of the GI Bill (see page 178) to complete their high school qualifications and go to college. Government programmes were designed to support schools faced with a flood of Indian children. Following **relocation** in the 1950s, many Indians lived in a world of urban

205 Below The carpentry shop at Carlisle Indian School, which was the first boarding school. It was started in 1878 by General Richard Pratt, who once wrote 'Hair, scalplock and paint will vanish like a dream before a neat suit of 'Confed' grey… [we must] kill the Indian and Save the Man'.

206 Below Jaune Quick-to-See-Smith, a **Salish** painter, shows her version of an Indian school in this 1992 pastel, *I See Red, One Little, Two Little…*. It refers to the **stereotypes** of Indians often found in schools, as in the common nursery counting song, 'One Little, Two Little, Three Little Indians'. She superimposes the rhyme over a blackboard, setting Indian miseducation to rights by covering the board in the Salish **language** rather than in the English language forced on Indian children in the schools.

207 Right Sam Ell studying at Sitting Bull College, Fort Yates, North Dakota.

reservations. The Civil Rights Movement was not yet a reality for Indians and relocation took place once again in an atmosphere of racism and discrimination. How Indians were treated in schools which segregated blacks and whites varied from place to place. Often it depended on how 'culturally identifiable' the Indians were. Thus, **Sioux** in Chicago went to 'white' schools, but Pamunkeys in Virginia went to 'black' schools, or, sadly, to no school at all.[48]

The demand for self-government and **self-determination** by Indians changed schooling. By 1998, few government boarding schools remained open. Monies guaranteed in treaties still partially support most Indians in a college education and some professional training. Today, most Indian students go to state schools. Others go to old **Bureau of Indian Affairs** schools, now run by tribes. Some independent, Indian-controlled schools operate in cities and on **reservations**. In the 1970s, tribally controlled community colleges brought higher education to the reservations. The colonial dream of educating Indian children is alive, but today that dream is one shared and often controlled by Indian parents and by tribes.

208 **Below** Bill Reid (1920–1997), a **Haida** artist, was one of the best-known sculptors in Indian Country. His huge pieces, carved from stone and cast in **metal**, draw on Haida and other traditional designs of the Queen Charlotte Islands of the **Northwest Coast**. This sculpture, *The Spirit of Haida Gwaii or Black Canoe* (on display at the Canadian Embassy in Washington, D.C.) is an abstract monument to the great seagoing canoes and **whalers** of the Haida past. The canoe carries 13 figures – **Raven**, Mouse Woman, Grizzly **Bear**, Bear Mother, **Beaver**, Dogfish Woman, **Eagle**, Frog, Wolf and a chief. Raven and **Wolf** represent the two **clans** in the Haida world.

Sculpture

Most indigenous people have some sculptural traditions in wood, stone, clay or **metal** carving and moulding, and even in the moulding of huge mound-like earthworks. In some cultures (among **Northwest Coastal** peoples, for example) those traditions produced monumental sculptures; in others, useful tools, religious artefacts and figurative carvings. With European tools came the possibility of carving and shaping larger and more refined works.

Early sculptors on the Plains, in the Southeast, in the **Arctic** and on the Northwest Coast produced **pipes** and pipe stems, clubs, speaker's staffs, **house posts**, architectural features of houses, eating bowls, spoons and ladles, **rattles**, animal and human figures and faces, bone and ivory carving, **pottery** and stone figures and **dance** sticks. In the early 20th century, artists combined Western/European and Native traditions and began to produce sculptural works of **art** in **metal**, stone, clay and wood.[49]

209 **Right** Bob Haozous is a contemporary **Apache** artist whose work can be a humorous well as a political commentary on Indian history. His father was the distinguished sculptor, Alan Houser, and Haozous puts his own history and that of the Apache people into this 1989 cast metal, painted piece, *Apache Soul House*. The *gaan* dancer on top, a spirit figure that comes during the Crown Dance of the Apache, represents a way of communicating with the spirit world.

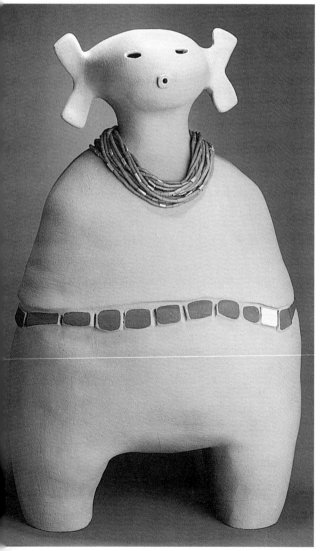

210 **Above** *Emergence of the Clowns*, 1988, by Roxanne Swentzell from Santa Clara Pueblo.

211 **Left** Nora Naranjo Morse, from Santa Clara Pueblo, and her niece, Roxanne Swentzell, have taken their traditional **pottery** toward sculpture in the large ceramic figures they produce. This sculpture, *Mudwoman*, refers to the connection between the origins of Pueblo people and pottery (see **adobe**) and to the mudhead **clowns** that often appear in Pueblo **art**, **dance** and mythology.

Self-determination, self-government

Along with **land claims**, the other major issue of concern for Native communities in Canada has been self-government. Native groups argue that they never gave up their right to self-government, but no-one agrees as to what is meant by 'self-government'. In the 1980s the Canadian Constitution was rewritten and the existing aboriginal treaty rights of Canada's Native people were recognized. In addition, a large proportion of Native people live in cities away from reserves and the question of how this affects self-government needs to be addressed.

A series of amendments to the Constitution on Native self-government were proposed, including naming the aboriginal government as one of the three orders of government in Canada. This amendment in the Charlottetown Accord was rejected in a national referendum. A second agreement, the Meech Lake Accord, was also unsuccessful because Elijah Harper (the Manitoba Native Member of the Legislative Assembly) went against it. The Meech Lake Accord would have allowed amendments to the Canadian Constitution that would have provided special rights and recognition for the province of Québec and for First Nations people. It was worked out at a meeting of provincial and Native leaders, and had to be approved by all the provincial governments within a two-year period. Many Native communities were not satisfied with the agreement because they felt it did not go far enough in recognizing Native rights. Native women felt it gave too much power to band councils, the same councils that supported women being excluded from the Indian Act if they married non-Native men. The province of Manitoba was the last to hold a vote on the issue. Elijah Harper used a little known legal clause to stall the vote until after the time limit ran out.

> **W**e're going to create political institutions that will reflect our beliefs and our thinking…. Native people will have much to contribute over the next century. It's our turn.
> *Georges Erasmus, former Grand Chief of the Assembly of First Nations*

Elijah Harper was born on a trap line in Northern Manitoba to **Cree-Ojibwa** parents.

He completed his high-school certificate and spent a year at the University of Manitoba studying anthropology. He was appointed as Chief of the Red Sucker Band and was later elected to the Manitoba government. He ran in the federal elections as a Liberal candidate and served one term. Harper is a good example of the efforts of present-day Canadian Indians to achieve self-government.

In the United States, the struggle for what Native people call self-determination can be seen in the call for the return of tribal lands to Native control. The people also want to be able to follow their Native religion, to use and preserve sacred lands and sites, to control education and healthcare, and to develop natural resources. The battles, mostly unsuccessful, for the return of Blue Lake to Taos Pueblo, Pyramid Lake to the Paiutes, the Black Hills to the **Sioux**, and large parts of the state of Maine to the Passamaquoddy and Penobscot, came to stand for Indian struggles for self-determination.

Tribal governments in the United States can now set their own priorities and goals for educational and social programmes and use the annual payments set out in **treaties** to operate their own **schools**, hospitals and law enforcement agencies. Most tribal governments, however, are too small, too poor and too dependent on the government to achieve the sort of ideal self-government they might hope for. Some fear that the move for self-determination is simply another way for the government to avoid its responsibilities toward Indians. Others fear that the efforts do not go far enough toward freeing tribal governments to function as **sovereign** nations.

212 Left The most famous image of Elijah Harper shows him holding an **eagle** feather for strength and guidance. Harper was unswerving in his opposition to the Meech Lake Accord.

Seminoles

The word 'Seminole' comes from the Spanish *cimarron*, meaning wild or runaway. Seminoles and Miccosukees are descendants of **Creek** Indians who fled to Florida from the coastal and interior South in the early 18th century. They included groups such as the Apalachi and Yamassee, who fled to North Florida after the Yamassee War in 1715 and the Upper Creeks who joined them in 1814 after the **Red Stick Wars**. The Seminoles followed Creek cultural and **economic** practices, organizing themselves into **matrilineal** villages, governed by chiefs. Living in the Everglade swamps of Florida, they have been and still are **hunters**, **farmers** and **fisherpeople**. The Second Seminole War in 1835–42 was as a result of Seminole resistance to resettlement and **Removal**. The majority of the Seminoles were removed to Oklahoma, although some managed to remain in Florida. They endured various further migrations to **Indian Territory** – one group of so-called Black Seminoles went to Northern Mexico (an area that became part of the state of Texas in 1848).

Florida Seminoles, because of their isolation, remained very traditional; most still speak the Muskogee **language**. They established three reservations in 1911, with an additional area for the Miccosukees who separated into the Everglades in South Florida. Although most Seminoles and Miccosukees remain poor, they pioneered the development of **tourism** in Everglades and swamps and eventually set up successful tribal museums. The Seminole women took up the sewing machine in the early 20th century, and their people are known for their superb ribbonwork, appliqué and patchwork clothing. In the 1980s, they led the way for other tribes in the development of high stakes **gambling** based on their status as a **sovereign** nation.

The Seminoles in Oklahoma (combined of Muskogee- and Hitchiti-speaking peoples) and the Black Seminole Freedmen (see **Africans**) are fairly indistinguishable from Creeks/Muscogees. Many still speak Muskogee, and keep their traditional ceremonial life, although they combine it with **Christian** practice as do most of the Southeastern tribal peoples in Oklahoma. Although they have been paid some money for the lands lost in Florida in the early 19th century, they have only 36,000 of the 347,000 acres of land originally set aside in Oklahoma. They lost most of this land through **allotment** and the 'land grab' period in Oklahoma Indian history.

Seneca

The original name for the Seneca means 'people of the big hill'. During much of the 18th century the Seneca were a powerful and wealthy Indian nation, the westernmost nation of the **Iroquois Confederacy**. Their traditional lands included a large part of present-day Western New York State and ranged into Ohio and Canada. They had acquired much of this territory through alliances and wars in the 17th century. Their vast domain enabled them to become major partners in the **fur trade** with the new European settlers. As the most numerous of the peoples in the Iroquois Confederacy, they were central figures in the territorial and political struggle between nations and cultures – European and Indian.

European **diseases** wiped out entire villages and weakened many Native peoples' trust in their religious leaders. In the 17th century the Senecas increasing involvement in the fur trade had led to **wars** against the Huron, the Erie and their French allies, and these hostilities persisted into the 18th century until a **treaty** was signed with the French and Indian allies in 1710. Other tribes in the Confederacy favoured alliances with the **British** or the rebellious American settlers. Missionaries pressured tribes to become **Christian** and Indian lands were given or sold to acquire European goods or to encourage friendly relations.

The Seneca reluctantly sided with the British in the American Revolution and so fell in defeat with their allies. In 1797 the Treaty of Big Tree established Seneca **reservations** in the state of New York. The Treaty of Fort Stanwix forced the Seneca to give up much of their land. By 1838, the four reservations of Buffalo Creek, Tonawanda, Cattaraugus and Allegany remained. From the 1830s, many Seneca and other Iroquois were removed from Ohio and New York to reservations in Kansas and Oklahoma. The Tonawanda Seneca later bought back most of their reservation. They restored a government by hereditary chiefs, whereas the Allegany and Cattaraugus Seneca have elected systems.

In the 1960s the Allegany Seneca lost one-third of the reservation to the Kinzua **dam** project. They received compensation, but the land was irreplaceable. At Tonawanda, 99-year leases to non-Indians by the **Bureau of Indian Affairs** on the Tonawanda Reservation ran out. The Tonawanda Seneca forced the government to acknowledge that they still retained the lands that they once bought back and that it had violated its trust agreement with the Seneca. Negotiations continue between non-Indian residents and Seneca who want the land back and compensation for territories that should not have been taken.

Sequoyah

The **Cherokees** became a literate people in the 1820s when Sequoyah (1790–*c*.1843), whose English name was George Guess, developed a method of writing the Cherokee language. Sequoyan is the only known, widely used written **language** invented by one person alone. By 1830, most Cherokees could read and write in their own language. In those years of turmoil, the creation of a written language gave Cherokees power. Sequoyan was a real form of resistance against white domination and a force for cultural revitalization.

The Cherokee Nation bought a printing press and two sets of type, one in English and one in the syllabary (set of characters) invented by Sequoyah. In 1828 the first issue of a bilingual newspaper, edited by **Elias Boudinot**, rolled off the presses. Cherokee hymnals, New Testaments and other publications soon followed, as did a flood of handwritten official documents, school lessons, correspondence, personal memoirs and record books.

Sequoyah, who had joined the 'Old Settlers' who had voluntarily moved to the Arkansas territory in the 1820s, tried to reunite the tribe in the West in the face of

213 Above A painting of 1828, by Charles Bird King, shows Sequoyah with a copy of his **Cherokee** syllabary in his hand. Sequoyah is dressed, like other Cherokee and Southeastern men of his time, in a cloth turban decorated with bird plumes, and a cloth European-style 'hunting jacket'. His clay pipe also speaks of European **trade** influences on Native practices, even though Sequoyah himself opposed the adoption of white ways.

146

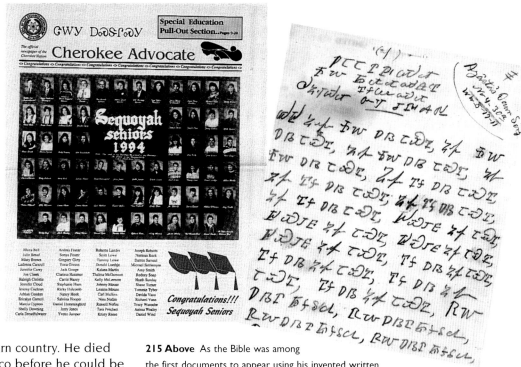

214 Right The front page of the newspaper, *Cherokee Advocate*. With its name in computer-generated Sequoyan script, it features the 1994 graduating students from Sequoyah High School in Tahlequah, Oklahoma.

enormous political unrest, violence and separation. When he was in his eighties, he and a band of followers went to the Texas territories and Mexico in order to visit other Indians and see something of the Western country. He died and was buried in Mexico before he could be reached by a messenger sent from the tribe to find him. Oo-*noo-leh*'s letter announcing his death to the Cherokee Council is evidence of the revolution in literacy caused by this extraordinary man.

215 Above As the Bible was among the first documents to appear using his invented written language, Sequoyah feared that his invention would be used to undermine **Cherokee** culture. However, his work was immediately used to preserve Cherokeean traditional culture. **Medicine** men and women (*disganawisdi*) began to write down many of their 'prescriptions', in the form of chants, prayers and formulae for plant medicines. This is part of a page with a 'dawn Song' in the Sequoyan script, from the writings of Ayasta, a female *disganawisdi* in the East.

Shells, shellwork

Molluscs were an important food source for coastal peoples. For centuries, people have also used sea and freshwater shells as currency (see **wampum**), decoration, religious objects, musical instruments and tools. Inland Natives (for example Pueblos) journeyed to the great rivers and to the oceans in order to obtain particular shells. They **traded** hides, **feathers** and other important objects for shells from faraway places. People from the Mississippi delta carved stories in and made gorgets from the whelk and freshwater pink mussel shells of their inland rivers.

Cherokee people today do the same. Pueblos, from

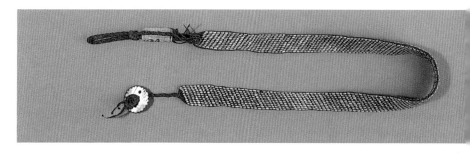

Santo Domingo, mirror the world in shell necklaces with the earth below in seashell and the sky above in turquoise. Plains people, far away from the sea, burn their cedar, sage and sweetgrass for prayers in abalone shells. Shells are used by many as **dance** rattles. They are connected with water, and so with the origin of life.

216 Above A shellwork necklace from Northern California.

217 Below A necklace of albalone shells made by Native people in California.

Sioux (Lakota, Dakota, Nakota)

The word 'Sioux', perhaps a mixture of **Ojibwa** and French words that may mean 'little snakes', has been used to describe at least 14 related groups of peoples speaking three different dialects. They occupied territories from Eastern Wisconsin to South Dakota to Montana as well as north to the Canadian plains. They included the Eastern Dakota (Mdewankânton or Santee, Sisseton, Wahpeton and Wahpekute), the middle territory Nakota (Yankton, Yanktonai, Assiniboine) and the Western Lakota (Oglala, Sicangu, Sihasapa, Itazipacola, Minneconjou, Hunkpapa, and Oowenupa). Most of these peoples (the Assiniboine broke off from the Sioux in the 1700s) formed a loose confederacy of members of the Sioux Nation (*Oceti Sakowin* or Seven Council Fires). They fished and gathered **wild rice** in the east, protected pipestone quarries and mined pipestone in the middle territories, and protected the Black Hills and hunted buffalo (*pte*) in the West. Living in small, family-centred groups called *tiyospaye*, they traded with each other and practised shared religious beliefs given to them by *Wakan Tanka* (the Creator) and White Buffalo Calf Woman long ago. Sioux lives and economies were revolutionized when the Spanish introduced the **horse** to America. The horse enabled them to hunt, travel and trade over vast areas. They were able to develop much more elaborate artistic traditions, especially beadwork, because of the extent of their trade in beads and hides. Later the French **fur trade** brought both peaceful interaction between Sioux and Europeans (including **intermarriage**) and the beginning of territorial disputes that escalated when American soldiers and traders arrived in the mid-nineteenth century. Dakota and Lakota had long-standing territorial arguments with Pawnees and **Ojibwa**, and the missionary intrusions into Sioux country and the seizures of Sioux land by the US army and settlers made the conflicts worse.

The **Treaty** of Fort Laramie in 1851 was meant to define protected territories, but it only split the Sioux into factions that supported or rejected the treaty, and further worsened relations between all Sioux and the government. The 1868 Fort Laramie Treaty confined all Sioux onto the Great Sioux Reservation, and the government forced them to sell the gold-rich Black Hills. (The Lakota never accepted the payments.) Armed resistance followed, leading to the Battle of the **Little Bighorn** when **Sitting Bull** and Crazy Horse defeated General Custer. Minneconjou, Hunkpapa, Oglala and other Lakota bands began to take part in the **Ghost Dance** movement. The murder of Sitting Bull and the massacre of Lakota at **Wounded Knee** in 1890 ended the so-called Indian Wars. The Sioux were confined to a reservation reduced by **allotment** and by new settlement by ranchers and farmers.

For the Seven Council Fires the twentieth century has been a continuing struggle to regain **sovereign** control over their religious practice, **language**, territory and government. The Sioux have continued to press their claims against the US government, trying to regain the resources that would allow them to be independent. In the 1970s they produced a ground-breaking educational system of community-based **schools** and tribal colleges much imitated by other Native nations.[50]

Sitting Bull

Sitting Bull was an Oglala Lakota holy man who became a war chief embodying all the virtues of his people. Known and feared as a warrior, both by whites and other Indians, he was a skilful political leader as well as a spiritual one. It fell on him to make the last resistance to the whites who wanted the Indians' land. However, neither his leadership nor his sponsorship of resistance could stop the final disaster for the **Sioux** people. Sitting Bull, after his time as a prisoner of war following the battle at the **Little Bighorn**, retired to the reservation to farm, raise cattle, send his children to white schools, and travel with Buffalo Bill Cody's Wild West Show.

Eventually, however, Sitting Bull could not hold back his opposition to land **allotments** under the Dawes Act nor his participation in the **Ghost Dance**. The Ghost Dance was intended to bring back the buffalo and to expel the whites from Indian lands forever. For Indians it was a last resort against assimilation into a non-Indian world. Trying to resist removal from the reservation, Sitting Bull was murdered by an Indian policeman in 1890, but his reputation is known around the world.

Sovereignty

We consider ourselves as a free and distinct nation and the government of the United States has no police over us further than a friendly intercourse in trade.
Cherokee statement, June 1818

The several Indian nations are distinct political communities, having territorial boundaries, within which their authority is exclusive, and having a right to all lands within those boundaries, which is not only acknowledged, but guaranteed by the United States.
US *Supreme Court Chief Justice John Marshall, in* Worcester v. Georgia, 1832

Indians have always insisted on their existence as sovereign, separable, free and independent governments – as nations. In the 1820s and the 1960s, Indians began to test their sovereignty in the courts, with cases on aboriginal rights and those laid down in **treaties**. Indian claims of sovereignty are involved in movements to regain alienated lands and aboriginal **hunting** and **fishing** territories, and most recently in the tribal development of the sale of **tobacco** products and the establishment of **gambling** activities on **reservations**. Although the courts and the government almost always uphold the legal principle of sovereignty, the actual attempts to practice it cause enormous conflicts both inside Indian communities and in their relationships with the outside world.

THE WHITE HOUSE

Office of the Press Secretary
For Immediate Release 29 April 1994
MEMORANDUM FOR THE HEADS OF EXECUTIVE DEPARTMENTS
AND AGENCIES

SUBJECT: Government-to-Government Relations with Native American Tribal Governments

The United States Government has a unique legal relationship with Native American tribal governments as set forth in the Constitution of the United States, treaties, statutes and court decisions. As executive departments and agencies undertake activities affecting Native American tribal rights or trust resources, such activities should be implemented in a knowledgeable, sensitive manner respectful of tribal sovereignty. Today, as part of an historic meeting, I am outlining principles that executive departments and agencies, including every component bureau and office, are to follow in their interactions with Native American tribal governments. The purpose of these principles is to clarify our responsibility to ensure that the Federal Government operates within a government-to-government relationship with federally recognized Native American tribes. I am strongly committed to building a more effective day-to-day working relationship reflecting respect for the rights of self-government due the sovereign tribal governments. In order to ensure that the rights of sovereign tribal governments are fully respected, executive branch activities shall be guided by the following...

WILLIAM J. CLINTON

Squash

Squash is one of the three major traditional Indian food plants (the 'Three Sisters'). The other two are **beans** and **maize**. The genus *curcurbita* includes all of today's edible and ornamental squashes, as well as pumpkins and gourds. Like most crops cultivated by American Indians before the arrival of Europeans, squash (an **Algonquian** word) is presumed to have originated in Mexico. By the 10th century, most **agriculturally** oriented tribes regarded squash as a staple **food**.

The blossoms, meat and seeds are edible. The seeds also provide an important source of oil. Slices or circular cuts of squash and pumpkin flesh were either sun- or fire-dried, making them ready to eat simply by rehydrating them. In the East, squashes were traditionally grown with beans and maize. This method of interplanting saved space and increased crop yield, and the large-leafed squash kept down weed growth and provided cover to the dry soil.

221 Left An early 19th-century **Cherokee** gourd **rattle**, probably used by **medicine** men (*disganawisdi*) in their prayers, songs and rituals.

Gourds are a type of squash and tribes made use of them in many ways. After removing the inner flesh of a gourd, the tough outer rind was made into objects such as bottles, bowls, cornmeal sifters, cups, funnels, ladles, spoons and strainers. Large gourds were used for storing and carrying water and as **fish** bait containers and fishnet floats. Two dried and hollow gourds around the body of a child learning to swim made a fine life jacket. Southeastern Indians also made gourd birdhouses which were placed on poles located throughout their fields of cultivated crops to attract insect-eating birds. Tribal peoples made hollow gourds into **rattles**, by placing seeds, small stones or shotgun pellets into them to create different sounds.

Squashes are mentioned in sacred songs of Southwestern tribes, such as the Pima and **Navajo**, and they appear in the **creation stories** of many Northeastern tribes such as the **Iroquois** and **Ojibwa**. There are four sacred plants in Navajo origin stories – maize, **tobacco**, beans and squash. The image of the squash plant appears in many Navajo weavings and the squash blossom in silver Navajo jewellery. The Tewa-speaking Northern Pueblo **clans** divide into winter and summer people or turquoise and squash people. The squash blossoms also appear in Pueblo **dance headdresses**, in traditional paintings and in designs on **pottery**.

218 Left Many different kinds of native squashes are held for recovery of their seeds at the Native Seeds/SEARCH. This group of biologists and agricultural specialists in Tucson, Arizona, works to restore traditional **agriculture** among native peoples of Mexico and the United States.

219 Right Frank Poolheco, a Hopi-Tewa artist from Albuquerque, makes beautiful gourd **rattles**, like this one, for **Buffalo Dances** at Hopi and Zuni. They call the **rain**, so that the crops will grow.

220 Left A feast day dance at Santa Clara Pueblo. The man in the foreground wears a **headdress** featuring squash blossom. The women wear *tablitas* with cloud and **rain** designs on them.

Truly in the East
The white bean
And the great corn-plant
Are tied with the white lightning.
Listen! Rain approaches!
The voice of the bluebird is heard.
Truly in the East
The white bean
And the great squash
Are tied with the rainbow.
Navajo chant

Status Indians, see **Federally recognized tribes**

Stereotypes

Picture these old scenes.

A young Indian woman throws herself into a ravine, because her father has forbidden her love for the young white man.

A handsome, strong warrior, dressed in buckskins, with flowing black hair, and a full war bonnet, raises his bow to the sky as he sings his death song.

An Indian with a raised tomahawk and scalplock, creeps from a grove of trees towards a small cabin in a clearing.

An old man, his long braids hanging forward over his shoulders, is slumped at dusk on a tired pony, his lance dragging the ground. It is the End of the Trail.

A beautiful dark-haired woman, throws her body over the kneeling and bound figure of a white man. Other Indians, fierce and hostile, loom over them.

Picture these new scenes.

On an American football field, a young white man dressed as a Plains war chief dances and shouts every time the team (the 'Braves' or the 'Redskins') scores, while the band plays a loud drumbeat.

Children on a suburban housing estate, dressed in cowboy hats and **feather** headbands, chase each other.

A spiritualist hands out flyers to passers-by advertising her service, which features an Indian spirit guide called Chief Red **Eagle**.

In stores in Santa Fe, white women dressed in turquoise and silver **squash** blossom necklaces buy designer clothes styled in the manner of the Old Indian West.

In a television advert an actor plays an Indian weeping over a polluted stream.

In the Black Forest of Germany, families visit a 'Sioux' encampment, spending the week dancing war dances, tanning hides and taking sweatbaths.

These figures are part of the mythology of Native American people – the Maid of the Mist, The Noble Savage, the Chieftain's Death Song, the Skulking Savage, the Poor Indian at the End of the Trail and the Tragic Half-Breed.

Particularly in New England and the Mid Atlantic, where Indians were no longer common, they were often romanticized in poems, songs, legends, Wild West Shows, medicine shows, circuses, films and artefacts.

Virtually all of these images, stories and stereotypes transferred themselves in a new form into the 20th century – Indian sports mascots dance on sports fields, 'New Age' 'shamans' lead white men and women through expensive healing **ceremonies** and children still play '**cowboys and Indians**'. Americans and Europeans still treasure their old ideas and images of Indians.[51]

Stickball

Stickball, played by **Cherokees**, is similar in some ways to lacrosse, particularly in its connection with ritual. Unlike lacrosse, it is played with two sticks. Although life among the Eastern Cherokees changed, many traditional beliefs, pastimes and ways of life were preserved as a result of their resistance to Anglo-American pressures. In the 1880s, the anthropologist James Mooney from the Smithsonian Institution visited the Eastern Cherokees to document surviving traditional aspects of their culture. He found the Cherokee **language** still written and spoken, many ancient religious beliefs and practices still followed, activities of daily life performed in traditional ways, and stickball playing and traditional **dancing** as popular as ever.

222 Above Cherokee men and women preparing for a game of stickball, *c.* 1885.

Stomp dance

Here's the scene. Night. A fire. A circle. Indians dancing around it. But something is wrong. Where are the beads? Only an occasional feather on a man's hat. Hats, jeans, overalls, cowboy boots. Calico dresses, regular clothes… . The music doesn't sound right either. No *dum-dum-dum-dum* drum. Just a high-pitched small drum. One man's voice calls out a line… . A small drum, the water drum, small enough to fit in one hand, makes the beat for this music. Creek songs are fast and crazy Cherokees like Creek singing. But if you don't watch it, the Creek men will charm you with that singing. Moving feet and rattles on the women's legs make the rest of the percussion for the call-and-response of the men's songs. The women make the rattles, called shackles, out of box turtles – sometimes condensed milk tins – sewn onto pieces of leather. Nowadays, they're just as likely to be sewn on the top parts of old cowboy boots… . The shackles are heavy and the people dance all night, but the shell-shakers keep the beat. Linda Hogan, a Chickasaw writer told it this way in a poem called 'Calling Myself Home'.

> There were old women
> who lived on amber. Their dark hands
> laced the shells of turtles
> together, pebbles inside
> and they danced
> with rattles strong on their legs.

In 1889, many [traditional] Cherokees reacted against changes in Cherokee society and resuscitated the Keetoowah Society. A Cherokee named Red Bird Smith formed a group known as the 'Nighthawk Keetoowah'. They not only sought to restore old practices and ceremonies such as the stomp dance, but actively, though unsuccessfully, opposed the allotment of Cherokee tribal lands. Stomp dances and other ceremonies continue today in Oklahoma. The members of the Keetoowah Society keep the stomp grounds because they keep the Sacred Fire. The Keetoowahs help the *Aniyunwiya* remember.

The people who belong to the stomp grounds sit under their seven brush arbors. Things begin when they are all represented, and everybody else rings around that huge circle. At particular celebrations, the people might play stickball and make a speech telling the history of the People and this stomp ground. After playing ball and sharing food, they dance. Some go back and forth to their arbors or trucks and cars and to lawn chairs and benches sitting with friends. People come from the outside rings and inside to join the counter-clockwise movement of a particular dance. The leader and the men turn their heads and hands toward the fire, honouring the fire. The people dance all night. There are lots of stomp dance songs; some are about animals, others about friendship, even love. These are always happy dances. Sometimes the song tells a funny story and laughter rises up in the middle of the dance. You should hear what Rabbit sang when he taught the wolves a new dance… . You will not see this dance at a pow wow, scarcely even when just Indians are gathering with each other, because this music and dance hasn't been widely shared with other people. Only those who know the songs, summer after summer, sing them… . At the end, Cherokees might say '*wado, wado*', 'thank you, thank you', because they have so appreciated the song and the dance.

Rayna Green, Cherokee folklorist

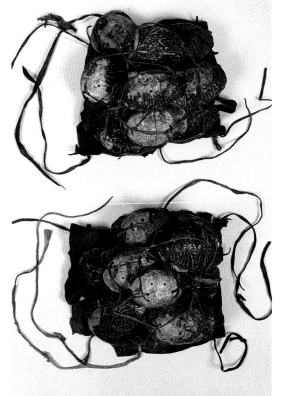

223 Left Southeastern Indian women (**Cherokee**, Choctaw, **Seminole** and **Creek**) make the rhythm for the stomp dance with the **turtle shells** they wear on their legs. Cherokees call the women 'shell shakers'.

224 Above These young Choctaw women in Washington, D.C., demonstrate a stomp dance. One woman wears shackles or 'turtles' made of tin cans.

For God said, if the Cherokees be destroyed and become extinct, then that will be the destruction of the whole world. This is the word of the forefathers of our own land.
Keetoowah Society of Cherokee Indians

Subsistence

Subsistence (subsistence **economies**), or living off the resources of the land, is a way of life – spiritual and physical. For most Native people in the **Arctic**, in the far Northwest and in Northern Canada, **hunting** and **fishing** are necessities, which have been undermined by sport, trophy and commercial fishing. Subsistence life is threatened by competition for resources, whether industrial, chemical,

legal or human. Thus, Native Alaskans, **Ojibwa** in Michigan, Wisconsin and Minnesota, and Puyallup and others in the state of Washington are now working to restore their hunting and fishing rights because of their physical and spiritual need for the subsistence lifestyle. As before, Native men and women need to know how to hunt, fish, grow and preserve their **food**, but today they also need to know how to protect it in the courts.

Our subsistence way of life is especially important to us. Among other needs it is our greatest. We are desperate to keep it.
Paul John, Tununak, 1984

Sun Dance

To Plains people, the Sun Dance was, and to some still is, their most important ceremonial event. Crow, Cheyenne, **Cree**, Assiniboine, Lakota, **Blackfeet**, Arapaho, Paiute, Shoshone, Bannock, Kiowas and Utes all shared the Sun Dance Religion. The dance was a target for **missionaries** and governments and so was banned (along with the **potlatch** and the **Ghost Dance**) by both Canada and the United States in the latter part of the 19th century. The Sun Dance, which requires that its believers work, pray and sacrifice for the good of all, has been revitalized in a number of places.

S un Dance
 Wakan tanka
when I pray to him, he hears me
Whatever is good,
he grants me.
Teton Sioux Sun Dance song

225 Above In this ledger drawing made by Bear's Heart, a Cheyenne, c. 1874, men and women gather in front of a Sun Dance Lodge to fulfil their pledge to dance. Sheets of paper from ledgers (large, bound inventory and accounts books used by traders and military men) were used by Indians to make drawings about their lives and histories.

Sweetgrass

This grass grows from Siberia to the Northern Plains of the United States and Canada and east to Nova Scotia. Many Indians use it to make **baskets** or as a kind of incense, that is a purifying smoke to accompany prayers and songs. Like sage, cedar and, to some extent, **tobacco**, the smoke from burning sweetgrass sends prayers to the spirits.

Sweetgrass
This sacred medicine, associated with the northern direction,
is made from hair of our mother, the earth.
…
Strength, Courage, Love,
Humbleness, Knowledge, Sharing and Respect,
The sweetgrass teaches us these gifts,
and helps us to embrace them in our prayers… .
Andrea Johnston

Sweetgrass is a link to remembering our past and a process of recovery… . Reclaiming, recovering and honouring the work and knowledge of these grandmothers is at the core of this effort.
Rebecca Baird

226 Left Barbara Kiyoshk with her sweetgrass **baskets** at the Six Nations **pow wow** in 1994.

227 Left In 1993 Rebecca Baird, a Canadian Native artist, produced this work called *A Time Within Memory*, together with traditional **basketmakers** such as Barbara Kiyoshk.

T

Tekakwitha, Kateri

The Blessed *Kateri Tekakwitha*, the 'Lily of the **Mohawks**' was an **Iroquois** woman who converted to Catholicism in the 1500s. She died of smallpox when nursing others with the **disease**. During the 20th century, she became a focal point of Indian national pride, with non-Catholic and Catholic Indians alike demanding that the Church declare her a saint.

228 Right A fringed and embroidered banner for *Kateri Tekakwitha*, from St Joseph's **Apache** Mission in New Mexico.

Termination

After the reorganization of the **Bureau of Indian Affairs** (BIA) in 1934 and the involvement of Indians in the **Second World War**, many felt there were clear signs of reform and progress for the Indian people. However, a new conservative movement in government demanded cuts to the budget. In 1953 some Congressmen proposed a policy of termination in order to end the government's relationship with Indians and to end their status as 'wards of the government'. Indian Commissioner Dillon Myers, in charge

of Japanese-American imprisonment during the Second World War put forward a plan to stop government Indian programmes. Congress passed a resolution 'freeing' tribes in California, New York, Texas and Florida from government supervision. Other Bills followed, terminating Menominee, Klamath, Siletz, Grande Ronde, some Paiute bands and all California rancherias from their federal **status**. Governments in a number of states took over the control of the administration and legal systems of some tribes. The US government was still responsible nationally for Indian education in the state and reservation **schools** and for Indian healthcare.

Within 10 years, the policy had proved a disaster (as had **relocation** to the cities). The termination policy was eventually rejected and a policy of **self-determination** for tribes was adopted. Many tribes had Acts passed to restore them to federal status. For example, the Menominee Restoration Act of 1973 returned Menominee land to trust status, re-establishing tribal authority and giving the tribe access to government services. A young Menominee woman called Ada Deer, who would 25 years later serve as head of the BIA, led the fight to restore her people. Even though the termination policy of the government was abandoned, some tribal peoples still remain terminated and unrestored.

One of the continuing themes that the majority culture never wants to hear is that Indians want to be Indians. Indians want to retain culture, want to retain the land, want to live as Indians live… despite the many policies of the federal government over the years, from Removal to putting people on reservations, to allotment, to assimilation [see acculturation], to termination, the continuing wish and desire of the Indians is to remain Indian, and this never seems to get across.
Ada Deer, Menominee

Tlingit

One of the Tsimshian language family, the Tlingit live along the islands in the archipelago of Southeast Alaska. Famed as seafaring **traders**, they exchanged goods with the **Haida**. They traded copper and mountain-goat wool for slaves and **shell** ornaments. They traded inland, taking European goods to the **Athabaskan**s in exchange for furs.

Their society is highly complex. The community is **matrilineal** and children are born into the mother's clan (either **Eagle** or **Raven**) and live in the mother's house. The **clans** govern social, political and **ceremonial** life. Members of houses joined to **hunt**, **fish** and trade. Today, Tlingit families live as nuclear families but hold ceremonial activities in the clan houses. These houses are filled with their clan symbols, such as the 'crests' that adorn houses, which tell stories of the history of the clans and serve as titles to land, and images carved onto **boxes**.

Land claims and hunting and fishing rights have occupied the Tlingits during the 20th century. Along with the Haida, they pursued their first **land claims** settlement in 1968. They were awarded US$7.5 million by the US Court of Claims, far short of their proposed settlement of US$80 million. This money was put into trust to help social and educational programmes. A second settlement in 1971 transferred large areas of land into communal ownership with other groups under the **Alaska Native Claims Settlement Act of 1971**.

Tobacco

Native to North America, tobacco is an important plant in the lives of Native North Americans and has been used for centuries for ceremonial and medicinal purposes. There is archaeological evidence of tobacco existing from 200 BC. Plains groups use tobacco in **ceremonies** in elaborately decorated **pipes** or *calumets*, to recognize important events such as **war**, peace, **trade**, death and birth. Among the **Cherokees**, tobacco is called 'grandfather'. Among many other nations, it is considered one of the four sacred **medicines** along with sage, sweetgrass and cedar. **Gifts** of tobacco, as a sign of respect, are given at naming ceremonies, healing ceremonies or special counsel from elders.

F or us Natives, most anything that lives and grows has a purpose and a spirit, for the purpose of communication in times of need and in appreciation in meeting those needs; it could be for food... or... medicine.... The medium we have been given for communicating with any spirit is Indian Tobacco.
Reg Henry, Cayuga head faithkeeper, from Six Nations

Tourism/tourist market

The enormous pressures that tourism put on Western and Southwestern tribal cultures undoubtedly created many features of Indian life we now regard as normal. Native Americans tried to respond positively to these developments by incorporating tourism into their patterns of living. Many Native women were forced into poverty when they lost access to traditional natural resources, and so converted their traditional skills into an artistry that allowed them to join in the cash **economy**. In the Midwest, Winnebagos and Menominees at Wisconsin Dells and in the Northeast at Niagara Falls, New York, **Iroquois basketmakers** and **beadworkers** developed entirely new **art** forms based on Iroquois traditions. In the Southwest too, women skilled at weaving, **pottery** and basketmaking produce goods for tourists (the new Conquistadors), who have built up a substantial demand for Indian goods. The shapes and sizes of pots and baskets changed and became smaller to suit the tourist market. European-style objects, such as picture frames, hats, ladies' purses and parasols are beaded, and it is this beadwork that makes these things 'Indian'.

W e didn't make fancy baskets until we were discovered.
Eunice Crowley, Mashpee Wampanoag, 1987

One of the most important cultural projects of the 1930s was the government's restoration of the ruins throughout the Southwest, especially in the Grand Canyon, Chaco Canyon and Pueblo Bonito. The United States was discovering its ancient Indian heritage. Thousands of Eastern tourists came by train to New Mexico and Arizona to 'see the Indians'. Various institutions, trade and art markets, and even **schools** were developed to capitalize on the beauties of American Indian land, craft and art. In this way, tourism made Pueblos and Hispanics into commodities (just

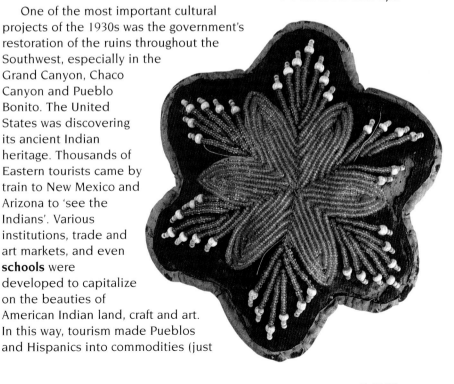

229 Below 'Fancies' or 'whimsies', such as this **Iroquois** pin cushion, represent an important point in the evolution and persistence of native **art** as it adapts to tourist demands and maintains its Indian style.

157

230 Above The Fred Harvey 'Indian Building' at the Alvarado Hotel in Albuquerque, New Mexico, in 1905.

like their crafts). The Pueblos adapted and transformed their production from goods for their own communities to those for the tourist market.

Private enterprise, such as the Fred Harvey Company, joined the government in promoting tourism in Indian Country. The Santa Fe Railroad delivered tourists to Harvey hotels, and tours offered a peaceful, safe, beautiful, exciting and exotic adventure, complete with affordable mementoes to take home. The Harvey Company also provided emerging US cultural institutions, such as fairs, expositions and **museums**,[52] with major collections of Indian artefacts and, sometimes, live Indians.

W ell, I can tell you more about the train because it ran right close back where the road is going down to the two rivers. And according to the thing I have heard my grandparents tell me about was the first time when it was going to run through there was a lot of people from the village that came to see it come, and because they had never see a train, they were relating it to *o'khua*, our *katsinas*. And I suppose of the sound that it made. And many of them came, I suppose all of them came with cornmeal. And when they heard the whistle just before it came into sight, they started throwing their cornmeal and told it to come in peace.
Estefanita (Esther) Martinez, San Juan Pueblo/Oke Okweenge, 1996

231 Above Gerald Nailor painted this humorous view of wealthy tourists shopping for **Navajo** rugs in 1937, while he was a student at Santa Fe Indian School.

232 Left Little beaded 'Comanche' **dolls** (so-called because Zunis learned **beadwork** from Plains Indians with whom they have always traded), such as this one called 'Tourist Girl', are a way of humorously commenting on the outsiders. They also make objects and symbols from the outside world into a **Zuni** way of thinking.

Indians in the Southwest and elsewhere developed special songs, dances and new instruments for the performances for tourists. This was partly to protect their religious dances from prying eyes and also to produce things that tourists wanted to see. In fact, *tse va ho*, the Tewa word for tourist, means 'someone not afraid to stare'. In some parts of Indian Country, the people who perform

233 **Right** Mary Adams, a **Mohawk** woman, made this 'wedding cake' fancy **basket** in the early 1990s. Fancy baskets of ash splint, as opposed to practical or work baskets, were first made for the tourist trade at Niagara Falls. With all sorts of amendments to common baskets (for example twists, curls and sweetgrass or paper twine), these baskets were produced in shapes and for uses that Anglo-Americans wanted, such as egg baskets.

for this market by dressing in costumes and posing with tourists for photographs are called 'show Indians'. Others, such as the Pueblos, use **humour** as a means of commenting on and controlling those forces that threaten to take over their land, culture and religion. Through ritual clowning, and verbal and visual joking, they deal with peoples and issues that disturb the order of the Pueblo world. Sacred or ceremonial **clowns**, for example, will often tease tourists attending **ceremonies** and even Pueblo members who have upset the order of things.

Nowadays, all over the United States and Canada, Native craft cooperatives and companies market Indian **art** and performance, just as the Harvey Company and Santa Fe Railway once did. Some cater for tourism, providing plastic tomahawks and photographs of tourists with 'Chiefs' in war bonnets. Others support economic development through the production of traditional art, and strive to manage the negative aspects of tourism.

Trade

Indian nations have long traded goods, such as **shells**, **feathers**, hides and **baskets**, with each other. They travelled from the Mississippi to the Gulf of Mexico, from the high desert Southwest to the Pacific Ocean, from the Northern Plains to the Pacific Northwest and from the Southern Plains to Central Mexico. Languages, such as Mobilian, Chinook 'jargon' and sign, were developed solely for the intertribal trade. Indian women had societies, such as quilling societies, that traded with each other across the Plains.

Trade with Europeans began with the Dutch in the early 1600s. Each group had products that the other wanted and needed, so their trade was useful for both groups. Whites wanted animal pelts, **food**, clothing and advice about survival in this new world. The **Iroquois** and **Algonquin** peoples in the Northeast and Southeast wanted European-made items, such as bells, mirrors, **metal** tools, thimbles, scissors, **blankets**, metal pots, guns, **horses**, cloth, buttons, horse equipment, **beads**, swords, coffee, sugar and **alcohol**. In the early 1700s, the European desire for Indian land and the Indian desire for European goods encouraged trade. Indians gave up traditional **quillwork**, skin

234 **Above** These knives show both traditional and imported technologies. The 18th-century blades, excavated at the Six Nations Reserve in Brantford, Ontario, are made of European **metal**, the wood and antler handles are **Seneca**.

235 Above These 18th-century trade **beads** are from Seneca country.

processing and **pottery** in favour of trade cloth, glass beads, metal pots and tools. Wooden utensils, such as spoons and cups and larger carved sculptural pieces became more common after the introduction of European knives and axes. Many goods used by Indians in the 19th century that came from Europe were adapted by Natives to suit their own needs.

Some day you will meet a people who are white. They will always try to give you things, but do not take them. At last I think that you will take these things that they offer you, and this will bring sickness to you.
Sweet Medicine, Cheyenne prophet

236 Left Wendat/Wyandotte women valued Paisley shawls, such as these, from Scottish mills. They also decorated European pouches, made of velvet and cotton, with seed **beads** and Venetian beads in a mix of European and **Iroquoian** floral designs.

237 Above Cattaraugus **Seneca** women of the 18th century wore trade cloth dresses, such as this red plaid dress with a white seed-beaded collar, over their tunics and leggings.

Traders and agents

When the Spanish arrived in the Southwest, they demanded that the Pueblo people give them **food**, **blankets** and **maize**. They forced Indians to make knitted stockings and provide tanned hides. At first, Indians valued most items made of **metal**, then things made of cloth and wool. Many things became valuable for both groups of people, but the balance quickly shifted, making Indians dependent on the European goods.

Commercial trade was often the basis for early **exploration** and **contact** with Indians. Sir Walter Raleigh made **tobacco** the source of a financial empire for England. Captain James Cook went to North America for the **fur trade**. By the mid 1780s, **British**, Spanish, French and Americans all competed for sea otter pelts, which they then took to China to trade. This intensive **hunting** brought about the extinction of the sea otter along the coast of British Columbia. Chiefs in this area built up great wealth due to this trade, redistributing it through the **potlatch**.

Traders were rarely interested in land, only in goods. The next major contact was for the land-based fur trade and the Hudson's Bay Company set up a trading post in Fort Langley in 1827.

238 Above This trading post at Fort Defiance or Camp Apache was established in 1873 before the development of the Southern Apache reservations. A few stores were later operated by Indians as government employees or licensed agents, and they often became the centre for most of the commercial exchange on the reservations.

Commercial agents in private business, often licensed by the British, Spanish, French and later the 'American' governments, entered Indian Country. The government sent agents to supply their troops, then to look after the government's business on **reservations** and in **Indian Territory**. The agents were supposed to fulfil the government's **treaty** obligations in goods and services – the 'annuities' that were guaranteed by treaty to Indians. The first stores and agents, established in forts, delivered flour, ploughs, salt, sugar, coffee, wagons, meat, tools and cloth. Often corrupt agents took the profits, delivered inferior goods or didn't deliver goods at all. Some agents were supposed to teach the Indians **farming** to carry out the government policy of '**civilization**'. Later agents, particularly in the Southwest, developed private companies and were extraordinarily influential in the development of Indian crafts, such as **Navajo** weaving and jewellery, Hopi **baskets** and Pueblo **pottery**, for the outside market. Trade items also enabled great leaps in artistic technology – with iron tools, artists could carve large house poles and figures.

161

Transport

The **Inuit dog**sled is as famous as the kayak and the canoe. Like its human-propelled cousin, the toboggan, it has largely become a **sport** for non-Indians. A major annual sporting event in Alaska, the Iditarod, is now built around a dogsledding competition.

In addition to the birch**bark** canoes, kayaks and large log canoes of the Northwest, Indians developed many types of vehicle, such as the *travois*, to transport goods.

In the far regions of the **Arctic** and Northwest Territories, Alaska and elsewhere, where distances are great and there is a need to travel quickly, the motorized snowmobile provides a faster and cheaper means of transport than dog teams and sleds. However, this form of transportation has made Inuit and others dependent on imported gasoline and machine parts.

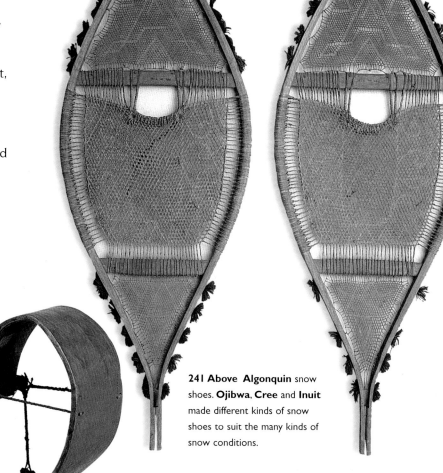

241 Above Algonquin snow shoes. **Ojibwa**, **Cree** and **Inuit** made different kinds of snow shoes to suit the many kinds of snow conditions.

239 Below A Woodlands toboggan.

240 Above An Inupiaq sled.

242 Above A motorized snowmobile used in the Arctic.

Treaties

Treaties, made between **sovereign** governments, were a main part of European **diplomatic** relations with the new territories. European governments treated Indian governments like those of other states, negotiating treaties with them in order to acquire more land. The treaty was a simple device. Indians gave up certain lands in return for peace, protection from their enemies and one-off or continuous payments. Treaties began the government-to-government relationships between the United States and the tribes and they set out the government's responsibility towards the tribes for 'as long as the grass shall grow and the waters flow' (according to the language of many treaties).

Treaties became the main instruments in the relationship between tribes and Britain France and the new US government. Although treaties are recognized by the US Constitution (the 'supreme law of the land'), there has been much conflict and different interpretations of what they mean for and to tribes, the government and states and what their responsibilities and obligations are to one another.

A Gold Chain

Chiefs and Warriors of the
Choctaw Nation of Indians

The President of the United States takes you by the hand and invites you and all the Nations of Red people within the territory of the United States to look unto him as their father and friend; and to rely in confidence upon his unvarying disposition to lead and protect them in the paths of peace and harmony, and to cultivate friendship with their Brothers of the same colour, and with the Citizens of the United States.

O the chain of friendship is now bright and binds us all together. For your and our sakes and for the sake of your and our children, we must prevent it from becoming rusty. So long as the mountains in our lands shall endure, and our Rivers flow, so long may the Red and White People dwelling in it live in the bonds of brotherhood and friendship.

In order that this friendship may be perpetual and to prevent... every cause which may interrupt it, it is hereby announced... that all lands belonging to you... shall remain the property of your Nation forever, unless you shall voluntarily relinquish or dispose of the same. And all persons Citizens of the United States are hereby strictly forbidden to disturb you or your Nation in the quiet possession of said lands.

The President of the United States sends you by your beloved chiefs, now present, a Chain. It is made of pure gold, which will never rust. And may the Great Spirit assist us in keeping the Chain of Friendship of which this Golden Chain is an emblem bright for a long succession of ages.

H. Dearborn
Indian Office of The United States
War Department
29 December 1803

Tribal governments

The Yup'iks had their own government for many years before the Indian Reorganization Act was introduced. Yup'iks had their own instructions from way back… that was government… and that whole idea is powerful and can be defined by one word by the white men – sovereignty.
Mike Albert, Tununak

Tribal government has existed from time immemorial. It was governing here in 1492 when Columbus supposedly discovered America. The elders say 'Re-establish your own governments, practice self-determination.'
Willie Kasayulie, Akiachak

Indians had many forms of government before **contact** with Europeans. These included large, formal and complex multi-tribal confederacies (such as the **Iroquois** and Wabenaki Confederacies). They ranged from governments based in religious structures (the Pueblos) to the loosely organized and leadership-based organizations (Plains tribes). All those forms of government, along with the groups of people themselves, had to change from the moment the European assault began on their old ways of life.

In the mid 19th century, many tribes from the Southwest and Midwest were moved west to **Indian Territory**. They faced tremendous difficulties in merging and existing in these new territories. **Removal** from their old homelands disrupted their traditional forms of government and lifestyles. In 1843, **Cherokee** Principal Chief John Ross called a meeting, a Council of tribes, at Tahlequah, which was the seat of government of the Cherokee Nation. For most tribes, a Council of adult men (and in some cases, women too) was the group that made decisions. Hundreds of representatives from numerous tribes removed to Indian Territory and those whose ancestral homes were in that region and a few US government officials attended the Council.

The Council's purpose was to 'preserve the existence of our race, to revive and cultivate friendly relations between our several communities, to secure to all their respective rights and to promote the general welfare'. The Cherokee Assistant Principal Chief George Lowrey spoke about the

243 **Right** This painting, *The Indian Council of 1843 at Tahlequah, Indian Territory*, is by John Mix Stanley, who was present during the Grand Council in 1843. The figure standing on the podium at the left is probably **Cherokee** Assistant Principal Chief George Lowrey, with John Ross to the far right. The very different forms of dress among the tribal delegates (including Cherokee, **Creek**, Chickasaw, Delaware, Wichita, Potawatomie, Chippewa and **Seminole**) indicates the different peoples who had been removed to Oklahoma. It also shows how important it was to them to wear tribal or 'citizen' clothing at this point in their histories.

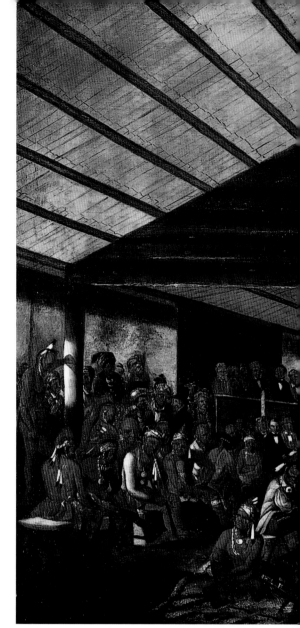

wampum belt given to the Cherokee by the **Seneca** in 1781. He brought it to the Council, where it was used to begin the proceedings. The belt portrayed two men shaking hands at the end of a path, showing the desire that 'the rising generation may travel in peace'. Some of these belts are still used by Cherokees in Oklahoma. The delegates agreed to remain at peace with each other and with the government. In order to please the government, they decided to encourage **agriculture** and education. The Council was one of the first attempts to restore tribal government and to find a way for Indians to speak to Washington and to each other with a unified voice.

Believing that a central government would help them retain control over their lives and their lands, Cherokees in the 1820s recorded

244 Above The 1849/1850 Constitution of the **Cherokee** Nation.

their first formal laws. They also established a national police force and created a Supreme Court. This movement away from local, communal government resulted in the Republican Constitution of 1828. It authorized a government like that of the United States, with a Principal Chief (for administration), a National Council (for laws and regulations) and a Supreme Court. This Constitution was published in Cherokee and in English and tried to unite several groups of Cherokee people and to present a united front to the forces demanding their Removal. Modelled on Southern state constitutions, it went against traditional Cherokee ideas of justice. For example, it legalized slavery and took away the power of Cherokee women who according to traditional law, controlled property and children.

We, The Members of the Cherokee Nation in Convention assembled, in order to establish justice, ensure tranquillity, promote the common welfare, and secure to ourselves and our posterity the blessing of liberty: acknowledging with humility and gratitude the goodness of the sovereign Ruler of the Universe, in offering us an opportunity so favourable to the design, and imploring his aid and direction in its accomplishment, do ordain and establish this Constitution for the Government of the Cherokee Nation.
Preamble to the 1827 Constitution of the Cherokee Nation

Modern tribes – like nations, states or provinces – adopted Constitutions that set out the principles and methods in which the tribe would be governed and operated, its legal and tax systems, its **citizenship** and its relationships with the US government, states and other political bodies. The Wheeler-Howard or Indian Reorganization Act of 1934 was intended to put tribal governments on an equal footing with other civilian forms of government in the United States. Under this Act, tribes would have their own, standardized Constitutions and elected governments. The **allotment** policy and the handover of land (with the '**civilization**' policy that went with it) were stopped. Enrolled members of tribes had two years in which to accept the Indian Reorganization Act. Some tribes insisted (and still do) that the Act was another way of forcing European ideas onto tribal cultures. However, some tribes were able to incorporate traditional forms of government into the standard Constitution. Although most tribes in the United States have very different forms of government, they do follow practices common to elected, civic governments throughout the world.

The story of Wilma Mankiller, a former Cherokee Principal Chief, demonstrates how tribal governments have developed and evolved in the late 20th century. Raised in Eastern Oklahoma by a **farming** family relocated to California in the 1950s, Mankiller stayed in California and received a better education than that available in rural Oklahoma. In the early 1960s, she became

245 Above Symbolic of **Cherokee** desire for unity and independence was the 1871 seal. It records the 1839 adoption of the Constitution of the Cherokee Nation in the West. This seal was imprinted on all documents until the Cherokee Nation was dissolved when Oklahoma was made a state in 1906. Today the seal is used once more by the Cherokee Nation of Oklahoma. The seven pointed star symbolizes the seven **clans** of the Cherokees and the seven characters of **Sequoyah**'s syllabary that mean 'Cherokee Nation' (*Tsalagi Ayili*). The wreath of oak leaves stands for the sacred fire of the Cherokee.

246 Left A 1994 poster urging the election of an individual for tribal chairman of the **Navajo** Nation.

VOTE for ZAH CHAVEZ
TEAM THAT UNDERSTANDS ROLE OF WOMEN AND FUTURE OF CHILDREN IN NAVAJO SOCIETY

involved in national politics and the Indian rights movement. As a local Indian community organizer, she participated in the takeover of Alcatraz (see page 121). She returned to Oklahoma and became involved in the development of her own Cherokee community. She was so successful at meeting the needs of rural, traditional communities with the methods of a new, progressive tribal government that Chief Ross Swimmer asked her to run for Deputy Chief of the Cherokee Nation (*Tsalagi Ayili*). Her later election as Principal Chief (*ugu*) of the second largest Indian nation in the country brought her national prominence and she received the Presidential Medal of Freedom.

Some of her opponents for election said women should not serve in public office. However, many Cherokees remembered women's importance in public affairs in the past and Outacitty's words to the **British** delegation: 'Where are your women?'. 'Mankiller' (*Outacitty* or *Asgayadihi*) was a distant relative of Wilma, whose family name still bears his military title. Some in the Cherokee Nation class Wilma Mankiller in the same category as **Nancy Ward** (*Nanyehi*), who

247 Above A 1992 tribal council meeting of the Eastern Band of **Cherokee** Indians, in North Carolina. On the ceiling of the meeting room are carved **masks** representing the seven Cherokee **clans**.

248 Above Modern elected tribal governments are responsible for education, economic development, housing, law enforcement and healthcare. The building of the Santa Clara Pueblo government, a combination of a new elected and traditional form of government, has meeting space for residents of Santa Clara, a basketball court, a community library and some offices of the tribal law enforcement.

was one of the last Beloved Women of the Cherokee. This is because they both defended the Cherokee people's **self-determination** so strongly. For many Native people, Mankiller's leadership embodies the old Indian prophecy that that women will lead Indian people into a new era.[53]

250 Above The Principal Chief of the **Cherokee** Nation, Wilma Mankiller, giving her inaugural speech in 1987.

Certainly I believe the ancient tribal cultures have important lessons to teach the rest of the world about the interconnectedness of all living things and the simple fact that our existence is dependent upon the natural world we are rapidly destroying. The traditional value systems that have sustained us throughout the past 500 years of trauma are those value systems that will bolster us and help us enter the 21st century on our own terms. Despite the last 500 years, there is much to celebrate. Our languages are still strong, ceremonies that we have been conducting since the beginning of time are still being held, our governments are surviving, and most importantly, we continue to exist as a distinct cultural group in the midst of the most powerful country in the world. Yet we also must recognize that we face a daunting set of problems and issues – continual threats to tribal sovereignty, low educational attainment levels, double digit unemployment, many homes without basic amenities and racism. We are beginning to look more to our own people, communities and history for solutions. We have begun to trust our own thinking again, not the Columbus myth. We look forward to the next 500 years as a time of renewal and revitalization for Native people throughout North America.
Wilma Mankiller

249 Above The tribal police uniform patches show the **sovereignty** of the nations they are connected with.

Turtle

According to the **Seneca** creation story, the original beings lived in a world above the sky. At their chief's request, they uprooted a large tree that stood near the chief's lodge. This made a large hole in the sky, revealing green waters in the world below. The chief's pregnant wife fell through the hole and landed on a turtle's back. With the soil she had grasped as she fell she created the earth and gave birth to the beings who became the Seneca people. Thus, for the Seneca and other **Iroquois**, the earth sits on Grandmother Turtle's back.

The Seneca story of how and why their people have a special feeling for the turtle is not uncommon among Native peoples. Iroquois and many Southeastern peoples value and look to the turtle as a creator. Many Indians also tell stories about the persistence, stubbornness and cleverness of the seemingly slow and weak turtle.

251 Below A late 19th-century turtle **shell** rattle with an **Iroquois** gourd and hickory **bark rattle** from the Six Nations Reserve in Brantford, Ontario, Canada. The turtle rattle, like this one used in the Cold Spring **Seneca** Longhouse in New York, is central to the most important Iroquois **ceremonies**. Gourd rattles were used in planting and harvesting ceremonies and the hickory bark rattle was used for social **dances**.

I told you I was little and can't run fast, but I can outsmart you. Wolf, wolf, your bones will be quivering, the flies will be quivering, the flies will be buzzing and buzzing around you.

Turtle's Song to the Wolf when he won the race, a Creek story-song similar to Aesop's fable The Tortoise and the Hare, as sung by Betty Mae Jumper, Seminole traditionalist and former tribal chairman

Tuscarora

The original Tuscarora lands are in Virginia and North Carolina, and the people are culturally and linguistically Iroquoian. They were a powerful **trading** nation.

Encroachment by Europeans led to conflict and then **war** in 1711. The British drove them from North Carolina and most fled north to Iroquois Country. A few stayed on a small **reservation** in North Carolina and some were sent into slavery. In 1720, the Tuscarora were officially adopted into the **Iroquois Confederacy** through their sponsoring nation, the **Oneida**.

During the American Revolution, Tuscarora and Oneida allied with the colonists. After the war, the Tuscarora were punished because the rest of the Iroquois nations had sided with the British. Once again without a home, they settled on a reservation near Lewiston, New York, and at Six Nations Reserve on the Grand River, Ontario. Many converted to **Christianity**, but some also retained the Longhouse traditions.

The Tuscarora resisted the construction of a reservoir on their lands by the New York State Power Authority in 1957, but lost that struggle and hundreds of acres of their New York reservation. Like other Iroquois, many have developed work in the construction industries, including high steel.

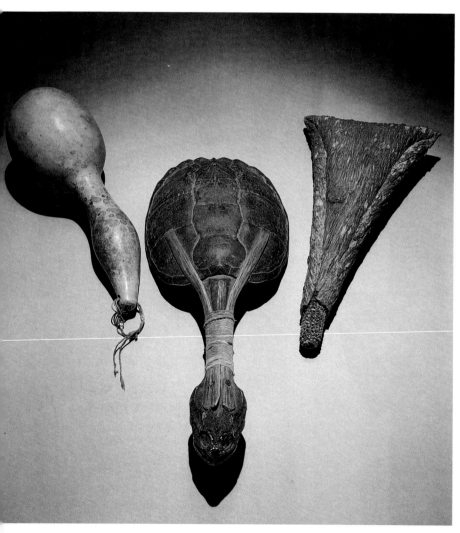

U

Ulu

This crescent shaped knife – similar to the Italian double-bladed knife called a *mezzaluna* (half moon) – is used by **Inuit** peoples in the **Arctic** for eating, cutting skins and cleaning fur and hair. Men make *ulus* from bone, antler, stone, **metal** and wood for their wives, daughters and other female relations. They are so distinctive and important to Inuit cultures that people now make jewellery in the shape of *ulus* and use their design on clothes, official communications and so on. Today, **tourists** and Inuit people buy commercially produced *ulus* made in Alaska and Greenland.

252 **Above** An Inuit *ulu* made from copper in the late 19th century.

Every woman has her own tools made with her own design. When an elder dies, her *ulu* is sometimes buried with her.
Ulayok Kaviok, Arviat, 1986

Urban Indians

255 **Below** Urban Indians.

The Great Depression and the **Second World War** affected Indian Country as deeply as the rest of the United States. During the period of the Dust Bowl on the Prairies, many Indians fled to California and other parts of the United States to escape the devastation. This was followed by forced **relocation** into cities by the **Bureau of Indian Affairs** (BIA) in the 1950s. The great migrations of the 1930s and 1950s created a population of 'urban' Indians living in cities such as Los Angeles, Phoenix, Cleveland, Minneapolis, New York City, Dallas, Buffalo, San Francisco and Chicago. In Canada, too, Indians migrated from 'the bush' to Toronto, Winnipeg and Ottawa. Over half of American Indians and over 30% of Canadian Indians now live in cities. Most of the urban areas developed 'Indian centres' – organizations which bring Indians together to share their cultures, languages and life histories. Many different tribal peoples met and worked together in the cities. This continued to form the characteristics of '**pan-Indian**', intertribal cultures which had begun in Indian **schools**. Furthermore, urban Indians have been at the centre of national Indian political activity. Despite their number, achievements and political influence, urban Indians still struggle for recognition (by Indians and non-Indians alike) as Native people.

Urban Indian population centres

Highest concentrations of Native Americans

Wampum

On his way to bring the Great Law of Peace to the Mohawks, the first of the Five Nations to receive it, the Peacemaker came to a small lake. While he was thinking how he would cross the lake, a flock of waterfowl lit on the water. He watched, and as they flew off the lake became dry and the bottom was covered with wampum beads. From these beads the Peacemaker made the first wampum belts to document the creation of the Great Peace – the League of the *Haudenosaunee*
Reg Henry, Cayuga faithkeeper, 1989

Wampum beads record important events and appear in a ceremonial context, as decorations and a symbol of status for chiefs and the **clan** mother. When the **Iroquois** confirmed treaties, offered condolences or made important statements, they gave **gifts** to acknowledge the seriousness of the occasion. By the late 18th century, the usual gifts were belts or strings of wampum made of whelk or quahog clam **shells**. The white beads can be carved from many different shells, but only the shell of the quahog clam gives purple beads. The Dutch used the belts and beads as currency, although the Iroquois did not, and they quickly began manufacturing wampum to use in negotiations with the Iroquois. Other Indians in Dutch areas also began to use the wampum as currency.

During the 18th century, wampum was woven into belts with particular designs of mnemonics and pictures to mark **treaties** or agreements. The *Gus-weh-tah* or the Two-Row wampum belt dating from 1664, shows perhaps the most important of these agreements – the **British**, Dutch or French and the Iroquois Confederacy. The two straight lines on the belt represent the peace, friendship and respect between the two nations. The two rows symbolize two boats travelling down the same river, neither interfering with the course of the other but abiding by each other's values.

Modern Iroquois believe that some wampum belts play an important role in how treaties are interpreted in legal cases today, because they symbolize attempts at relationships that failed. Ironically, until recently, these most powerful symbols of the Iroquois Confederacy and its relationships with other peoples were rarely in Iroquois hands. Wampum is symbolically very important to Iroquois leadership, therefore Indian agents removed many belts and chief's strings from reservations and communities and sold them to **museums** and collectors. Some have been the subjects of long disputes over their ownership and others have been loaned to tribal museums or to members of the Iroquois Grand Council for use in ceremonial recountings of the events where the belts were first given. In recent times, Iroquois have launched legal battles to have these important artefacts returned to communities as they are symbols of nationhood.

254 Below A late 18th-century wampum belt, with a **turtle**.

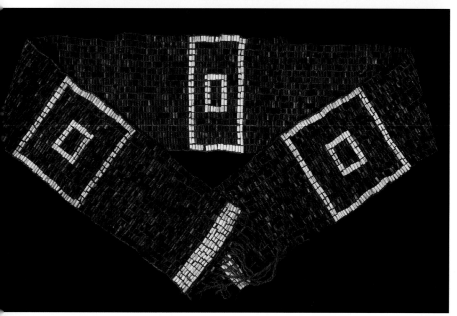

255 Left A late 18th-century purple **shell** wampum belt. Coastal **Algonquin** peoples in the Southeast made and used trade bead shells (*roanoke*) made from mussel shells and peak (*wampumpeak*), the purple part of clam shells, and the other parts of whelk shells.

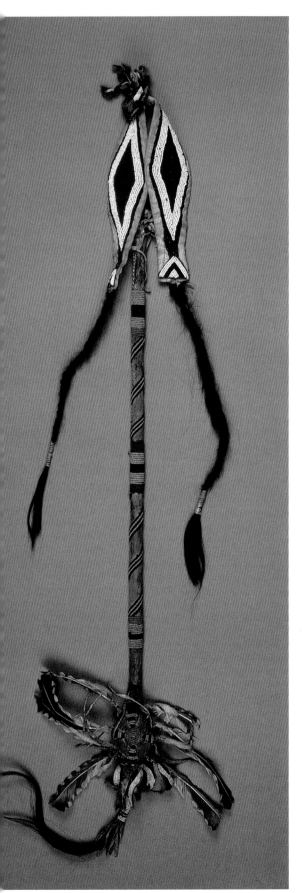

256 Left A late 19th-century Blood coup stick, with its wrist straps covering the handle.

257 Below This work, *Counting Coup*, by Gerald McMaster (Plains **Cree**) is taken from 'Cowboy and Indian Show' in 1991. McMaster is Curator of Contemporary Indian Art at the Canadian Museum of Civilization. He uses 'humour as a tool, as a weapon. For him, it is 'another way of being serious'.

War

War was common between Native peoples, but what it actually consisted of and what actually took place varied among different groups, in different places and at different times. War could be short concentrated periods of armed aggression between large groups or periodic outbursts of violence over a longer time.

For some, war consisted of a number of raids over time on one set of people by small groups of others. Acts that caused war included the taking of captives (women and children), acts of violence, the stealing of **horses** and encroachments on **hunting**, **fishing** and water resources.

For many Plains peoples, acts of bravery by warriors could include striking or touching an enemy with a *coup* (French for 'blow' or 'strike') stick, or killing or wounding with one. An experienced warrior might have a *coup* stick with paintings or carvings of how many times he had struck the enemy, thus giving rise to the notion of 'counting *coup*'.

Until guns and bullets made it useless, men (and **horses**) carried and wore reinforced and painted hide armour for protection against arrows and spears. Often the designs on shields and other hunter's and warrior's equipment came from **dreams** and visions and were meant to be protective.

258 Below The cover for a painted buffalo hide Pawnee shield, c. 1820–25.

Ward, Nancy

The early Indian **Removal** period before 1830 cannot be characterized better than in the life and actions of Nancy Ward (Nanyehi). Having earned the title of 'Beloved Woman of the **Cherokees**' and 'War Woman of Chota', she was the governor of the Women's Council during **war** with the **Creeks**. She could speak for the women on matters of peace, war and community life.

At first, Nanyehi believed that the way to survive was by accommodating the new ways of the whites and trying to live with them. There are many stories of her intervention in the fate of whites who had intruded on the Cherokee people. Others believed that Native peoples could not peacefully co-exist with the intruders.

She married an Irish trader called Brian Ward, after her first husband, a Cherokee named Kingfisher, died. Now known to whites as Nancy Ward, she became wealthy, with land, slaves and some power. When Americans declared war on the **British**, the Cherokees were dragged into armed conflict with them. Although she had often defended British settlers even against the wishes of her own people, she could not prevent the war that followed, which devastated Cherokee lands and resources. Trying to save what remained, the Cherokees were the first tribe to sign a treaty with the new US government. She was present at the Peace Commission in 1785, presenting strings of **wampum** to the Peace Commissioners on behalf of the Women's Council. For a while, peace seemed to come to the Cherokee people, and they adopted many of the ways of the whites that now populated their land.

More settlers came and wanted more Cherokee land. Many Cherokees felt that they should simply go to the proposed **Indian Territory** and give up dealing with these people who were never satisfied. Others, such as Nancy Ward, felt that they could never leave their homelands and their sacred grounds.

Native men also made and carried war clubs for war, hunting and for ceremonial purposes. In the Northeast, traditional war clubs were often 'ball-headed', often with **clan** animals or other symbols of power carved into the handle and ball. Others were carved from roots with the root nodule left intact on the end of the club. On the Plains, the clubs were often carved from or in the shape of a rifle stock or like a tomahawk. They were then etched, carved in designs or (as in the root clubs and Plains dance sticks) shaped into human, animal or bird heads or feet. When the clubs were replaced by rifles, men carried them as part of their ceremonial dress. In the 19th century, some carved them for the **tourist** trade. Men carry them today in the Northwest and the Plains, more often as 'dance sticks' than as war clubs, as part of the ceremonial dress worn by 'straight **dancers**'.

259 Above A Woodlands ball-headed club with otter.

Cherokee mothers do not wish to go to an unknown country; we have raised all of you on the land which we now inhabit. We have understood that some of our children wish to govern the Mississippi, but this act would be like destroying your mothers. We beg of you not to part with any more of our land…. The Cherokee ladies now being present at the meeting of the Chiefs and warriors in council have thought it their duties as mothers to address their beloved Chiefs and warriors now assembled…. [W]e know that our country has once been extensive but by repeated sales has become circumscribed to a small tract and never have thought it our duty to interfere in the disposition of it till now, if a father or mother was to sell all their lands which they had to depend on, which their children had to raise their living on, which would be bad indeed and to be removed to another country. We do not wish to go to an unknown country which we have understood some of our children wish to go over the Mississippi but this act of our children would be like destroying your mothers. Your mother and sisters ask and beg of you not to part with any more of our lands. *Nancy Ward's message to the Cherokee National Council, 1817*

Yet no matter what Nancy Ward, the Women's Council and many in the Men's Council felt, things had changed forever. A new form of government had been shaped through a new Constitution and had been adopted by the Cherokees and other tribes. This deposed the Women's Councils and substituted a legal system modelled on white governments. In the **Removal** that followed, as many as 6,000 died on the Trail of Tears, and Nancy Ward's beloved homelands were lost. Moreover, the system which supported government by both men and women was also disbanded. Today, Cherokees often cite Nancy Ward's leadership as a model for restoring of the old ways of government.

260 Below An early Coastal **Salish** spindle whorl, used for spinning **dog** and mountain goat hair into wool. The wool was then used to make capes, blankets, and ceremonial dress.

Water rights

Concern about water rights is common to indigenous peoples everywhere. Access to water is the basis for survival. For economic development, water resources – often from lands previously given or dammed – are essential. Many tribes, particularly those in the dry West, are trying to regain access to valuable waters which have been given over to commercial interests and states. They are challenging the government and corporations in court, quoting **treaty** agreements that promised them access to water 'as long as the grass shall grow and the water flows'.

Weaving

Weaving is probably one of the oldest of skills among peoples of the world. The **Navajo** weavings have stories of their own about its origin. White Shell Woman came upon a dark hole in the ground, apparently the home of Spider Woman. She was busy creating designs. Spider Woman invited White Shell Woman in and taught her how to weave a Navajo dress.

There is a Navajo phrase, *aashi bi' bohlii*, which means, it's up to you. When my mother uses this term, she says there are no formulas in weaving. Weaving allows us to create and express ourselves with tools, materials, and designs. It is up to you – the weaver. D.Y. *Begay, weaver*

261 Above A Chilkat **blanket**, made of dyed mountain goat wool, with cedar **bark** sewn and woven into it. These woven textiles were the dancing blankets of high-ranking people of the **Northwest Coast** in the 19th century. The designs on the weaving – the same designs and figures that appear on **house posts** and on painted walls, **drums** and **masks** – represent the crest of the wearer. They also tell the stories of the original crest and the way in which it obtained power and position.

The use of reeds and grasses, wood splints and animal hair and fur to make containers, small animal pens, bedding, seating and clothes is an ancient and complex craft. For most Native people, the invention and export/import of mass-produced, machine-weaving in the 18th century marked the end of hand weaving. Indians still weave **baskets** and ceremonial clothing for the **tourist** market and for use in their own communities. The variation and complexity of different kinds weaving, among Pueblos, **Northwest Coastal** peoples and Navajos in wool, cotton and fur is as remarkable as basket weaving in the Northeast, Southeast, California and Plateau regions.

Oh, Mother the Earth, Oh Father the Sky... .
Then weave for us a garment of brightness,
May the warp be the white light of morning,
May the weft be the red light of evening,
May the fringes be the falling rain,
May the border be the standing rainbow.
Tewa song

263 Above *Beeldléi* (meaning 'wearing **blanket**') **Navajo** woven bla

262 Left A **Tlingit** woman putting the raised border on the Chilkat **blanket** she has twined, *c.* 1995.

264 Above A weaving by the Hopi textile artist Ramona Sakiestewa, from her Katsina Series, No. 11, 1991. The strips of colour represent the *katsinas*, the spirits of ancestors who return annually to bless the people. They are alive and undefeated, not banished to the past, as the conquerors wished. She says, 'I cannot bear one more book or exhibit that calls Indians vanishing, enduring, the last of anything. I'd rather be described as persistent and annoying.' So these *katsinas* 'dance in the homes … of those who wished them gone'.

Whale

For peoples on the **Northwest Coast** (including the **Inuit** and Makah) the whale provided physical and spiritual sustenance to the people who hunted him.

The whale – the largest mammal – was dangerous to hunt because he was clever and treacherous. It took great skill, bravery and special powers to hunt whales. Thus, a good hunter needed elaborate **ceremony** and ritual clothing.

In the Kwakwaka'wakw story, the hero *Siwidi* (Paddled-to) becomes part killer-whale. He can find and visit the undersea creatures.

Then Born-to-be-Head-Harpooner started, and he told his people to get ready. Then he loaned to Paddled-to a small canoe, and Born-to-be-Head-Harpooner told Paddled-to to try to spout. Paddled-to went aboard the new little canoe. As soon as he went aboard, the small canoe became a killer-whale, and Paddled-to did well with his spouting.
A Kwakwaka'wakw story about whales and men

The Kwakwaka'wakw people carve feast dishes shaped like killer-whale. Whale hunters wear hats with references to the stories of great spirit whales and whale hunters. Vancouver Island is full of carved whale figures. The great **Tlingit** whale houses represent the men with the power to hunt whales. The whale shrines of Nuu-chah-nulth, filled with the figures of famous whaling hunters and dedicated to ritual purification of hunters, attract whales to shore.

Wild rice

'Wild rice' refers to a grass species, possibly from Asia originally (*Zizania*), which grows in the wild in the fresh waters of North America and Asia. The common grass has long been used as **food**. Some lakes are completely covered with rice in season and the harvesting beds are huge. Wild rice stands can be damaged by a few fungi, some competing plants, birds, animals, insects, and hail and floods. Rice failures brought famine to entire groups of **Ojibwa** in the 19th and early 20th centuries.

Wild rice was harvested and eaten by Ojibwa, by Dakota **Sioux** in the Northern Woodlands, and later in the 19th century by the Osage, Omaha, Ponca, Menominee, Potawatomi and Winnebago. It also became a major cash crop in **trade** throughout the world. The nutritional value of wild rice is high – it is rich in carbohydrates, low in fat and contains essential proteins, vitamins and minerals.

Wild rice was an important part of Ojibwa nutrition, being the principle staple, along with hunted meat, maple sugar and gathered fruits. The Ojibwa have many stories that explain the role of wild rice (*manoomin*) in their lives and its ceremonial and medicinal uses. They speak of its discovery by *Wenabozhoo* (Nanabush, Manbozhoo), their cultural hero and spiritual founder, who then gave them sugar, **fish** and other staples of the diet and culture. As well as describing the origin of rice and its gift to the Indian people, the stories tell how to use rice, how to make sure it keeps growing and how to protect it. They also suggest how its abundance or disappearance can be explained. Wild rice is used in child naming, curing and other religious **ceremonies**, such as those of the Midéwiwin (the Grand Medicine Society of the Ojibwa). Ojibwa believed that ceremonies helped preserve the rice beds and rice growth, ensuring good harvests. Even today, **pow wows** have some place for the prayers for and consumption of wild rice.

The rice was harvested traditionally by poling canoes (like punts). Then smaller, flat bottomed wood **boats** were used. The rice is gathered with two long sticks, one to bend the rice and the other to thresh the rice kernels into the canoe. Called 'knocking' the rice, this process caused much of the rice grain to fall in the water, thus providing reseeding for the coming years. Whereas in the 19th century it was an activity for women and younger children, today men are more involved. It is now an entire family enterprise, with men poling boats, women knocking rice and the whole family processing. People go to the rice camps in August and September for two-week periods. These times are great social occasions with entertainment and **games** as well as work.

After harvesting, rice is dried, either in the sun or by fire-drying. It is then scorched or parched and hulled to remove the close-fitting chaff next to the kernel. The old-fashioned way of preparing rice was to place it in a bag of some kind, traditionally deer or mooseskin, in a wood lined pit. Then men and children, wearing moccasins, would

265 Right In this 1946 photograph from Minnesota **Ojibwa** country, two women are parching and drying wild rice in birch**bark** trays (*nooshkaachinaagan*) and galvanized tin tubs. They are under a wigwam frame against which a baby in a **baby carrier** leans.

266 Above An Ojibwa couple knocking rice from a flat-bottomed skiff canoe in 1987. The canoes or flat-bottomed **boats** used in the Great Lakes don't harm the roots of rice, and the pointed end of the raft hardly bends the stalks.

'dance', 'jig' or tread the rice. Songs often accompanied this part of the process. Some people hulled the rice using a large mortar and pestle. Finally, rice was winnowed to rid the rice of the chaff. This was done by putting it onto a birch**bark** tray and tossing it so that the heavier kernels remained in the tray and the chaff would fly out. The rice was then stored. Although there are now many shortcuts and new techniques, many Ojibwa still like to prepare rice in the old ways.

Rice is cooked by boiling in water or broth. It is sometimes eaten as a sort of porridge or used to thicken meat, vegetable and fish stews. A flour can be made from rice and a type of bread baked from it. Children made popped rice by frying the rice like popcorn, then sweetening it or eating it plain. Gathered berries, animal fats and maple products were often used to flavour rice.

Nothing can equal the aroma of a ricing camp. Wood fires burning, rice drying and the dewy fresh air drifting in from the lake. A contented feeling of well-being filled the camp. The first grain of the season had been offered for blessing from the Great Spirit. The time had come to partake of the gift. Boiled with venison or with ducks or rice hens, it was nourishing and delicious.
Lolita Taylor, Ojibwe, c.1988

Although still harvested as an important cash and cultural crop by Ojibwa people and others, it is now considered a gourmet crop throughout the world. Thus, commercial rice production in paddies from Michigan to California is common. As traditional ricing areas are turned to commercial production, the amount of land devoted to traditionally harvested and grown rice is reduced. Competition from non-Indian grown paddy rice has negatively affected the economy of Native people. Nowadays, industrial and agricultural development means there are fewer and more polluted rice beds and **dams** cause variable water levels.

176

Wolf

The wolf – related to **dogs** and **Coyote** – is highly esteemed by many Native peoples. Indians called on his protective spirit. There are many wolf **clans** among tribal peoples including the **Cherokee** and **Iroquois**. Indians speak of the wolf in terms of his close relationship to humans, even of his ability to transform into a human.

267 Above A **Northwest Coast** wolf **headdress**, probably Nuu-chah-nulth from Vancouver, used in a **dance** which referred to a story or stories involving the wolf.

World War, Second

The Second World War had a huge impact on American Indians, taking large numbers of volunteers off the **reservations** and out of the boarding **schools** and putting them with other Americans in the war effort. By doing so, for the first time since becoming citizens in 1924, many Indians gained the respect of their fellow Americans for their courage and patriotism. The kind of racism experienced by black soldiers worked in reverse for American Indians. They were not separated into all-Indian units, and stereotypes about their warrior-like capabilities worked to their benefit. They were successful. The **Navajo** Code Talkers who served in the Pacific Theatre – Marines who used the complex Navajo language to communicate – offered the only code unbroken by the Japanese. Ira Hayes (a soldier and Pima hero) raised the US **flag** at Iwo Jima, when the US military recovered a major battle site from the

268 Above Horace Poolaw, a Kiowa who served as an aerial **photographer** during the Second World War, took this photograph of himself and Gus Palmer, another Kiowa and a tail gunner, in a B-29 nose cone.

Japanese in the South Pacific.

Many Indian women also participated in the war effort, and the war was a revolutionary moment for Indian people when they became involved in mainstream society. Women from the reservations and rural ranching and **farming** areas worked in the cities in industrial and war-related jobs, such as in aircraft factories, asbestos plants, Army ordinance depots and shipyards. Most, like the white and black women, lost their jobs to returning veterans or when the work finished at the end of the war. Many went to work in Indian schools, as matrons, cooks or caretakers, or in urban areas as semi-skilled

177

labour, home helps or waitresses.

The Second World War also created a growing number of educated and experienced new leaders for tribal nations. The GI Bill of Rights in 1944 offered some the chance for higher education. For others, the skills gained during the war propelled them into different positions. However getting jobs on reservations was not easy, as most had little opportunity for work. So, many Indians who ended their military service in a large city stayed there – in Chicago, Los Angeles, Atlanta, Dallas or San Francisco. This created the first pool of **urban Indians** which was added to by the **relocation** of the 1950s. The mainstreaming Indians experienced after the War was important in promoting the virtues of education and middle-class values in a way that the Indian schools had not. A new generation of tribal leaders was born out of the war.

Curiously, participation in the Second World War also revitalized traditional Indian ways. Warrior and War Mothers' societies returned to Indian Country. All the traditional ceremonial attention once paid to the honouring of veterans and warriors began again and continued in tribes everywhere.

The warriors, they went overseas. The war is over now. They're all coming back, and we're all happy, we're proud and we're honoured that they fought for us, these men and women in uniform, to fight for our freedom and we're singing for joy.
Anita Anquoe George, a Kiowa woman's War Mothers' song

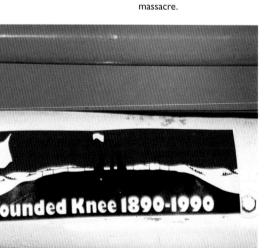

269 Below A car sticker, which shows the outline and gate of the graveyard at Wounded Knee, issued during the centennial of the massacre.

Wounded Knee, 1890 and 1973

One of the most famous and most horrifying **photographs** of the 19th century shows the mass grave into which Army soldiers pushed Indian men, women and children after the deadly battle at Wounded Knee Creek in 1890. The massacre of **Sioux** by the government troops, after the government had assured peace to Red Cloud and his people, occurred because the Sioux continued to hunt in lands the government had closed off to them and opened to white settlement. The Sioux continued the **Ghost Dance** that they believed would defeat the whites and they continued to judge criminal cases in their traditional way. So, in 1885, the government passed the Seven Major Crimes Act in order to gain legal control over the reservations for certain crimes.

According to the Sioux, the government ignored their **treaty** again and again. Their protests ended in the arrest and murder of **Sitting Bull** and the actions at Wounded Knee against virtually unarmed people. Big

Writing systems

The earliest known written works in a Native language were documents produced by Native **Christians** and town officials and a Bible printed in the **Algonquian** language in Massachusett in 1663. Christian Indian and white collaborators developed most early writing systems to encourage literacy, so that people could read the Bible. Only **Cherokee** has a system invented entirely by an Indian person (the Cherokee **Sequoyah**), and Cherokees have used that writing system to their own benefit. Writing systems were developed for the Mohican, Delaware, **Mi'kmaq**, Maliseet-Passamaquoddy, Western **Abenaki**, Northern **Iroquois**, Fox (Mesquakie), Sauk, Kickapoo, Ottawa, Potawatomi, Winnebago, **Cree**-Montagnais and **Ojibwa**, **Athapaskan** and Eskimo-**Aleut**. Most have made and continue to make limited use of these writing systems.

A number of tribal peoples now use recently developed writing systems (mostly based on the English alphabet) in order to revitalize their language through the schools. Ojibwa, Cree and **Inuit** have developed writing systems to help communication between tribes, for example in school materials and

270 Above January 1891, the scene at Wounded Knee, South Dakota, after the massacre of Big Foot and his followers on 20 December 1890.

Foot and his people, about 350 starving, ill and cold Minneconjou Sioux, joined by the now leaderless followers of Sitting Bull (all Ghost Dancers), gathered in late December a short distance from the Pine Ridge Agency. The Army decided to surround and disarm them. Someone fired a shot. Although many of the Sioux tried to resist, the larger and better-armed Army forces killed 153 men, women and children. Twenty-five soldiers died. The dead Indians were buried in a mass grave at Wounded Knee.

In 1973 at Wounded Knee there was a 70-day armed confrontation between activists of the American Indian Movement, residents of the Pine Ridge Reservation community, the tribal officials of the Pine Ridge Reservation and government authorities (the Federal Bureau of Investigation). The confrontation resulted in the death of two Indians and two federal agents, and years of court cases and debate over the incidents. Like the massacre nearly 100 years earlier, the confrontation drew public attention to Native issues previously ignored by the general public.

271 Above Steven Ross, Eastern Band **Cherokee**, writes his name using *Tsalagi* characters during a cultural class at the Cherokee Elementary Tribal School in North Carolina, 1992. Cherokee is not a language threatened with extinction. Although the writing system has been useful in teaching and maintaining Cherokee as a spoken language, there are few opportunities to use it as a written language. In classrooms in Oklahoma and North Carolina, however, Cherokees still use the **Sequoyan** system to teach the language.

newspapers. Computer software has been developed so that tribal newspapers and other materials can be printed in the Native language. Additionally, a number of tribal linguists now work in their own communities to develop written materials and other strategies for **language** preservation.

Pat Ningewance will be contributing her column to Wawatay News semi-monthly. *staff photo*

Our lands offer us a lifestyle.

Boreal West
Suite 221, 435 James St. South
Thunder Bay, ON P7E 6S8
807-475-1251
Fax: 807-473-3023
BWRT@webmail.mnr.gov.on.ca
http://www.mnr.gov.on.ca

273 Above A page from the *Wawatay News*, 12 March 1998, in English and Cree.

272 Above A **Cree** newspaper, *Wawatay News*, 12 March 1998, from Sioux Lookout, Ontario, Canada, in Inuktitut syllabics.

Y

Yurok

The Yurok people live next to their Hupa neighbours in the Redwood forests of Klamath River Valley along the Pacific Coast. They have **fished salmon**, **hunted** and harvested acorns there for centuries. Attempts at **treaties** and land settlements with the US government, following the 1849 Gold Rush into their country, were left unresolved until the 1990s, when at last they established a Yurok **reservation** and enrolled several thousand people. Before that time, their **economies**, lands, rights and interests were combined with those of the Hupa.

Yuroks have been at the forefront of Native political action to restore traditional Native subsistence and hunting methods (such as spearfishing and gillnetting), land management and resource protection, and **ceremonies**. For example, along with Hupa, Karok and other Northern California peoples, they have organized environmental clean-ups of areas where basketmakers would gather materials for ceremonial **baskets** and basket hats.

Z

Zuni/A:shiwi

By 1,000 AD the ancestors of the present-day Zuni had migrated to the Southwestern river valley they occupy today. They were among the first Native peoples recorded to have **contact** with the Europeans (in 1539). For five centuries, they have struggled to maintain their unique **language**, their **matrilineal clan** and religious government and ceremonial systems. Although they now are part of the US tribal trust system operated by the **Bureau of Indian Affairs**, with an elected civil government, tribally controlled schools and hospital and modern housing, much of their daily and ceremonial life is governed by religion. Most Zunis speak the Zuni language, alongside English and Spanish.

Known for their traditional **pottery** and innovative, distinctive silver-and-stone jewellery, they have maintained the ancient crafts as part of their religion, although the crafts are also the centre of their family based **economy**.

Information sources

1 For more information on tribal culture areas and specific tribal histories in North America, see *The Handbook of North American Indians*, vols 4 (*History of Indian White Relations*, 1988), 5 (*Arctic*, 1984), 6 (*Subarctic*, 1981), 7 (*Northwest Coast*, 1990), 8 (*California*, 1978), 9 and 10 (*Southwest*, 1979, 1983), 11 (*Great Basin*), 1986), 12 (*Plateau*, 1998), 15 (*Northeast*, 1978), 17 (*Languages*, 1998), Washington, D.C.: Smithsonian Institution Press. See also Taylor, Colin F. and William C. Sturtevant (consultants), *The Native Americans: Indigenous Peoples of North America*, New York: Smithmark Books, 1996; and the series, *Indians of North America*, by Chelsea House Publishers, New York (Abenaki, Crow, Apache, Arapaho, Aztec, Cahuilla, Catawba, Cherokee, Cheyenne, Chickasaw, Chinook, Chipewyan, Choctaw, Chumash, Coast Salish, Comanche, Creek, Crow, Eskimo, Hidatsa, Huron, Iroquois, Kiowa, Kwakiutl, Lenape, Lumbee, Maya, Menominee, Modoc, Montagnais-Naskapi, Nanticoke, Narragansett, Navajo, Nez Perce, Ojibwa, Osage, Paiute, Pima-Maricopa, Potawatomi, Powhatan, Pueblo, Quapaw, Seminole, Tarahumara, Tunica-Biloxi, Wampanoag, Yakima, Yankton Sioux, Yuma, Urban Indians, American Indian Literature, Women in American Indian Society, Archaeology of North America and Federal Indian Policy). For Natives in Canada, see Olive Dickason, *Canada's First Nations: A History of Founding Peoples from Earliest Times*, Norman: University of Oklahoma Press, 1992. On Indians in the twentieth century, see Hirschfelder, Arlene and Martha Kreipe de Montaño, *The Native American Almanac: A Portrait of Native America Today*, New York: Prentice Hall, 1993; and Davis, Mary B., *Native America in the Twentieth Century: An Encyclopedia*, New York and London: Garland Publishing Co., 1996. See also Johansen, Bruce E. and Donald A. Grimble, Jr, *The Encyclopedia of Native American Biography*, New York: DaCapo Press, 1998.

2 For excellent information on African-Americans and Native Americans, see Forbes, Jack D., *Black Africans and Native Americans: Colour, Evolution and Class in the Evolution of Red-Black Peoples*, Oxford, England: Basil Blackwell Publishers, 1988.

3 Hoxie, Frederick E. (ed.), *Encyclopedia of North American Indians*, Boston and New York: Houghton Mifflin Company, 1996, 7–11.

4 For information cited throughout this encyclopaedia and for other references on American Indian women, see Green, Rayna, *Women in American Indian Society*, New York and Philadelphia: Chelsea House Publishers, 1992.

5 Hoxie, 1996, 19–21.

6 For extensive information on Native architecture, see Nabokov, Peter and Robert Easton, *Native American Architecture*, New York and Oxford: Oxford University Press, 1989.

7 For more on contemporary Native art, see Archuleta, Margaret and Rennard Strickland, *Shared Visions: Native American Painters and Sculptors in the Twentieth Century*, Phoenix, A.Z.: The Heard Museum, 1991; McMaster, Gerald and Lee Ann Martin (Mi'kmaq), *Indigena: Contemporary Native Perspectives*, Hull, Quebec: Canadian Museum of Civilization, 1992; Coe, Ralph T., *Lost and Found Traditions: Native American Art, 1965–1985*, New York: American Federation of Arts, 1986; and Nemiroff, Diana, Robert Houle and Charlotte Townsend-Gault, *Land Spirit Power: First Nations at the National Gallery of Canada*, Ottawa: National Gallery of Canada, 1992. On earlier art, see Coe, Ralph T., *Sacred Circles: Two Thousand Years of North American Indian Art*, London: Arts Council of Great Britain, 1976; and King, J.C.H., *Thunderbird and Lightning: Indian Life in Northeastern North America, 1600–1900*, London: British Museum Press, 1982.

8 Northrup, Jim (Anishinabe), 'Fond du Lac Follies', *News From Indian Country*, Mid-August, 1997, 10B.

9 Hassrick, Royal B., *The Sioux: Life and Customs of A Warrior Society*, 1964, xiii, 42.

10 Hill, Tom (Seneca) and Richard Hill Sr (Tuscarora), *Creation's Journey: Native American Identity and Belief*, Washington, D.C.: Smithsonian Institution Press, 1994, 73.

11 Jones, Suzi (ed.), *Pacific Basketmakers: A Living Tradition, Catalogue of the 1981 Pacific Basketmaker's Symposium and Exhibition*, Fairbanks, A.K.: University of Alaska Museum, 1983, 34.

12 Hill and Hill, 1994, 118–119.

13 Hill and Hill, 1994, 138.

14 Fitzhugh, William W. and Susan Kaplan, *Inua: Spirit World of the Bering Sea Eskimo*, Washington, D.C.: Smithsonian Institution Press, 1982, 286.

183

15 *The Papers of Sir William Johnson*, 16 vols, Albany: State University of New York Press, 1925–1965, III, 707–708.

16 For more on Native calendars and astronomy, see Williamson, Ray, *Living the Sky: The Cosmos of the American Indian*, Boston: Houghton Mifflin, 1984.

17 Gilman, Carolyn and Mary Jane Schneider, *The Way to Independence*, Minneapolis: Minnesota Historical Society Press, 1987, 224.

18 For more on Indians and the Civil War, see Hauptmann, Lawrence M., *Between Two Fires: American Indians in the Civil War*, New York: The Free Press, 1995.

19 For more on Native dolls, see Lenz, Mary Jan, *The Stuff of Dreams: Native American Dolls*, New York: Museum of the American Indian, 1986. On *katsina* dolls, see Secakuku, Alph H., *Following the Sun and Moon: Hopi Kachina Tradition*, Flagstaff, A.Z.: Northland Publishing in co-operation with the Heard Museum, 1995.

20 Diamond, Beverley, M., Sam Cronk and Franziska von Rosen, *Visions of Sound: Musical Instruments of First Nations Communities in Northeastern America*, Chicago and London: University of Chicago Press, 1994, 33.

21 'Lakota Flute Song', Green, Rayna and Howard Bass, producers. *Heartbeat: Voices of First Nations Women*. Smithsonian Folkways SF CD 40415, 1995.

22 Fitzhugh, William W. and Aron Crowell, *Crossroads of Continents: Cultures of Siberia and Alaska*, Washington, D.C.: Smithsonian Institution Press, 1988, 203.

23 Lowie, Robert, 'Plains Indian Age Societies: Historical and Comparative Summary', *American Museum of Natural History, Anthropological Papers* 11, pt 10, 1916, 279.

24 MacDowell, Marsha L. and C. Kurt Dewhurst (eds), *To Honor and Comfort: Native Quilting Traditions*, Santa Fe, N.M.: Museum of New Mexico Press, 1997, 166.

25 Ewers, John C., *The Horse in Blackfoot Indian Culture*, BAE Bulletin 159, Washington, D.C.: Smithsonian Institution, 1955.

26 Ewers, 137.

27 Jonaitis, Aldona (ed.), *Chiefly Feasts: The Enduring Kwakiutl Potlatch*, Seattle: University of Washington, Press, 1991, 25.

28 See Fagg, William (ed.), *Eskimo Art in the British Museum*, London: Trustees of the British Museum, 1972.

29 Hoxie, 1996, 219–220.

30 Golla, in Davis, 1996, 311.

31 Davis, 1996, 311.

32 For more on modern Native literature, see Green, Rayna (ed.), *That's What She Said: Fiction and Poetry by Native American Women*, Bloomington, Indiana: Indiana University Press, 1984; Brown Ruoff, Lavonne, *American Indian Literature*, New York: Chelsea House Publishers, 1991; and read novels by Leslie Silko (*Ceremony, Storyteller*), James Welch (*Winter in the Blood*), N. Scott Momaday (*House Made of Dawn, The Way to Rainy Mountain*), D'arcy McNickle (*The Surrounded, Wind From An Enemy Sky*), Louise Erdrich (*Love Medicine*), Susan Power (*The Grass Dancer*), and poetry by Simon Ortiz (*Going for the Rain, From Sand Creek*), Elizabeth Woody (*Luminaries of the Humble, Seven Hands, Seven Hearts*).

33 For more on Northwest Coast masks, see King, J.C.H., *Portrait Masks From the Northwest Coast of America*, New York: Thames and Hudson, 1979; also Jonaitis, 1991.

34 Wayman, M.L., J.C.H. King and P.T. Craddock, *Aspects of Early North American Metallurgy*, London: Trustees of the British Museum, 1992.

35 For more on the Métis, see Harrison, Julia D., *Métis: People Between Two Worlds*, Vancouver/Toronto: Glenbow-Alberta Institute with Douglas and McIntyre, 1985.

36 For more on Native Americans and museums, see Ames, Michael, *Cannibal Tours and Glass Boxes: The Anthropology of Museums*, Vancouver: University of British Columbia, British Columbia Press, 1992; Cole, Douglas and Ira Chaikin, *An Iron Hand Against the People: The Law Against the Potlatch of the Northwest Coast*, Seattle: University of Washington Press, 1990; and King, J.C.H., *Artificial Curiosities from the Northeast Coast of America: Native American Artefacts in the British Museum Collected on the Third Voyage of Captain James Cook and Acquired Through Sir Joseph Banks*, London: British Museum Publications, 1981.

37 Stine, Jeffrey, 'Oil From the Arctic: Building the Trans-Alaska Pipeline', An Exhibition at the National Museum of American History, Smithsonian Institution, 1998.

38 Fitzhugh, 1982, 221.

39 See Green, Rayna, 'Rosebuds of the Plateau: Frank Matsura and the Fainting Couch Aesthetic' and other Native writers on Indians and photography in Lucy R. Lippard, *Partial Recall: Photographs of Native North Americans*, New York: The New Press, 1992, 47–54; also Richardson Fleming, Paula and Judith Luskey, *The North American Indians in Early Photographs*, New York: Dorset Press, 1988. 160 Neihardt, John G., *Black Elk Speaks: Being the Life Story of a Holy Man of the Oglala Sioux*, Lincoln: University of Nebraska Press, 1961, 3–4.

40 For more on Native pipes, see King, J.C.H., *Smoking Pipes of the North American Indian*, London: British Museum Publications, 1977.

41 Green, Rayna, 'The Pocahontas Perplex: The Image of Indian Women in American Culture', *The Massachusetts Review* XVI, no. 4, 1975, 698–714.

42 A superb account of Indian activism can be found in Warrior, Robert and Paul Chaat Smith, *Like a Hurricane, The Indian Movement from Alcatraz to Wounded Knee*, New York: New Press, 1996.

43 Diamond, 1994, 68.

44 Hill and Hill, 98.

45 A fine source for understanding the Indian history told through ledger drawings is Berlo, Janet Catherine (ed.), *Plains Indian Drawings, 1865–1935: Images From A Visual History*, New York: Harry Abrams, 1996.

46 King, 1991.

47 Green, Rayna, 'Kill the Indian and Save the Man: Indian Education in the United States', in Mary Lou Hultgren and Paulette Fairbanks Molin, *To Lead and To Serve: American Indian Education at Hampton Institute, 1978–1923*, Virginia Beach, V.A.: Virginia Foundation for the Humanities, 9–14.

48 Green, 1989.

49 Davis, 570–574.

50 Hoxie, 590–593.

51 Green, Rayna, 'Poor Lo and Dusky Ramona: Scenes From An Album of Indian America', in Jane S. Becker and Barbara Franco, *Folk Roots, New Roots: Folklore in American Life*, Lexington, Massachusetts: Museum of Our National Heritage, 1989, 77–102. For more on American Indian stereotypes and images in American and European culture, see Doxtator, Deborah, *Fluffs and Feathers: An Exhibit on the Symbols of Indianess: A Resource Guide*, Brantford, Ontario: Woodland Cultural Centre, 1988; and Green, Rayna, *Handbook of North American Indians*, IV, Washington, D.C.: Smithsonian Institution, 1979.

52 An excellent source of information about Indians and tourism can be found in Weigle, Marta and Barbara Babcock (eds), *The Great Southwest of the Fred Harvey Company and the Santa Fe Railway*, Phoenix, A.Z.: The Heard Museum, 1996.

53 Mankiller, Wilma and Michael Wallis, *Mankiller: A Chief and Her People*, New York: St Martin's Press, 1993 (Mankiller's autobiography).

Picture credits

Abbreviations:
Courtesy of the Trustees of the British Museum, photo copyright The British Museum hereafter abbreviated **BM** (catalogue/accession numbers in parentheses);

Courtesy of the Smithsonian Institution, **SI** (accession/catalog numbers, photographers, numbers of photographic negative reproductions, where available, in parentheses);

National Anthropological Archives **SI/NAA**,

National Museum of American History, **SI/NMAH**,

National Museum of Natural History, **SI/NMNH**,

National Museum of the American Indian, **SI/NMAI**,

Center for Folklife Programs and Cultural Studies, **SI/CFPCS**,

National Portrait Gallery, **SI/NPG**,

National Museum of American Art, **SI/NMAA**,

SI Libraries, **SI/L**;

Courtesy of Rayna Green, **RG**.

Introduction maps drawn by James Farrant.

1   (BM 1949 AM 22.141);

2   (BM 1987 AM 9.3);

3   (SI/NAA 14891, photograph by J. Pankratz , neg. #76-14891);

4   (SI/NAA 53.378, photograph by Jesse Hastings Bratley);

5   (Courtesy of National Woman's Christian Temperance Union, photograph by Richard Strauss, SI);

6   (Courtesy of Nebraska State Historical Society, RG 2026.PH: 00067 (L164);

7   (photograph by Annie Sahlin);

8   (photograph by Annie Sahlin);

9   (SI/NAA 1169-A);

10   (SI/NAA 74-3623);

11   (BM 1949 Am 22.13, 1949 Am 22.19);

12   (SI/NMAH Division of Cultural History, neg. #94-202);

13   (photograph by Annie Sahlin);

14   (courtesy of MALAK Photographs, Limited, neg. #240Q-8M-294);

15   (SI/NMNH Department of Anthropology, no #, photograph by Jeff Tinsley and Hugh Tallman, neg. #97-8705A);

16   (BM 5211);

17   (BM 1979 Am 9.1);

18   (BM SI 2040);

19   (Courtesy of A Poolaw Photo, photograph by Horace Poolaw);

20   (SI/NMAI 2667, photograph by M.R. Harrington);

21   (SI/NMAH Hands on History Room, photograph y Richard Strauss);

22   (RG, photograph by Rayna Green);

23   (SI/NMNH Department of Anthropology 18809, photograph by Eric Long, neg. #87-11773);

24   (BM 6976);

25   (BM Q85 AM 352 (7262);

26   (BM NWC 48);

27   (BM SL 1218);

28   (SI/CFPCS, photograph by Barbara Strong, neg. #FAF 78-18037-8);

29   (SI/CFPCS, photograph by Kim Nielsen, neg. #FAF 85-150-78-5);

30   (BM 1954 W Am 5.947);

31   (RG, photograph by Rick Vargas, SI, neg. #98-164, strip 2);

32   (RG, courtesy Marjorie Bear Don't Walk, photograph by Rick Vargas, SI, neg. #98-162, strip 1);

33 (BM +5930);

34 (Courtesy of the Maxwell Museum of Anthropology,
    University of New Mexico, Albuquerque 82.52.1,
    photograph by Eric Long, SI);

35 (BM 1962 Am 4.1);

36 (BM Sl 758);

37 (BM 2583);

38 (RG, photograph by Richard Strauss, SI);

39 (BM 1859.11-26. 79);

40 (BM +228);

41 (Courtesy of the New York Public Library,
    neg. #N-124781);

42 (BM 5205);

43 (BM 1944 Am 2.197);

44 (BM Van 190);

45 (BM);

46 (SI/NMAI 15/8002);

47 (BM 1981 Am 17.1);

48 (SI/NMAH Graphic Arts Collections 8116,
    neg. #97-8319);

49 (SI/NMAA 1979.144.24, neg. #6208135T);

50 (SI/NMAH Hands on History Room, courtesy of
    Dennis Fox, Jr);

51 (SI/NMAH Hands on History Room, courtesy of
    Georgianna Old Elk and Anna Old Elk);

52 (SI/NMAI 25951, photograph by Edward H. Davis);

53 (BM 1942 Am 7.2);

54 (Courtesy of Jimmy Dick);

55 (SI/NMAH Division of Cultural History, photograph
    by Eric Long, neg. #92-5031);

56 (RG, photograph by Richard Strauss, SI);

57 (SI/CFPCS, photograph by Rick Vargas, neg. #FAF
    92-7321/2);

58 (SI/NMAH Division of Cultural History Collections
    1991.6035.03, photograph by Richard Strauss,
    neg. #92-5013);

59 (SI/L PM 784 B5 1860);

60 (SI/NMAH Division of Cultural History Collections,
    photograph by Rick Vargas, neg. #92-5032);

61 (Courtesy of Oren Lyons and M. and T. Bank,
    Syracuse, New York);

62 (SI/NMAH Division of Cultural History Collections
    1991.3192.01, courtesy of Lois Gutierrez de la
    Cruz, photograph by Eric Long, neg. #92-5037);

63 (photograph by Owen Seumptewa);

64 (RG, photograph by Rick Vargas, SI, neg. #98-168,
    strip 2);

65 (BM Q86 AM 11);

66 (Permission of the artist, Jaune Quick-to-See-
    Smith, photograph by Richard Strauss, SI);

67 (Library of Congress, Prints and Photographs
    Division USZ62-1030);

68 (photograph by Joel Grimes);

69 (SI/NMAA 1979.144.77);

70 (Courtesy of Harry Fonseca and The Heard
    Museum, Phoenix, Arizona IAC1758);

71 (SI/NMAH Division of Cultural History, photograph
    by Richard Strauss);

72 (Courtesy of Melanie Fernandez, artwork by
    Bill Powless, photograph by Richard Strauss, SI);

73 (National Archives of Canada C-092418);

74 (BM Q85 Am 21);

75 (SI/NMAH, National Numismatics Collection
    1990.0466.01, photograph by Douglas Mudd);

76 (BM 1921.10-14.84);

77 (SI/NAA 55-664);

78 (BM 78 D.b 2);

79 (BM 1891.6-12-25);

80 (SI/NMAH Hands on History Room, photograph by Dane Penland);

81 (SI/NMNH Department of Anthropology,421274 and 421275, neg. #87-11784);

82 (photograph by Owen Seumptewa);

83 (BM 1949 AM 22.145);

84 (SI/CFPCS, neg. #FAF 78-3483-7);

85 (RG, photograph by Rayna Green);

86 (SI/NMAH Division of Cultural History, photograph by Laurie Minor-Penland);

87 (SI/NMAA 1979.144.2);

88 (BM 1970 Am 9. 4);

89 (SI/NMAI 54496, 108164, 1371, 8847, 2585, 8141);

90 (RG, photograph by Rick Vargas, SI, neg. #98-162, strip 3);

91 (BM 1930.20);

92 (SI/NMAI 15.2393, photograph by David Heald);

93 (BM 1933. 11-29.1);

94 (RG, photograph by Rick Vargas, SI, neg. #98-165, strip 2);

95 (BM 1949 Am 22 35);

96 (SI/NAA);

97 (Courtesy of Great Lakes Indian Fish and Wildlife Commission, photograph by Charlie Otto Rasmussen);

98 (SI/NMAH, Military History Collections 4104, photograph by Hugh Tallman, neg. #98-3869);

99 (SI/NMAI 19.3217, photograph by David Heald);

100 (RG, photograph by Rick Vargas, SI, neg. #98-165, strip 1);

101 (BM 5004);

102 (SI/NMAH, Division of Cultural History, photograph byLaurie Minor-Penland, neg. #87-16622-4);

103 (Courtesy of the Seneca-Iroquois National Museum, Salamanca, NY 81.0001.0003, photograph by Rich Strauss, SI);

104 (Courtesy of Thomas Vennum, photograph by Jim Leary);

105 (Library of Congress, American Folklife Center 22862, photograph by Michael Crommett);

106 (RG, photograph by Richard Hill, Sr);

107 (SI/NMAI 6.8343, 24.1544, 2.7101, 14.3357, 19.7123, 21.1921, 24.3362, 19,6341, 2.5985, 24.4386, 2.2202, 20.5948, 20.5868, 22.8991, 7.1079, 12.2127, 18.2199, 20.5877, 16.2326, 22.9638, 25.2635, 21.994, 21.3539, 20.8703, 8.4686, 2.1312, 2.7386, 24.1092, 15.4471, 10.4450, 19.3690, and 16.4122, photograph by David Heald);

108 (SI/NMAI 23.9267, photograph by David Heald);

109 (RG, photograph by Rick Vargas, SI, neg. #98-166, strip 1);

110 (RG, photograph by Rayna Green);

111 (Courtesy of the Mashantucket Pequot Nation, photograph by Gary Thibault/Tebo Photography);

112 (Courtesy of Tudjaat, photograph by Joseph Kugielski);

113 (BM 5168 and 5169);

114 (Courtesy of the Arizona Historical Society, Tucson, Arizona AHS 8847);

115 (BM 1976 AM 3. 94);

116 (Notman Photographic Archives, McCord Museum of Canadian History, Montreal 1-29099, photograph by William Notman);

117 (BM 1958 AM 4.1 and 2);

118 (SI/CFPCS, photograph by J. Ploskonka, neg. #FAF 84-9104-34A);

119 (SI/NAA);

120 (SI/NMAI 1993.6052, neg. #1/3303, photograph by Pam Dewey);

121 (SI/NMAI 2.1673, photograph by David Heald);

122 (Courtesy of Michigan State University Museum, Lansing, Michigan 02.1997:60.1:4);

123 (SI/NMNH Department of Anthropology 380991, 380992, photograph by Eric Long, neg. #85-11261);

124 (SI/NMA 20.5318);

125 (RG, photograph by Rayna Green);

126 (BM 5216);

127 (BM 1929.12-16.7);

128 (BM 1949 AM 23 1);

129 (BM 1944 AM 2.293 and Q 87 AM 5);

130 (SI/NMAI P13584);

131 (Courtesy of Bob Haozous and The Hood Museum of Art, Dartmouth College, Hanover, New Hampshire, purchased through the Joseph B. Obering '56 Fund);

132 (BM NWC 42);

133 (BM NWC 6);

134 (BM Van 194);

135 (Map drawn by James Farrant);

136 (BM Sl 1842);

137 (SI/NMAI 8.2719);

138 (Courtesy of the Woodland Cultural Centre);

139 (BM 1983 AM 37.1, courtesy of Richard Glazer Danay);

140 (Map drawn by James Farrant, after Francis Paul Prucha, *Atlas of American Indian Affairs*, Lincoln and London: University of Nebraska Press, 1990, maps 14, 17, 20 and 22);

141 (Courtesy of Joy Harjo, photograph by Hulleah Tsinhnahjinnie);

142 (Courtesy of Tomson Highway, photograph by Micheal Cooper);

143 (BM 1980 AM 32.1);

144 (RG, photograph by Rayna Green);

145 (photograph by Joel Grimes);

146 (Courtesy of Pablita Abeyta and RG, photograph by Richard Strauss, SI);

147 (Courtesy of the Seneca-Iroquois National Museum, Salamanca, NY 81.0001-1560-1, photograph by Richard Strauss, SI);

148 (BM 1976 Am 3.79);

149 (Courtesy of Atlatl Inc., National Service Organization for Native American Arts and Kristopher Beck);

150 (Courtesy of Atlatl Inc., National Service Organization for Native American Arts and Lillian Pitt);

151 (BM 1976 Am 3.15);

152 (photograph by Annie Sahlin);

153 (BM 1900.4-11.30);

154 (SI/NMAH, Social History Collections 1981.1030.1. and 1981.1030.2, neg. #82-1456);

155 (BM 1932 3-7.16);

156 (National Library of Canada C-007625);

157 (National Archives of Canada C-079643);

158 (SI/NMAH, Division of Cultural History RSN 81668U00, neg. #8711783);

159 (Courtesy of James Luna);

160 (BM Van 196);

161 (BM Sl 2065);

162 (BM Sl 1730);

163 (Courtesy of James Luna);

164 (RG, photograph by Rick Vargas, SI, neg. #98-168, strip 1);

165 (Map drawn by James Farrant);

166 (Courtesy of Michigan State University Museum, Lansing, Michigan 02.1997: 60.1: 76);

167 (BM 1855.11-26.266);

168 (SI/NMNH Department of Anthropology, no acc. #, photograph by Hugh Tallman and Jeff Tinsley, neg. #97-8706);

169 (BM 1842.12-10.46);

170 (silver print by Greg Staats);

171 (photograph by Shelley Niro);

172 (Courtesy of A Poolaw Photo, photograph by Horace Poolaw);

173 (BM 1921.10.14.07);

174 (BM 1991 Am 9.1);

175 (BM 1924.10-9.7);

176 (SI/NPG, 65.61);

177 (Courtesy of Murv Jacob and RG, photograph by Richard Strauss, SI);

178 (SI/NMAH, Photographic History Collections 69.236.105, photograph by Gertrude Kasebier, neg. #85-7213);

179 (BM 1939 AM 9.1);

180 (BM Q83 Am 330);

181 (BM 1951 Am 8.2);

182 (Courtesy of The Heard Museum, Phoenix, Arizona RC 1312/C, photograph by Edward S. Curtis);

183 (SI/NMAH Division of Cultural History 1991.3029.02, courtesy of Russell Sanchez, photograph by Laurie Minor-Penland, neg. #92-97);

184 (photograph by Shan Goshorn, from the series Challenging Indian Stereotypes);

185 (Courtesy of the Indian Pueblo Cultural Center, Inc., Albuquerque, NM 88.3.6);

186 (Courtesy of Murv Jacob);

187 (SI/NMAH, Division of Cultural History 1991.3123.01, photograph by Richard Strauss, neg. #92-5009);

188 (photograph by Annie Sahlin);

189 (BM 1944 Am 2125);

190 (SI/CFPCS, neg. #FAF 76-142 49-26);

191 (BM 1991 Am 11.2);

192 (RG, photograph by Rick Vargas, SI no neg. number);

193 (SI/NMAI photograph by Eric Long, neg. #85-12395);

194 (Collection of The New-York Historical Society 1893.1);

195 (BM 7479(i));

196 (photograph by Joel Grimes);

197 (Map drawn by James Farrant);

198 (SI/NAA 988-A, neg. #45-876);

199 (Courtesy of Zuni Pueblo, photograph by Diane Nordeck, SI, neg. #92-1240);

200 (Courtesy of the Woodland Cultural Centre, photograph by Tim Johnson);

201 (SI/NMAH, Graphic Arts Collections 8111, neg. #97-8329);

202 (Courtesy of Robert Houle, photograph by Greg Staats);

203 (SI/NAA 1063-0);

204 (unidentified);

205 (Library of Congress, Prints and Photographs Division 45805/262-26790, photograph by Frances Benjamin Johnston);

206 (Permission of the artist, Jaune Quick-to-See-Smith);

207 (Courtesy of Sitting Bull College);

208 (Courtesy of the Canadian Embassy, Washington, D.C., photograph by Bo Polatty);

209 (Courtesy of Bob Haozous);

210 (Courtesy of Roxanne Swentzell and The Heard Museum, Phoenix, Arizona IAC 2344, photograph by Craig Smith);

211 (SI/NMAH Division of Cultural History 1991.3058.01 a-b, courtesy of Nora Naranjo Morse, photograph by Laurie Minor-Penland, neg. #91-19814);

212 (photograph by Ed Prokopchuk);

213 (SI/L, Dibner Library. Thomas A. McKenney. *The Indian Tribes of the United States*);

214 (Courtesy of Cherokee Advocate, photograph by Rick Vargas, SI);

215 (SI/NAA MS2287-b, 4-30a, WW, 8-7-11);

216 (BM Van 209);

217 (BM 2004);

218 (RG, photograph by Rayna Green);

219 (RG, photograph by Rick Vargas, SI, neg. #98-167, strip 1);

220 (photograph by Annie Sahlin);

221 (BM SI 1237);

222 (SI/NAA Cherokee 1044B, photograph by James Mooney);

223 (SI/NMAI 1/8239);

224 (SI/CFPCS, photograph by S. Sweezy, neg. #FAF 75-14251-32);

225 (SI/NMAH Graphic Arts Collections 8118, neg. #97-8321);

226 (Courtesy of Rebecca Baird, photograph by Rebecca Baird);

227 (Courtesy of Rebecca Baird *et al.*, photograph by Rebecca Baird);

228 (SI/NMAH Division of Cultural History 1991.6035.02, Courtesy of St Joseph's Apache Mission, photograph by Jeff Tinsley, neg. #92-5000);

229 (BM 1979 AM 22. 65);

230 (Courtesy of Museum of New Mexico, Santa Fe, New Mexico, photograph by Hance and Nast, neg. #1507);

231 (Courtesy of Courtesy of Museum of New Mexico, Santa Fe, New Mexico, Museum of Indian Arts and Culture/Laboratory of Anthropology, Dorothy Dunn Kramer Collection 5140413, photograph by Blair Clark);

232 (SI/NMAH, Division of Cultural History 1991.3042.02, photograph by Eric Long, neg. #92-5039);

233 (SI/NMAA 1989.30.1 a-e);

234 (Courtesy of Cranbrook Institute of Science CS 2118 and 2117, photograph by Rick Vargas, SI);

235 (Courtesy of the Seneca-Iroquois National Museum, Salamanca, NY 81.0001.1112-1129, 81.0001.0231-40, 81.0001.0260, 81.0001.0391, no. neg. #, photograph by Eric Long, SI);

236 (SI/NMAI 24/7279, 24/1358, 16/9757, photograph by Rick Vargas);

237 (SI/NMAI 14/4989, photograph by Rick Vargas);

238 (SI/NAA Coll. 78, photograph by Timothy H. O'Sullivan);

239 (BM 1944 Am 2.208);

240 (BM 1855.11-26.354);

241 (BM 1988 Am 4.1);

242 (BM 1986 Am 10.107);

243 (SI/NMAA 1985.66. 248, 934B);

244 (SI/NAA BAE 7344, neg. #92-8895);

245 (RG, photograph by Richard Strauss, SI);

246 (RG, photograph by Rayna Green);

247 (photograph by Shan Goshorn);

248 (photograph by Annie Sahlin);

249 (SI/NMAH Division of Cultural History, photograph by Rick Vargas, neg. #98-163);

250 (Courtesy of Wilma Mankiller, photograph by Cherokee Nation Communications Department);

251 (SI/NMNH, Department of Anthropology 380935, 380918, 381395);

252 (BM St 748);

253 (Map drawn by James Farrant);

254 (BM 1931.12);

255 (BM 1949 Am 22.119);

256 (BM 1903.81);

257 (Courtesy of Gerald McMaster);

258 (BM 5202);

259 (BM 1949 Am 22 146);

260 (BM 1861.3-12.62);

261 (BM 1976 Am 3. 28);

262 (SI/CFPCS, neg. #FAF 84-9087-29a);

263 (BM 1948 AM 17 21);

264 (SI/NMAH Division of Cultural History 1991.3195.01, courtesy of Ramona Sakiestewa, photograph by Jeff Tinsley, neg. #98-5005);

265 (Minnesota Historical Society, photograph by Monroe Kelley);

266 (Courtesy of Thomas Vennum);

267 (BM 1939 Am 11 3);

268 (Courtesy of A Poolaw Photo, photograph by Horace Poolaw);

269 (RG, photograph by Rayna Green);

270 (SI/NAA 3200-B-15, photograph by George Trager);

271 (photograph by Shan Goshorn, from the series *Reclaiming Cultural Ownership*);

272 (photograph by Richard Strauss, SI);

273 (photograph by Richard Strauss, SI).

Quotation acknowledgements

Page 3

Gattuso, John, *Circle of Nations: Voices and Visions of American Indians, North American Native Writers and Photographers*, Hillsboro, O.R.: Beyond Words Publishing Company, 1993, 60. Reprinted by permission of Beyond Words Publishing Company.

Page 4

Trimble, Stephen, *The People: Indians of the American Southwest*, Santa Fe, N.M.: School of American Research Press, 1993, 44. Reprinted by permission of the School of American Research Press and Steven Trimble.

Page 5

Between Sacred Mountains: Navajo Stories and Lessons From the Land. Sun Tracks: An American Indian Literary Series, vol. 11, Tucson, A.Z.: University of Arizona Press, 1984, 23. Copyright *c.* 1984, the Arizona Board of Regents. Reprinted by permission of the University of Arizona Press.

Page 6 top

Smohalla, the Wanapum prophet, *c.* 1880, reported by an army officer. *Fourteenth Annual Report of the Bureau of American Ethnology*, pt 2, 1896, 720–721.

Page 6 bottom

Wilson, Gilbert, Field Report, vol. 13, 1913, in *Wilson Papers*, Minneapolis, M.N.: Minnesota Historical Society, 109–110.

Page 7 top left

In Rayna Green and Rick Tejada Flores (co-directors), *Corn Is Who We Are: The Story of Pueblo Indian Food*, 20-minute colour documentary film, Smithsonian Productions and Alturas Productions, 1995. Printed by permission of the film directors, Smithsonian Productions and Alturas Productions.

Page 7 bottom left

Berger, Thomas R., *Village Journey: The Report of the Alaska Native Review Commission*, New York: Hill and Wang, 1985, 6. For more on land issues in Canada and the Arctic, see Alden Cox, Bruce (ed.), *Native Peoples, Native Land: Canadian Indians, Inuit and Métis*, Ottawa: Carlton University Press, 1988.

Page 7 right

Berger, 1985, 15.

Page 8

Diamond, Beverley, M., Sam Cronk and Franziska von Rosen, *Visions of Sound: Musical Instruments of First Nations Communities in Northeastern America*,

Chicago and London: University of Chicago Press, 1994, 164. Reprinted by permission of the University of Chicago Press, *c.* 1984. Reprinted in Canada by permission of Wilfrid Laurier University Press.

Page 10

Karen Loveland, producer and Rayna Green, writer, *We Are Here: 500 Years of Pueblo Sovereignty*, 15-minute colour documentary film, Smithsonian Productions, 1992. Printed by permission of Rayna Green and Smithsonian Productions.

Page 11

Maxidiwiac (Buffalo Bird Woman, Waheenee), *Waheenee: An Indian Girl's Story: Told By Herself to Gilbert Wilson*, illus. by Frederick N. Wilson, St. Paul: Webb Publishing Co., 1921. Reprint: Bison Books. Lincoln, Nebraska: University of Nebraska Press, 1981, 45.

Page 14 top left

Radulovitch, Mary Lou Fox, Ojibwe Cultural Foundation.

Page 14 bottom left

Momaday, N. Scott, *The Names: A Memoir*, New York: Harper and Row, Publishers, 1976, 35.

Page 14 right

Gattuso, 1993, 89. On earlier art, see Information sources, Coe, 1976, and King, 1982

Page 16

Michelson, Truman, 'Narrative of an Arapaho Woman', *American Anthropologist* 35, no. 4, 1933, 595–610.

Page 18

Jones, Suzi (ed.), *Pacific Basketmakers: A Living Tradition, Catalogue of the 1981 Pacific Basketmaker's Symposium and Exhibition*, Fairbanks, A.K.: University of Alaska Museum, 1983, 33. Reprinted by permission of the University of Alaska Museum.

Page 20 left

Winch, Terrence (ed.), *All Roads Are Good: Native Voices on Life and Culture*, Washington, D.C.: Smithsonian Institution, 1994, 197. Reprinted by permission of the National Museum of the American Indian and the Smithsonian Institution Press.

Page 20 right

Tewa song, translation by Herman Agoyo, San Juan Pueblo, to Rayna Green, 1995.

Page 21 left

Green, Rayna, 'Red Earth People and Southeastern Basketry', in Linda Mowat, Howard Morphy and Penny Dransart, *Basketmakers: Meaning and Form in*

Native American Baskets, Oxford, England: Pitt Rivers Museum, University Of Oxford, 1992, 11–18. Reprinted by permission of the Pitt-Rivers Museum.

Page 21 top right

Teit, James, 'The Salishan Tribes of the Western Plateaus', in Franz Boas (ed.), *45th Annual Report of the Bureau of American Ethnology for the Years*, 1927–28, Washington, D.C.: Smithsonian Institution, 1930, 23–396, 392.

Page 21 bottom right

Teit, 1930, 328.

Page 23

Adapted from 'Tepary Beans and Human Beings at Agriculture's Arid Limits', in *Gathering the Desert* by Gary Nabhan. Copyright 1985 the Arizona Board of Regents. Reprinted by Permission of the University of Arizona Press.

Page 24

Boas, Franz (1858–1992), *Kwakiutl Ethnography*, in H. Codere (ed.), Chicago: University of Chicago Press, 1966, 100.

Page 26 top left

Excerpts from *The Native American Perspective on the Trade Blanket: A Woman's Experience* by Rain Parrish, is reprinted with the permission of Gibbs Smith, Publisher (Salt Lake City, 1992), from the book *Language of the Robe*, by Robert Kapoun, with Charles Lohrman, 3.

Page 26 bottom left

Excerpts from *The Native American Perspective on the Trade Blanket: A Man's Experience* by Bob Block, is reprinted with the permission of Gibbs Smith, Publisher (Salt Lake City, 1992), from the book *Language of the Robe*, by Robert Kapoun, with Charles Lohrman, 3–5.

Page 26 right

Pitseolak, *Pictures Out of My Life*, Seattle: University of Washington Press, 1971.

Page 27 left

Boudinot, Elias, *An Address to the Whites. Delivered at First Presbyterian Church, May 26, 1826, Philadelphia*, printed by William F. Geddes, 1826; see also Perdue, Theda (ed.), *Cherokee Editor: The Writings of Elias Boudinot*, Knoxville, T.N.: The University of Tennessee Press, 1983.

Page 27 right

Boudinot, cited in Walker, Robert Sparks, *Torchlights to the Cherokees*, New York: The Macmillan Company, 1931.

Page 29

Domine Pater or Good Peter, a Seneca-Cayuga orator, 1788. In the Papers of Sir William Johnson 1715–1779, 16 vols, Albany: State University of New York Press, 1921–1965, III.

Page 33

Davis, Mary B., *Native America in the Twentieth Century: An Encyclopedia*: New York and London: Garland Publishing Co., 1996, 84. Reprinted by permission of Garland Publishing Co.

Page 34

In Kennedy, Michael S., *The Assiniboines*, Norman, Oklahoma: University of Oklahoma Press, 1961. Reprinted by permission of the University of Oklahoma Press.

Page 35

From an interview with Tessie Naranjo (Santa Clara Pueblo), 1997 for Rayna Green, writer, producer and director and Tessie Naranjo, researcher, From *Ritual to Retail: Native Americans, Tourism and the Fred Harvey Company*, 20-minute colour documentary video, The Heard Museum, Phoenix, Arizona, 1997. Printed by permission of the Heard Museum, Tessie Naranjo and Rayna Green.

Page 36

Waubagesgig (ed.), *The Only Good Indian: Essays By Canadian Indians*, Toronto: New Press, 1970. Reprinted by permission of Stoddard Publishing, North York, Ontario.

Page 37 top left

In Keegan, Marcia, *Southwest Indian Cookbook, Pueblo and Navajo Images, Quotes and Recipes*. Santa Fe: Clearlight Publishers, 1996. Reprinted by permission of Clearlight Publishers.

Page 37 bottom left

Truman. Joel, photographs and Betty Reid, text, *Navajo: Portrait of a Nation*. Eaglewood, Ca: Westcliffe Publishers, 1992. Reprinted by permission of Betty Reid.

Page 38 top

Vision experienced by three Cherokees, 1811.

Page 38 centre

Resolution of the Georgia Legislature, December 1827.

Page 38 bottom

John Ross to Lewis Cass, 14 February 1835, US House of Representatives, Memorial and Protest of the Cherokee Nation, Document 286 (serial 292), 129–133, 1835.

Page 41
 Davis, 1996, 84.

Page 42 right
 In Perdue, 1980, 7–8, from interviews conducted
 in the 1930s under the US Works Progress
 Administration, papers at the University of
 Oklahoma.

Page 43 top
 Trimble, 1993, 122.

Page 43 bottom
 Benton-Banai, Eddie, *The Mishomis Book*,
 Minneapolis: Indian Country Press and
 Publications, 1979, 74.

Page 44
 Winch, 1994, 78.

Page 48 left
 Nabhan, 1982, 83. Adapted from 'Tepary Beans
 and Human Beings at Agriculture's Arid Limits' in
 Gathering the Desert by Gary Nabhan. Copyright
 1985 The Arizona Board of Regents. Reprinted by
 Permission of the University of Arizona Press.

Page 48 top right
 Rayna Green and Howard Bass, producers,
 Heartbeat: Voices of First Nations Women, 1995.
 Smithsonian Folkways SF CD 40415. Printed by
 permission of the producers and Smithsonian
 Folkways Recordings.

Page 48 bottom right
 Stories of the People, Washington, D.C.: National
 Museum of the American Indian and Universe
 Publishing, 1997, 68. Reprinted by permission of
 National Museum of the American Indian and
 Universe Publishing.

Page 49
 Gilman and Schneider, 1987.

Page 52
 Diamond, 1994, 164.

Page 55
 Malotki, Ekkehart with Michael Lomatuway'ma,
 Earth Fire: A Hopi Legend of the Sunset Crater Eruption,
 Flagstaff, A.Z.: Northland Press, 1987, 154.
 Reprinted by permission of Ekkehart Malotki and
 Northland Press.

Page 56 from top left
 Vennum, Thomas, Jr, Wild Rice and the Ojibwa
 People, St Paul, M.N.: Minnesota Historical
 Society Press, 1988, 58. Reprinted by permission
 of the Minnesota Historical Society Press. Original
 quote in Eva Lips, *Die Reisernte der Ojibwa-Indianer:
 Wirtschaft und Recht Eines Erntevolkes*, Berlin:

Academie Verlag, 1956, 55, 65.
 John Fire Lame Deer and Richard Erdoes, *Lame
 Deer, Seeker of Visions*, New York: Simon and
 Schuster, 1972, 155–160.

Diamond, 1994, 177.

Diamond, 1994, 160.

Diamond, 1994, 35–38.

Green and Bass, 1995.

Page 59
 Stung Serpent, *c.* 1720, cited in Ballentine, Betty
 and Ian Ballentine (eds), *The Native Americans: An
 Illustrated History*, Atlanta, G.A.: Turner Publications,
 1993, 274.

Page 60
 Densmore, Frances, 'Teton Sioux Music', *Bureau of
 American Ethnology Bulletin*, 61, 1918.

Page 61
 Hill, Tom and Richard Hill Sr, *Creation's Journey:
 Native American Identity and Belief*, Washington, DC:
 National Museum of the American Indian and the
 Smithsonian Institution Press, 1994, 89. Reprinted
 by permission of National Museum of the American
 Indian and the Smithsonian Institution Press.

Page 63 top
 Katz, Jane (ed.), *Messengers of the Wind: Native
 American Women Tell Their Life Stories*, New York: One
 World Books, 1995, 147–169. Reprinted by
 permission of Ramona Bennett.

Page 63 bottom
 United States of America 1837 Treaty with the
 Chippewa, Article 5.

Page 64
 Herbst, Toby and Joel Kopp, *The Flag in American
 Indian Art*, New York State Historical Association,
 University of Washington Press Seattle, University
 of Washington Press for The New York State
 Historical Association, 12–13. Reprinted by
 permission of the New York State Historical
 Association.

Page 65 left
 Reprinted with permission from *Native American
 Dance, Ceremonies and Social Traditions*, National
 Museum of the American Indian and Charlotte
 Heth, General Editor, *c* 1992, Fulcrum Publishing,
 Inc./Starwood Publishing, Golden, Colorado. All
 Rights Reserved. See also *Drumbeat … Heartbeat: A
 Celebration of the Pow Wow*, Minneapolis: Lerner
 Publications.

Page 65 right
Stories and Legends of the Palm Springs Indians, Los Angeles: Times-Mirror Press, 1943, 25.

Page 66 left
Adapted from 'Tepary Beans and Human Beings at Agriculture's Arid Limits', in Gathering the Desert by Gary Nabhan. Copyright 1985, the Arizona Board of Regents. Reprinted by Permission of the University of Arizona Press, 101.

Page 66 top right
Keegan, Marcia, 8; books for young people on Native food tradition include Clambake: A Tradition; Ininlatig's Gift of Sugar; Traditional Native Sugarmaking; The Sacred Harvest; Wild Rice Gathering, Minneapolis: Lerner Publications.

Page 66 bottom right
Tallmountain, Mary, There is no Word for Goodbye, Marvin, S.D.: Blue Cloud Quarterly Press, 1982.

Page 68
Ackerman, Lillian (ed.), A Song to the Creator: Traditional Arts of Native Women of the Plateau, Norman: University of Oklahoma Press, 1996, ix. Reprinted by permission of the publishers, the editor and Barbara Coddington for the Plateau Project.

Page 70 top
Winch, 1994, 135.

Page 70 bottom
Green and Bass, 1995.

Page 72
Chona, Maria, Papago Woman, Edited by Ruth Underhill, Orlando, FL: Holt, Rinehart and Winston/Harcourt Brace, 1979.

Page 75 top
Ghost Dance Song, believed to be sung by Kicking Bear, the Minneconjou Sioux leader. Oral tradition.

Page 75 bottom
Ghost Dance Song. Oral tradition.

Page 76 left
McDowell, Marsha and C. Kurt Dewhurst (eds), To Honor and Comfort: Native Quilting Traditions, Santa Fe, N.M.: Museum of New Mexico Press and the Michigan State University Museum, 1997. Reprinted by permission of the Michigan State University Museum.

Page 76 top right
Ackerman, 1996, ix.

Page 76 bottom right
Chrystos, Not Vanishing, Vancouver: Press Gang Publishers, 1988.

Page 78 left
Excerpt from an English version of the traditional Thanksgiving address, gawi'yo, given in part by Reg Henry, Cayuga faithkeeper, at the Six Nations Reserve, Canada, in 1996.

Page 78 right
Gattuso, 1993, 88–89.

Page 83
Thomas Jefferson to the Western Indians, 5 May 1808.

Page 85 left
Oakes, Jill and Rick Riewe, Our Boots: An Inuit Women's Art, London: Thames and Hudson, 1996, 17. Reprinted by permission of Thames and Hudson.

Page 85 right
King, J.C.H. (ed.), The Living Arctic: Hunters of the Canadian North-A Report and Catalogue, London: British Museum Press, 1989, 17; see also King, J.C.H., Arctic Hunter: Indians and Inuits of Northern Canada, London: British Museum Press, 1987.

Page 87
A Treaty Between Great Britain and the Iroquois, 1794.

Page 88 top right
Trimble, 1993, 45.

Page 88 from centre left
Attakullakulla, c. 1769 in Davis, K.G. (ed.), Documents of the American Revolution, 1770–1773, 15 vols, Shannon: Irish University Press, 1972.

Oral tradition.

Loveland, 1992.

Stories of the People, Washington, D.C.: National Museum of the American Indian and Universe Publishing, 1997, 68. Reprinted by permission of National Museum of the American Indian and Universe Publishing, 43.

Green and Tejada Flores, 1995.

Page 89
King, J.C.H. (ed.), The Living Arctic: Hunters of the Canadian North – A Report and Catalogue, London: British Museum Press, 1989, 17.

Page 91 top left
Diamond, 1994, 164.

Page 91 bottom left
Indian Education, pt 1, US Congress, Special Senate Subcommittee on Indian Education, Hearings, 91st Congress, 1st Session, 1969.

Page 91 bottom left
    Trimble, 1993.

Page 92
    Joy Harjo and Poetic Justice. *Letter From the End of the Twentieth Century*. Silver Wave Records, SD/SC 914, 1996. Reprinted by permission of Joy Harjo, 1994.

Page 93
    Humfreville, J. Leo, *Twenty Years Among Our Savage Indians*, Hartford: Hartford Publishing Co., 1897.

Page 94
    Barboncito, 28 May 1868 at a council convened on the subject of Navajo Removal.

Page 95
    Keegan, 1977, 14.

Page 96 from top right
    Green and Tejada Flores, 1995.

    Maxidiwiac (Buffalo Bird Woman, Waheenee), *Waheenee: An Indian Girl's Story: Told By Herself to Gilbert Wilson*, Illus. by Frederick N. Wilson, St Paul: Webb Publishing Co., 1921, 175. Reprint: Bison Books. Lincoln, Nebraska: University of Nebraska Press, 1981, 45.

    Green and Tejada Flores, 1995.

    Grimes and Reid, 1992.

Page 98
    Fitzhugh, William W. and Aron Crowell, *Crossroads of Continents: Cultures of Siberia and Alaska*, Washington, D.C.: Smithsonian Institution Press, 1988, 333. Reprinted by permission of the Smithsonian Institution Press.

Page 99
    Hungry Wolf, Beverley, *The Ways of My Grandmothers*, New York: William Morrow and Company, 1980, 140–141. Reprinted by permission of William Morrow and Company.

Page 105 top
    Hammond, George P. and Agapito Rey (eds and trans.), *Don Juan de Onate: Colonizer of New Mexico, 1595–1628*, Albuquerque: University of New Mexico Press, 1953, 675–676.

Page 105 bottom left
    Oral tradition, Rayna Green.

Page 108 from top left
    Gante, Edna (Catalogue ed.), *Circle of Life: Cultural Community in Ojibwe Crafts*, Duluth: St. Louis Historical Society, Chisholm Museum and Duluth Art Institute, 1984, 5. Reprinted by permission of the publishers and Fred Benjamin.

Keegan, 1977, 14.

Green and Bass, 1995.

Oral tradition, Rayna Green.

Page 111 left
    Grimes and Reid, 1992, 119.

Page 111 right
    Grimes and Reid, 1992, 122.

Page 116
    Lewis, Richard, *I Breathe A New Song: Poems of the Eskimo*, New York: Simon and Schuster, 1971.

Page 118 top
    Katz, Jane (ed.), *This Song Remembers: Self-Portraits of Native Americans in the Nineties*, N.Y.: Houghton Mifflin, 1980.

Page 118 bottom
    Reprinted from *Black Elk Speaks*, by John G. Neihardt, by permission of the University of Nebraska Press. Copyright 1932, 1959, 1972, by John G. Neihardt. Copyright 1961, by the John G. Neihardt Trust, 3–4.

Page 124 top
    'Nan Chu Kweejo' (Clay Mother) from *Mudwoman: Poems From the Clay* by Nora Naranjo-Morse. Copyright 1992 Nora Naranjo-Morse. Reprinted by permission of the University of Arizona Press, Tucson.

Page 124 bottom
    Cited in Morrison, Howard *et al. American Encounters. An Exhibition Book*. Washington: National Museum of American History, 1992.

Page 125
    Martin, Christopher (ed.), *Native Needlework: Contemporary Indian Textiles From North Dakota*, Fargo: North Dakota Council on the Arts, 1988, 13–14. Reprinted by permission of the North Dakota Council on the Arts.

Page 126
    Loveland, 1992; for a good history of the Pueblo peoples from a Pueblo perspective, see Sando, Joe S., *Pueblo Nations: Eight Centuries of Pueblo History*, Santa Fe, N.M.: Clear Light Publishers, 1992.

Page 127 left
    Gattuso, 1993, 49.

Page 127 right
    Ackerman, 1996, 126.

Page 128 left
Oral tradition, Rayna Green.

Page 128 right
Hill and Hill, 1994.

Page 131
In William L. Stone, *The Life and Times of Sa Go Wat Ha*, New York: Wiley and Putnam, 1841.

Page 133
Colonial Records of North Carolina, X, 763–785, Henry Stuart, a letter to John Stuart, 25 August 1776.

Page 134
Evan Jones' journal, 16 June 1838, at the Baptist Historical Society, Rochester, New York; see more McLoughlin, William G., *After the Trail of Tears: The Cherokees' Struggle for Sovereignty, 1839–1880*, Chapel Hill: University of North Carolina Press, 1994.

Page 135 top
Foreman, Grant, *Indian Removal: The Emigration of the Five Civilized Tribes of Indians*, Norman: University of Oklahoma Press, 1932, reported from interviews conducted in the 1930s under the Works Progress Administration, papers at the University of Oklahoma.

Page 135 bottom
Gen. John Ellis Wool, Commander of the United States troops in the Cherokee Nation, 1836. Wool to Cass, 10 September 1836, US Senate, *Report From the Secretary of War … In Relation to the Cherokee Treaty of* 1835, Document 120 (serial 315), 29–30.

Page 139 left
Katz, 1995, 250–251. Reprinted by permission of Vi Hilbert.

Page 139 right
In Smyth, Albert Henry (ed.), *The Writings of Benjamin Franklin, American History*, no. 47, 10 vols, New York: Haskell House, X, 1969, 98–99.

Page 141 top
Sekaquaptewa, Helen, 'School to Keams Canyon', in *Me and Mine: The Life Story of Helen Sekaquaptewa* as told to Louise Udall, 93. Copyright 1969 the Arizona Board of Regents. Reprinted by permission of the University of Arizona Press.

Page 141 bottom
John Howard Payne Papers. Letters from Brainerd Mission, Sally Reece Letter to Reverend Daniel Campbell, 25 July 1828, Newberry Library, Chicago, Illinois.

Page 144
Georges Erasmus, *Maclean's Magazine* (14 July 1986).

Page 149 top
Cherokee Statement to the Secretary of War, June 1818. Papers of the War Department, US National Archives

Page 149 bottom
US Supreme Court Chief Justice John Marshall, in *Worcester v. State of Georgia*, 1832.

Page 150
Keegan, 1977, 58.

Page 152
Green, Rayna, *Cherokee Stomp Dance: Laughter Rises Up*, Reprinted with permission from Native American Dance, Ceremonies and Social Traditions, National Museum of the American Indian and Charlotte Heth, General Editor, 1992, Fulcrum Publishing, Inc./Starwood Publishing, Golden, Colorado. All Rights Reserved, 177.

Page 153 left
Keetoowah Society of Cherokee Indians.

Page 153 right
Berger, 1985, 5.

Page 154
Densmore, 1918, 140.

Page 155 top
Brant, Beth and Sandra Laronde (eds), *Sweetgrass Grows All Around Her*, Toronto: Native Women in the Arts, 1996, 4. Reprinted by permission of Native Women and the Arts.

Page 155 bottom
Brant and Laronde, 1996. Reprinted by permission of Native Women and the Arts.

Page 156
Berger, 1985, 129.

Page 157 left
Diamond, 1994, 26.

Page 157 right
Lester, Joan A., *We're Still Here: Art of Indian New England*, Boston, M.A.: The Children's Museum, 1987, 25.

Page 158
Green and Naranjo, 1997.

Page 160
Sweet Medicine, Cheyenne Prophet.

Page 164 top
Berger, 1985, 140.

Page 164 bottom
Berger, 1985, 137.

Page 165

Laws of the Cherokee Nation: Adopted at Various
Periods, Printed for the Benefit of the Nation.
Tahlequah, Oklahoma: Cherokee Advocate, 1852.

Page 167

Reprinted by permission of Wilma Mankiller.

Page 168

Green and Bass, 1995.

Page 169

Oakes and Riewe, 1996, 22.

Page 170

Council Fire: A Resource Guide, Brantford, Ontario:
Woodland Cultural Centre, 1989, 1. Reprinted by
permission of the Woodland Cultural Centre.

Page 173

Nancy Ward.

Page 174 top

Bonar, Eulalie H., *Woven By The Grandmothers:
Nineteenth Century Navajo Textiles From the National
Museum of the American Indian*, Washington, D.C.:
Smithsonian Institution Press, 1996, 25. Reprinted
by permission of National Museum of the
American Indian and the Smithsonian Institution
Press. See also Roessel, Monty (Navajo), *Songs
from the Loom: A Navajo Girl Learns to Weave*,
Minneapolis: Lerner Pubications.

Page 174 bottom

Keegan, 1977, 39.

Page 175

Boas, Franz and George Hunt, 'Kwakiutl Texts',
Second Series Publications of the Jesup North
Pacific Expedition 10, American Museum of
Natural History, 1906, 63.

Page 176

Lolita Taylor.

Page 178

Green and Bass, 1995.

Authors' acknowledgements

Rayna Green is Director of the American Indian Program, National Museum of American History, Smithsonian Institution. Of Cherokee ancestry, she holds a PhD in Folklore and American Studies, and is the author of several books and many articles and a producer of many museum exhibitions, films and audio recordings on American Indians.

Abundant thanks and gratitude go especially to Sarah Grogan, Research and Production Assistant, whose fine mind, considerable organization and good company kept Rayna Green productive; to Penny Bateman, whose good idea it was we should produce this book; to Jonathan C.H. King, Keeper, North American Collections, British Museum, Museum of Mankind, who made the museum's collections and his good advice available to us; and to the National Museum of American History and the Smithsonian Institution, for financial, legal and intellectual support for this project.

Many thanks for excellent photography go to Rick Strauss, Jeff Tinsley, Eric Long, Alan Hart and Rick Vargas in the Office of Printing and Photographic Services and to Pam Dewey, National Museum of the American Indian, Smithsonian Institution; and to Paula Fleming in the National Anthropological Archives, Bill Yeingst, Helena Wright, Joan Boudreau, Susan Myers, Sue Ostroff, Jennifer Locke, Lisa Graddy, Howard Bass and Doug Mudd at the National Museum of American History, for collegial support as well as object and picture research; to Ann Kidd, Linda Quinn and Michael Lell, research interns; to colleagues at ORBIS Associates for material on Native plant medicine, and to Helene Quick for final production support and extraordinary patience.

Melanie Fernandez is Community Arts Officer and Acting First Nations Officer at the Ontario Arts Council.

Over time, I have had the privilege to be supported by many people who assisted me through the writing and research processes. Many thanks go to: Dr Trudy Nicks of the Royal Ontario Musuem (ROM), Ethnology Department, for arranging access to ROM resources and to Judy Rittersorn, of the ROM Library, for her enthusiastic assistance; family and friends, Sheila, Jules, Ian, Sandra, Roma, Anna, Diane, Sue, Penny and Ruth for their encouragement and support through this project and past ones; my colleagues at the Ontario Arts Council, who were understanding while I was trying to juggle projects; and, most importantly, the staff, former and current, of the Woodland Cultural Centre in Brantford, Ontario, Alice, Renee, Winnie, Shiela, Tom, Amos and especially Reg Henry, for helping me to truly understand First Nations culture and perspectives, past and present.

Special thanks go to Dave Agar, Mike Rowe and Saul Peckham of The British Museum Photographic Service.

General Index

stickball 17, 37, 50, 71, 72, 73, 151; *see also* games and sports
stomp dances 10, 50, 76, 138, 152, 153, 166; *see also* dance
stories/storytelling 14, 21, 32, 37, 48, 49, 81, 84, 91, 97, 100, 101, 105, 114, 116, 120, 127, 128, 129, 173, 175, 177
Subarctic 13, 9
subsistence 7, 8, 59, 62, 63, 66, 67, 69, 85, 96, 112, 113, 153
sugar 5, 66, 113
Sun Dance 6, 138, 154
sunglasses 85
Supreme Court of Canada 90, 104, 112
Suqpiaq 7, 8
sutures 18
sweathouse/sweatlodge 11
sweetgrass 147, 155, 157, 159
symbols 33, 38, 43, 53, 58, 61, 64, 71, 96, 99, 100, 102, 114, 128, 170, 172

t

Tanaina/Denaina 14
technologies 3, 11, 85
Termination 33, 132, 136, 156
Thanksgiving 78
theatre 14, 93; *see also* plays, playwrights
Three Sisters 22, 66, 78, 150
thunder 57, 128, 150
thunderbirds 57, 58, 61, 113
Timuacan 90
tipi 11, 13, 15, 32, 49, 93, 127
Tlingit 11, 12, 24, 28, 77, 111, 122, 156, 174, 175
tobacco 7, 30, 66, 95, 96, 118, 150, 155, 157
toboggans 49, 110, 162
Tohono O'odham/Papago 22, 23, 66, 69, 72, 73
Tolowa 129
tomahawk 31, 46, 53, 151
tools/utensils 15, 17, 18, 19, 21, 29, 43, 69, 82, 100, 101, 102, 104, 129, 143, 150, 159, 169
'totem poles' 80
tourism 3, 11, 20, 21, 38, 49, 51, 77, 145, 157, 158, 159, 174
trade beads/silver 17, 23, 29, 104, 160, 170
trade blankets/cloth 17, 27, 69, 160
trade languages 90, 115
trade/traders 7, 11, 15, 17, 20, 23, 25, 26, 30, 31, 32, 33, 34, 37, 38, 39, 45, 49, 59, 60, 61, 69, 78, 84, 85, 102, 104, 108, 115, 131, 146, 147, 149, 159, 160, 161, 168, 170, 175
trading posts 31, 39, 49, 161
Trail of Tears 38, 39, 134, 135, 173
train 35, 158
transport 18, 26, 49, 50, 54, 67, 77, 84, 104, 113, 139, 143, 162, 175, 176; *see also* canoes, sleds
treaties 6, 25, 27, 30, 34, 35, 36, 38, 40, 41, 47, 50, 51, 63, 82, 86, 90, 93, 104, 114, 123, 131, 132, 133, 134, 136,

140, 144, 145, 146, 148, 149, 161, 163, 170, 173, 178
Treaty Party 27, 134
Tree of Peace 58, 114
tribal colleges 138, 142, 148
tribal government 3, 14, 34, 85, 86, 90, 103, 111, 123, 145, 146, 149, 156, 164, 165, 166, 167; *see also* sovereignty, treaties
tribal membership 36, 40
trickster 23, 81, 104, 120, 127, 129
trust relationship 33, 156, 163; *see also* Bureau of Indian Affairs, treaties
Tsimshian 77, 101, 111, 122, 156
tuberculosis 44, 54, 85
Tulalip 139
Turtle 37, 43, 55, 81, 97, 114, 118, 152, 153, 168, 170
Turtle Mountain Chippewa 103
Tuscaroras 5, 69, 85, 86, 114, 140, 168

u

United States of America 1, 2, 5, 9, 10, 11, 34, 37, 38, 39, 40, 41, 51, 52, 74, 87, 89, 90, 109, 111, 135, 149
US Cavalry 22, 38, 74, 92, 178, 179
US Constitution 111
US Supreme Court/Constitution 40, 89, 105, 110, 134
ulu 169
umiak 27, 84; *see also* canoes, transport
Unangan 8
Upper Kuskokwim 14
urban Indians 51, 132, 142, 144, 169, 178
Utes 20, 70

v

Vancouver Island 2, 79, 175, 177
Vermont 2, 94
veterans 58, 61, 64, 178
Viking 24
Virginia 119, 139, 168
visions *see* dreams

w

Wabenaki Confederacy/Alliance 2, 104
walrus 98
Wampanoags 92, 94, 159,
wampum 52, 59, 86, 136, 164, 170, 172
Wanapum 6
War Department of US Government 33, 163
War of 1812 131
war/wars/warfare 2, 14, 23, 24, 25, 29, 30, 31, 36, 37, 38, 46, 50, 54, 69, 71, 74, 86, 93, 104, 105, 108, 112, 113, 114, 116, 122, 130, 131, 133, 136, 141, 145, 146, 148, 168, 171, 172, 178, 179
warriors 14, 22, 30, 35, 58, 61, 64, 126, 131, 148, 151, 171, 173, 177
Wasco/Warm Springs Reservation 7, 14, 57, 68, 70, 76, 78, 98

Index of Individuals

Thorpe, Jim 72
Trahant, Mark 3
Turkey Legs 54
Two Hatchet, Leroy 57
Tyler, Leonard 54

v
Van Buren, President Martin 134
Vanderburg. Agnes 68
Velarde, Pablita 66
Victoria, Queen of England 30, 46, 53
Victory, Cleaver Warden 54

w
Wallulatum, Sylvia 57
Wanatee, Don 91
Ward, Helma 128
Ward, Nancy 167, 172
Washington, George 30
Waska, Peter 7
Watie, General Stand 27
Watt, Nettie 21
Weir, Robert 130
Welch, James 91
West, Benjamin 137
Wettlin-Larsen, Georgia 65
White, Elmer 125
Whycocomaugh 53
Wied, Prince Maximillian of 60, 106
Wild Horse 54
Williams, Alice Olsen 114
Wolf, Beverley Hungry 99
Wolf Chief 135
Wolfe, General 137
Woody, Elizabeth 14, 76, 68
Wool, Gen. John Ellis 135
Worcester, Reverend Samuel 28, 40, 105
Wovoka/Jack Wilson 32, 74
Wurtemburg, Prince Paul of 60

y
Yellow Bear 54
Yellow Eyes 54
Young Chief 46